The Link With Home

The Link With Home

SIXTY YEARS OF FORCES RADIO

Alan Grace

Foreword by David Hatch CBE

A BFBS Production for the SSVC

First published in the United Kingdom in 2003
A British Forces Broadcasting Service production for the Services Sound and Vision
Corporation.

British Library Cataloguing in Publication Data.

A catalogue record for this book is available from the British Library.

ISBN 0-9522135-1-6

For June, Rory and Pat and all members, both past and present, of the
Forces Broadcasting Service.

Front Cover:
Soldiers in the North African Desert, listening to the news from home.
(© IWM: E12950)

Back Cover:
Glen Mansell, the producer, presenter of 'Calling the Balkans' with one of his youngest
listeners. *(© Private Photograph)*
Ivor Wynne-Jones, one of the FBS veterans from Palestine with Richard Astbury in the
latest Forces Broadcasting Studio in Chalfont. *(© Private Photograph)*

Inside Front and Back Cover:
A Selection of Forces Radio Times

Printed in Great Britain by:
Lamport Gilbert Limited
3 Darwin Close
Reading
Berkshire RG2 0TB

Design and Typesetting by:
JS Typesetters
2 Tofrek Terrace
Reading
Berkshire RG30 2JS

Contents

Insignia worn by the
Forces Broadcasting Service
1943 to the present day

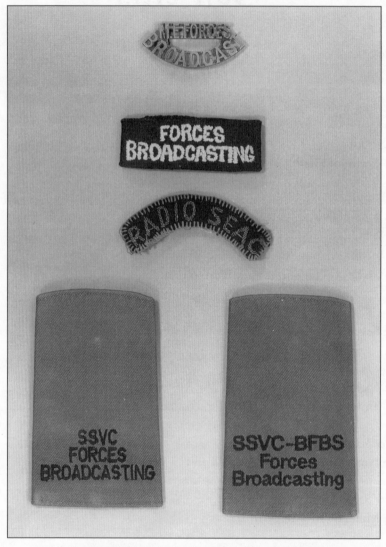

Top: Middle East Forces Broadcast – Cairo 1943/44
Forces Broadcasting – Palestine 1946/48
Radio SEAC – 1946/47
SSVC Forces Broadcasting and SSVC – BFBS Forces Broadcasting
currently worn in the Balkans

Introduction

HRH The Duke of York

Patron of the Services, Sound and Vision Corporation

BUCKINGHAM PALACE

The British Forces Broadcasting Service has enjoyed a long and proud history since its establishment in North Africa during the Second World War.

Over the past 60 years BFBS Radio – and more recently BFBS Television – have been a link with the UK for millions of Servicemen and women, and their loved ones, either whilst separated due to conflict or when serving together overseas.

Although largely hidden from view at home, BFBS continues to fill a vital need with integrity and panache in some 23 countries where our forces are currently serving. In doing so it has set standards and created a loyalty that is the envy of many other broadcasting organisations.

This book tells how BFBS' undoubted success has been achieved, and I congratulate all those who have played a part in this remarkable story.

The Gurkha broadcasters of BFBS Church Crookham. *(© Crown Copyright: FBS 1563)*

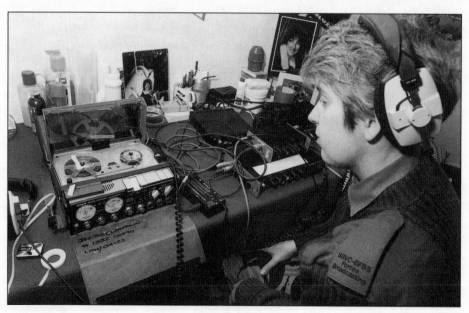

Cathy Pearson editing tapes in Bosnia – 1995. *(© Private Photograph)*

Foreword

By David Hatch CBE

For BFBS to be celebrating their 60 years anniversary is a major achievement as their first 30 years passed in a constant struggle for survival.

The first challenge was one of ownership. The War Office, having endorsed the need for a wartime radio service for Britain's forces as they fought through Africa, Europe and Asia, lacked the will to see the concept through when the war ended. The BBC, however, declined to assume responsibility for the new broadcaster, leaving the War Office, reluctantly, in charge.

Since BFN Germany's transmitters radiated on 247 metres, the same frequency as the Light Programme, replacing the BFBS service tailored for the British Army of the Rhine with a homogeneous BBC relay was a constant theme of discussion. That the service was left intact to welcome rock 'n' roll in the fifties and the first buds of today's forces radio is a tribute to the foresight and tenacity of our representatives.

The presentation of pop music on BFN was only accomplished in the Sixties by fighting off a vociferous band of officers who felt that it was not appropriate to the needs of the British fighting force. At the same time, National Service ended and audiences diminished, forcing BFBS to adapt.

Then Government intervened in the Seventies to challenge the existence of BFBS with savage cuts in successive defence reviews. Staff numbers were reduced, presenters' pay fell behind the industry average and BFBS faced collapse from within. These were troubled times.

But the need for BFBS prevailed against all the odds. In the midst of these punishing cuts, BFBS Cyprus, for example, proved its worth as the only beacon of news and information during the Turkish invasion in summer 1974.

The struggle against the reactionary elements of the BFBS audience reached a head in 1977 as the service struggled to modernise. Out went plays, features, comedies and BBC World Service relays and in came back-to-back pop in the style of BBC Radio 1 and commercial radio. Audiences picked up, but vocal minorities remained critical of the change. In the Eighties, a new radio service grew on spare frequencies - BFBS 2. Initially locally run in Gibraltar and Cyprus it became an essential service from the UK, shifting the gaze of the pop channel's detractors as they now had separate access to plays, features and relays of BBC Radio 4.

Another ownership challenge arose with the merger of BFBS (then a department of the Ministry of Defence) and the Services Kinema Corporation (SKC – a charity) in 1982/3. The bitter forced marriage produced a number of casualties, but 20 years later the resultant Services Sound and Vision Corporation (SSVC) manages BFBS's successful survival.

BFBS then needed to prove that it could embrace the new technology of the Eighties and Saddam Hussein's invasion of Kuwait in 1990 presented the opportunity. A studio was installed in Saudi Arabia in time for the outbreak of the first Gulf War and BFBS was the first forces broadcaster to transmit in the newly liberated Kuwait. In 2003 the investment in flexible staff and up-to-date technology paid off once again as BFBS broadcast during the second Gulf War. Within 10 days of the end of hostilities a BFBS studio was broadcasting live from the new Iraq.

The Grand Staircase in the Musikhalle, the home of BFN Hamburg.

(© Private Photograph)

Acknowledgements

One of my former colleagues had a simple philosophy: "I enjoy today, I look forward to the future, but I have forgotten the past." Such principles are admirable, but they do not help a writer, who is trying to reflect the history of an organisation that, in 60 years, operated 92 Radio Stations stretching from Belize to Hong Kong, Athens to Basra.

When Charles Foster and Marc Tyley asked me to produce a book to commemorate 60 years of Forces Broadcasting, I had no idea just how many stories would come to light. Some of the early ones were cloaked in nostalgia and sometimes a little biased towards the teller of the tale.

Many of the pioneers and architects of the original Army Broadcasting Service have long since left us, but I was lucky enough to have access to some of their letters and files and occasionally listened to recordings they had made many years ago. They made setting up a Radio Station close to the front line, or scrounging equipment to keep a station on the air, appear perfectly normal.

For a book to be able to convey the story of how the Forces Broadcasting Service operated you need more than text, you need photographs. I am indebted, therefore, to the Ministry of Defence for allowing me to use photographs taken by their photographers around the world and to Hilary Roberts, the Curator of Photographs at the Imperial War Museum, for her advice and counsel. The Forces Broadcasting Archive is now held in the Imperial War Museum.

To Julie Snelling at the BBC Written Archives Centre in Caversham and to Chris Horrocks, the Editor of Soldier Magazine.

To Pat Pachebat, a veteran of 40 years, whose encyclopaedic knowledge of Austria, Cyprus, Nairobi and Aden was invaluable and to Bruce Turner, my golfing partner at North Hants Golf Club, who used his Daily Telegraph expertise to sort out my commas and colons.

The recollections, comments and help of the members of the Forces Broadcasting Service have been vital in the writing of this book, and I wish to thank them all:

Michael Anderheiden, Richard Astbury, Peter Attrill, Leslie Austin, Jonathan Bennett, Neil Carter, Charles Chilton, Kay Donnolly, Aidan Donovan, Roger Dunn, Patrick Eade, Bob Egby, Tony Fawcett, Susie Ferguson, Helen Finch,

Charles Foster, Avril and Hector Frendo, John Grist, Simon Guettier, Bryan Hamilton, John Harris, Rory Higgins, Peter Holwill, Roger Hudson, Richard Hutchinson, Sarah Kennedy, Alan Kumm, Charly Lowndes, Glen Mansell, Bob Martin, Peter McDonagh, Dusty Miller, Nicky Ness, Pat Pachebat, Alan Phillips, Chris Pratt, Dave Ramsay, Dave Raven, Sean Ridley, Mike Robertson, Chris Russell, John Russell, Tom Singleton, Guy Thomas, Mike Townley, Marc Tyley, Damian Watson, Patrick Watts, Ian Woolf and Ivor Wynne-Jones.

And finally to my wife, June, who mastered the art of the computer, a skill I doubt I shall ever achieve.

Alan Grace joined BFN Cologne in 1957 as a Sport Reporter/ Announcer. In a broadcasting career that spanned 37 years, he held various posts with BFBS in Germany, Aden, London, Cyprus and Hong Kong. On his retirement in 1994, he became the Archivist/ Historian of BFBS. He is a keen golfer and military historian and lives in Hampshire.

CHAPTER ONE

The Forties

The Hour in English

From a harem in Algiers to a container in Umm Qasr, Iraq – in the past 60 years, the members of the Forces Broadcasting Service have operated in 92 different locations: they were the nomads of radio.

Jonathan Bennett was a young airman serving in Gibraltar when he became a volunteer presenter with BFBS Gibraltar in 1979. Three years later he was taken on by BFBS and posted to Cologne. The next 20 years would take him to a variety of stations, including Al Jubyal in 1991 and Arifjan in Kuwait in 2003.

"My initial thought on landing at Kuwait Airport in March 2003 was how much better it looked," he said. "Last time I'd seen it was in 1991. The Iraqis had only left (forcibly) three days before and it was in a sorry state. On arriving back, 12 years later, the airport may have been pristine but the tension was palpable. It was March 17th, the UN Inspectors had left, war was a certainty and my flight only came in because it was taking the UK diplomats out. Along with the handful of others on the flight, we walked past the boarding gate full of the diplomats and their families waiting to go out. They all looked at us as if we were mad. In many ways, I suppose we were.

"The similarities to the first Gulf War were considerable (it all looked and smelt the same for a start!) but there were differences, the most notable being the broadcast technology. Gulf War 1 had propelled us into the satellite era, albeit with dishes the size of Jodrell Bank. Twelve years on and the receive dishes were no bigger than Sky dishes back home, and just about as easy to set up. On top of that was the VSAT (Very Small Aperture Terminals) technology, which enabled us to have our own up-link, as in Bosnia and Kosovo. This meant we could transmit our own programmes from just about anywhere: all we needed was a generator, some diesel, and life-support and off we went. We even had our own accommodation; that of the breakfast show presenter (me at the time) being a bed in the corner of the studio, which also doubled as the office. At least it gave me the shortest ever commute to work I'll ever get, all of 10 feet."

How different it had all been 60 years earlier.

The front cover of the Forces Magazine called 'The Hour in English', which featured the Forces Broadcasting programme in Iceland. Corporal Norman Spires reading one of his short stories for 'The Hour in English'.
(© BFBS Archive)

The Second World War was well under way before Forces Broadcasting, on a wide and effective scale, could be contemplated for the benefit of British Troops.

The Russians and the Germans had tackled the problem aggressively and with success. The Germans, especially, used radio on a massive scale. With characteristic thoroughness, they planned their Forces broadcasts with an eye to military strategy, and during the Battle of France, to quote from Brigadier M. C. Morgan's official history of Army Welfare 1939-45, broadcasting was "elevated to the position of the fourth fighting service". Long before the British had even experimented with such a service, the enemy was sending out news, fiery political talks, patriotic message programmes, sports bulletins, martial music and entertainment.

By 1942, the Russians too, were broadcasting regularly to and from the front –
and never at any time was the value of propaganda overlooked. A feature, 'Letter
from the Front', was transmitted thrice daily, with family messages spiced with
political and patriotic slogans. Once a day, a special 55-minute programme was
broadcast to the soldiers containing statistics and production records from
factories. These were considered at the time to be more important than sports
news! The object was to present the civilian workers as industrial warriors.

The Americans had also realised the vital importance of direct broadcasts to
their troops. Their mobile transmitters, generously staffed and equipped, were
regarded as an essential part of the U.S. fighting machine. They were in operation
within days, if not hours, of their troops arrival in Africa.

The War Office was much slower on the uptake. A report on 'Educational
Welfare and Recreational Needs of the Army' in May 1940 made no mention of
broadcasting, either as education or recreation.

When 3,500 servicemen arrived at Reykjavik, the capital of Iceland, in May 1940
they quickly discovered that it was impossible to receive any BBC programmes.
The men obviously wanted some news and, if possible, a link with home. Major
Roberts-Wray of the Royal Indian Army Service Corps decided to ask the War
Office to fund a special programme on Icelandic Radio. His proposal already had
the backing the GOC Iceland.

With little or no drama available to Major Roberts-Wray's team, it was decided
that the men themselves would have to produce a series of short stories. Corporal
Norman Spires had always been fascinated by the work of A.J.Allen who wrote
and broadcast short stories for the BBC, usually late in the evening and always
giving his story a twist in the tale. Soon Norman had written 'Extension
Thirteen', 'The Man Who Came Back', 'The Lighthouse' and 'The Ghost in
Studio One'.

The Services in Iceland had a good Forces Orchestra, which was conducted by
Corporal Eddie Braden, who played at concerts, dances and in the pit of the
interestingly named 'Fish Shed Theatre'. His vocalist was the crooner Corporal
Sam Costa.

Another volunteer with time on his hands was LAC Frank Muir, an RAF
photographer. He offered to write scripts for 'The Hour in English' and soon was
introducing some shows. Norman Spires recalled Frank's first visit to the studios:
"He was intrigued with the Icelandic word for 'recording studio', which was
Rikisutvarpssalur. The Iceland Forces Programme was his first opportunity to
become involved in radio. He was soon acting as a compere to our band and gave
the concerts a touch of humour." Years later, in an interview for Forces

Broadcasting, he recalled his early days: "There was a music programme I created called 'Once Upon A Time' in which I linked the musical numbers the band wanted to play with adult fairy stories of a shaggy-dog nature. If I remember correctly, they were read by a Naval officer. There was also a piano programme called 'Ivory Interlude' and a music-cum-comedy sketch show called 'Roadhouse' in which I ad-libbed most of the roadhouse's staff and guests. We also did little comic serials inspired by strip cartoons in the Daily Mirror (I think we forgot to ask their permission!)."

The Adjutant General, Sir Ronald Adam, who throughout his term took a close interest in radio, formed an Army Broadcasting Committee, which in March 1942 set up the Army Broadcasting Section under Major A.A. Mocatta and Major Eric Maschwitz.

The preamble to the charter of the Broadcasting Section reads: "The functions and organisation of the new broadcasting section will be to keep continuous close liaison between the Army and the BBC and to do everything possible to improve the Forces Programme and make fuller use of it as far as the Army is concerned."

The first meeting of the Army Broadcasting Committee also noted the desperate need to give troops receivers so that they could hear the programmes made for them.

Maschwitz also advised that the Adjutant General should recommend the appointment of specialist broadcasting officers and that the Army Broadcasting Section in the War Office should be responsible, and lay down rules, for the guidance for local stations.

However, by the time the Army Broadcasting Committee had approved Maschwitz's report in March 1944, the British Forces Experimental Station in Algiers was fully operational and some of its broadcasters were already on their way to Italy.

The Middle East Command was one of the first to grasp the potential of broadcasting. It had had its own Middle East Broadcasting Unit (MEBU) from 1941 and local programmes were beamed out regularly from Cairo, Jerusalem, Beirut and Baghdad.

But a new Forces station was about to be launched further along the North African coast. BFES Algiers was described by Maschwitz as a "historic scrounge". The men responsible were Lt. Colonel Gale Pedrick-Harvey, the new chief broadcasting officer of Central Mediterranean Force (CMF), who had been Gale

Brigadier Newth, Welfare Office of the CMF with Douglas Young, Nan Kenway and Tommy Trinder, who were touring with an ENSA party, at the opening of the BFES studios in Algiers – January 1944.   *(© Crown Copyright: FBS 1545)*

Pedrick, journalist, playwright and critic in civilian life; Major Philip Slessor, a former BBC announcer, and Major Emlyn Griffiths, formerly a well-known theatrical agent. They made a strong team.

Within weeks, they had built their first studio, audaciously named 'Studio 3A' after the famous studio in Broadcasting House in London. Unlike its namesake, however, 'Studio 3A' Algiers was a tangle of string, cigarette tins, paper clips, and lengths of wire; all the paraphernalia of the pre-war radio ham.

The transmitter was a German model captured in Tunisia. It was so dirty and neglected that they had to scrape off the sand by hand before erecting it in a pigeon loft at El Bair, the highest part of the city. To earth it, they used a drainpipe.

Pedrick-Harvey and his team launched the British Forces Experimental Station, Algiers, on January 1st, 1944.

Excited as they were, none can have realised that this was the birth of a Broadcasting Service that six decades later would still be bringing its own programmes to British Forces around the world.

To Philip Slessor went the honour of making the first announcement: "This is the British Forces Experimental Station, Algiers. The time is 6.30 a.m. on Saturday January 1st, 1944." The signature tune on that first morning was 'Lili Marlene', the song that had followed the Desert Armies across the North Africa; but later, following a complaint from headquarters, it was changed to 'Rule Britannia'.

Recruiting and training staff went on as fast as possible, though it was not easy. This was the start of the Italian campaign and staff officers were more concerned to get troops into the frontline rather than into the broadcasting studio.

However, 'General Routine Orders' of early 1944 carried the following:

1. The Army Broadcasting Service has been set up in this theatre with the object of improving broadcasting conditions and material from the point of view of British Troops.

2. Officers not above the rank of Captain and ORs not above the rank of Sergeant are urgently required. They should have had at least three years' experience of studio engineering, recording and programme building with the BBC, the Gramophone Company, or any of the Commercial Broadcasting Companies. They should not be above medical category B1. Also, they had to be over the age of 30.

Gradually, the service drew in would-be broadcasters from all branches of the Army – wounded infantrymen, guards, pioneers, gunners and a few precious recruits from the Royal Corps of Signals. Almost all had just finished a period of strenuous active service and they knew what their audience wanted. A great variety of accents were heard, but this was exactly what the listeners wanted. It amused them to hear speakers from Tyneside, Glasgow, Cardiff and County Cork. The only thing that puzzled them at first was that one could be an announcer without being an officer!

This BFES Station was the prototype of many more which would follow the armies northwards through Italy, and the staff were busy devising crash programmes to train a far greater number of broadcasters and engineers than would be needed in Algiers.

Apart from the stations designed to cover specific areas of the Italian campaign, it was essential that at least two stations should be mobile and travel with the First Army, the Eighth Army and the Desert Air Force. They were built as frontline stations and each consisted of three Army trucks, which housed studios, gramophone library, office and transmitter.

In the next two years, B 3 and B 4, the Mobile Stations, were to be the spearhead of Forces Broadcasting, sometimes only three miles from the fighting line, sharing the same hardships and dangers, but still managing to provide a service. By April 1944, the Army Broadcasters were also operating a static station in Bari.

The Mobile Stations were soon on the move. B 3, with Captain David Lambert, drove to Campobasso, a hilltop town in the Apennine Mountains. Corporal Norman Spires drove the transmitter truck, an American Chevrolet, which towed the petrol generator. The rest of the personnel were in a three-ton truck with all the stores.

The Mobile Station was sited in the large square and garden in front of a monastery and began its daily programmes with three sessions (morning, midday and evening). Early in the morning, and again around six in the evening, the bells of the monastery tower accompanied B 3's live continuity announcement. The Father Abbot was loathe to suspend calls to prayer so, after some discussion, the broadcasters decided to ignore the occasional peal on the grounds that the enemy knew all about Campobasso.

Life was spartan there. Members of the station staff were under canvas for a while, but they were able to make better arrangements later. Norman Spires shared a monastic cell with the technical sergeant and, in the evenings, the monks would welcome them into the Refectory.

The equipment in the transmitter van was elementary. The two turntables and the pick-up arms were of 'radiogram quality' and there were no groove locators. But there was a large box of steel needles.

When Cassino fell, the bells of Santa Maria peeled joyously and B 3 made ready to move. Two officers decided to go forward and select a new location nearer the frontline and agreed to signal Norman Spires to move the Station. "I closed down that evening and much of the apparatus was packed up ready for departure," he said. "The next day was 6th June, 1944 and we awaited the signal to commence the move. What we did not know was that this was D-Day! There was I, in temporary charge of a Mobile Radio Station, seemingly unable to transmit the momentous news that was pouring in from the BBC. I decided to forget my instructions and put B 3 back on air. The officers arrived back at 10.00 a.m. and, fortunately for me, agreed the disposition. That night, we closed down for the second time and made ready for the move.

We arrived on the outskirts of Rome about five in the afternoon to find that the British troops had gone ahead and the Americans had not yet arrived. We camped, and were given instructions to move to the Villa Camillucia on the Monte Mario the next day. It was here that B 3 became static and assumed the status of a real radio station."

The first primitive Radio Times produced by the Station was headed "Your Own Radio Station... in Rome". On a single sheet of A3 paper, the Station publicised itself as follows: "This is the British Forces Station in Rome... When you hear this Station call on your radio, you'll know that your own Service Radio Station, operated by the Army Broadcasting Service, is on the air. It's your own station, and it's here in Rome."

Another delight of the early days in Rome came when the water supply failed and, for several days, the entire staff were 'forced' to drink wine.

Meanwhile the other Mobile Station, B 4, had moved to Riccione and was parked in a rather muddy farmyard.

The miniature studio had the basic requirements. It was made of matchboard lined with hessian and the inevitable army blankets. It had two turntables and two microphones made from obsolete AA sound locator sets, one on a stand that used to support an Italian bedstead. An old cocoa tin was the only microphone shield. Paper clips were used to keep the wiring in place. The position of B 4 was always close to the fighting troops, which meant that a large number of the Eighth Army were regularly within earshot of the makeshift station. It was their link with

Lieutenant Leslie Perowne reading the local news in the studio of B 4, the Mobile Forces Radio Station in Italy. The engineer on duty is Sergeant Clifford Davis, the well-known Fleet Street journalist – 1944.   (© *Crown Copyright: FBS 907*)

home because it was impossible to pick up the BBC except on short wave. The British troops in Italy had had no programmes of their own until the Forces Broadcasting Stations opened.

B 4 had now acquired the name of Gladys. Norman Bailey remarked in later years: "You have to understand that, at the time, the Mobile Studio was our main focal point; soldiers tended to humanise equipment and Gladys seemed a dependable and affectionate name."

By now B 4 was transmitting 13 hours per day, with five news bulletins as the key points. However, for most servicemen, their favourite programme was 'Music As You Like It'. In their programme guide called 'The Forward Forces Radio Times', the station emphasised that: "It is your programme. If you are in hospital, get the orderly to send us a list from your ward." Another popular programme was called 'The Frontline Story', a weekly commentary by Fred Redman on the Eighth Army News.

Just as they were getting used to Riccione, B 4 was on the move again and arrived in Cesena almost as soon as the town had been liberated. It was 'on air' five days after the Germans had left.

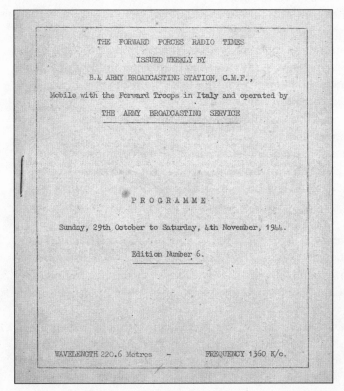

A rare copy of the Forward Forces Radio Times, printed in the field by B 4, November 1944.
(© BFBS Archive)

The station was only three miles behind the frontline and, being in an advanced 'forward' position, was able to announce the capture of both Forli and Farnia by the Eighth Army before even the BBC carried the story. Eyewitness accounts followed of the entry into all the important towns, including Ravenna.

A few days after the fall of Forli, two of the B 4 team, Clifford Davis and Raymond Raikes, were in the Station's 15 cwt truck on their way to Forli to collect essential items. On the way back, the driver of the truck thought his vehicle was backfiring. Instead, the noise turned out to be machine gun bullets splattering the road from an enemy fighter overhead.

This attack followed a certain amount of enemy propaganda directed against B 4 and the 'Voice of the Eighth Army' transmitter, through the medium of Axis Sally broadcasting from three German transmitters located in Northern Italy and Germany itself.

In May 1945, the Mobile Station B 4 came to rest in what had been the Fascist Headquarters for Northern Italy in Udine. The previous occupants had only just left. Telephones were still ringing and the rooms were scattered with personal belongings. However, for many of the team it was their first decent accommodation since leaving North Africa.

From its position just north of Venice, the Station at Udine was a natural link with the troops in Austria and, soon after the ceasefire, the unit commandeered a high-powered transmitter at Klagenfurt, which Hitler had used to send orders to Rommel in the Western Desert. With a landline to this transmitter and another to Trieste, and later Padua, Udine was soon the focal point of what became the British Forces Network, Northern Italy.

For many of the broadcasters, Udine was the end of the road. Some moved to other broadcasting stations in Italy. Some, like Raymond Raikes, had already returned to the Broadcasting Section's headquarters in Eaton Square in London to help train the men and women who would replace the broadcasters who had campaigned through Italy and were high on the list for demobilisation.

FBS Trieste started life as a mere relay station, an offshoot of British Forces Network Northern Italy. It was simply a couple of rooms in a flat near the transmitter situated on a hillside above the city. It had a facility for rudimentary programmes should the landline from Udine break, a not uncommon occurrence because covetous eyes were eager for the copper content of the cable.

After the initial Italian peace treaty was signed on 15th December, 1947, FBS Trieste became a fully operational station, the sole survivor of what had been the largest broadcasting network of any theatre of war, the Central Mediterranean Force. At various times, it covered 13 locations as its mobile studios and transmitters pushed their way up Italy in the wake of the advancing armies. There was a northern network based on Udine, and a southern network on Naples.

The ripening into a full-blown station entailed a move from the first premises to a 19th century villa, set high on a hill overlooking the Adriatic. But the villa had a horrific wartime history. It had been the headquarters of the Gestapo, and the prison for women. It was known locally as the Villa Triste - the house of sadness. None of the Italian staff would take the steep stairs down into the basement where the Germans had interrogated prisoners, and where some had been tortured to death. They claimed that, although no one had seen a ghost, the basement had bad vibrations. Even the young servicemen agreed that there was an aura of evil in the basement. John Jacob recalled that his first bedroom was a white-tiled apartment, which the Italian cleaner claimed had been used for water torture.

Almost no one on the station had any broadcasting experience beyond the brief induction course at Eaton Square. It was learning by trying. When a recruit arrived, he was told: "This is how you switch on a mike; this is how you play a record; this is when we shut down." After that, the newcomer taught himself. If he was unable to acquire a self-critical faculty, he never improved. Most did, but occasionally a newcomer would arrive secure in the belief that he knew it all. He would fit uneasily into a set-up that depended upon camaraderie and a passionate conviction that "the programme came first." Soon he would disappear, off-loaded to a more military activity. One such casualty forgot to wind the clock on his first announcing shift and caused all British clocks to go progressively slower until FBS had to make correction 'breaks' every five minutes. He never broadcast again.

FBS Trieste had no money, few experienced broadcasters, and little equipment – the entire Outside Broadcast microphone stock was one BBC ribbon mike with 85 ft of cable and one Ferrograph tape recorder - but it went from strength to strength in the years to come.

February 1945 saw Captain Leslie Perowne, an old Algiers hand, and Driver Albert Ellis driving a truckful of records on to a ship at Taranto bound for Greece to open Station A 4 for British and Indian troops serving in Greece.

The idea of covering Athens with a Broadcasting Unit from the Central Mediterranean Force arose out of a visit by Brigadier Newth of Army Welfare and Philip Slessor a few months before, and an agreement with the Greek Radiophonicus Strathmos Athenon to give British Forces 1–1½ hours a day of airtime.

Captain Leslie Perowne and
Captain James Hanson, later
Lord Hanson, the ABS Athens
Jazz expert – 1946.
(© Crown Copyright: FBS 1567)

The Forces Broadcasters had the use of one small studio fitted with a single microphone and twin turntables, already old, and the use of a larger studio for concerts. There was one transmitter left intact by the retreating German Army for both the Greek and British audiences, which meant that while English language programmes were being transmitted, the Greek Service was off the air.

The Station's first broadcast, made two weeks after Perowne arrived, was a scoop. It opened with a recording of Winston Churchill and Anthony Eden with the Greek Prime Minister and the Regent, from outside the Old Palace where Churchill, who had just returned from the Yalta Summit, addressed a vast crowd.

The presentation of record programmes was not easy. The Telefunken turntables revolved at 80 rpm instead of 78 rpm, which meant that all the pre-recorded programmes ran a little short of the time given on the cue sheet.

Dennis Scuse succeeded Perowne as Station Manager until the Station was transferred to the charge of the Middle East Command. The turnover of staff

continued and Sergeant Eric Newman arrived from FBS Jerusalem towards the
end of 1946.

Eric Newman knew little Greek but, as they were operating through the
generosity of the Greek Radio Station, he felt it a courtesy to greet Greek
listeners in their own language. They wrote out the phrase phonetically, and
would open with: "This is your Forces Broadcasting Service from Radio Athens
broadcasting on a wavelength of 499 metres 601 kilocycles. To our Greek listeners
we say: Ethaw E'Raddio. Fonikes E'Pressia Ton V'Tanikon the Namion
Herateasaman Tous Elenas Akroatasmas." At Greek parties, it became Newman's
most popular party trick.

As 1946 drew to its close, the number of British and Indian troops in Greece
began to decline and the Athens Station became a remote outpost for which
nobody seemed eager to take responsibility. With Cairo so far away, when
difficulties occurred over living accommodation they simply made up beds in the
office rooms and lived as an autonomous unit.

When Eric Newman left Athens in 1947, Jack Cottrell took over. He
had joined Forces Broadcasting in the early Algiers days and worked his way
round Italy from Bari to Naples, to Rome, and then to Milan before arriving
in Athens. Three months later, he made the last announcement and closed
the Station.

A few days earlier, the Broadcasting Section in London had written to the staff:
"You have assisted in no small measure in the entertainment and education of the
troops and have been a big factor in helping to maintain their morale."

Lt. Colonel Dickie Meyer arrived in Cairo in December 1943 to take over the
new Middle East Broadcasting Unit. Forces Broadcasting in the Middle East had,
of course, been on the air since 1941. The unit's programmes had been broadcast
on Egyptian State Broadcasting, Radio Levant, the Palestine Broadcasting Service
in Jerusalem, and Radio Baghdad in Iraq. But he did not take long to decide that
services were inadequate. He put it baldly: "Most of the troops couldn't hear
them anyway, so that didn't get us very far." In February 1944, he was back at the
War Office asking for authority to start his own network.

That same month, the first Middle East Forces station opened at Quastina in
the Gaza Strip.

Some of the announcers on E.S.B. (Egyptian State Broadcasting) were service
volunteers. Among them was Raymond Baxter, who made his first broadcast in
Cairo reading the NAAFI News.

With everything in short supply, improvisation was vital. An engineer who
could adapt a hi-fi pick-up arm to take the standard gramophone needles of the

Major Leslie Knight conducting a Planning Conference in the Jerusalem Studios. Here new ideas were submitted and present programmes criticised. Left to right: Captain John Gordon, Leslie Knight, Tom Moffat and Staff Sergeant Peter White – 1947.   *(© Crown Copyright: FBS 706)*

time was more valuable than a man with a top-class degree in electronics. The studio clock, their only accurate time check, had come out of a Hawker Hurricane.

Another problem for the staff operating in Cairo was what became affectionately known as the Cairo signature tune. This was the loud braying of donkeys, particularly prevalent around dawn. The FBU studios were not well soundproofed and when the braying reached its loudest crescendo, there was nothing to do except turn off the microphone. It was later claimed that the Cairo announcers were taught a measure of verbal economy by the donkeys.

Following the start at Quastina, Beirut, Basra and Damascus came on stream at monthly intervals and by the end of the year the initial network was almost complete, with out-stations at places such as Baghdad and Khartoum.

The Cairo programme unit was now in charge of the complicated job of Programme Control, which included scheduling, production and the movement of recorded programmes around the Stations. It was quite a headache as each Station took a certain number of BBC relays as well as its own local productions and also used recorded programmes from ORBS (Overseas Recorded Broadcasting Service) and the BBC. With British Summer Time and Double Summer Time, plus a variation of times between Egypt and other Middle Eastern Stations, they had to juggle the schedules.

The programmes were "bicycled" round the Stations, so that a batch of programmes would set off on a route round the Network. It would play Cairo in Week 1, move to Jerusalem during Week 2 for transmission in Week 3, then on to Lebanon, and finally to Baghdad and Basra.

Basra was not an easy place to work. The temperature in summer hovered around 110 degrees Fahrenheit, and 90 degrees was cold. It was administered by the Indian Army and the Forces broadcasters shared the camp at Magul outside the town with their Indian counterparts, living in 'dobi' huts and eating a largely vegetarian Indian diet. On Indian Independence Day 1947, the representatives of the British Raj and those of the country they were handing back celebrated with great gusto.

Apart from the headquarters unit at Cairo, Jerusalem was the biggest and most formal of the Middle East Stations, taking Cairo's programme schedules. They also ran an alternative service, JCKW, transmitted on short wave, which provided a Radio 3 style of programmes at certain times of the day.

With troops of many nations in the area, Jerusalem also broadcast in Hindustani and special programmes for soldiers from East and West Africa, and Ceylon. Once a week after normal close down at midnight, a Polish soldier presented a programme introduced by Chopin's Polonaise in A. Occasionally, one studio was used for Arabic programmes.

There were also changes at the top. In 1946, Major Leslie Knight took over from Dickie Meyer when he returned to civilian broadcasting. Almost immediately, the headquarters of Forces Broadcasting moved to Jerusalem.

Rising tension in Egypt was behind the move. Indications that the Egyptians might abrogate the treaty with Britain made it prudent to have Forces Broadcasting's headquarters in a territory where Britain still held a Mandate.

There were other changes. In April 1946, as the British Forces in the Lebanon were reduced to a handful, the Beirut Station closed. It went off the air at midnight and the staff began to pack everything into trucks for the 15-mile drive down the coast to Haifa, on the other side of the Palestine border.

By the end of 1946, the studio in Jerusalem had a day and night Arab Legion guard and all Forces personnel were ordered to live in a cantonment behind barbed wire.

Hugh Myers, formerly of FBS Beirut, opened a new Station JCCA, No 5 FBU in Benghazi, which continued until 1967. It was a small rectangular two-storey, sand-coloured building on the edge of what had been an Italian military airfield.

The record library at FBS Jerusalem – 1946.   *(© Crown Copyright: FBS 694)*

The airfield had a hard time during the African campaigns and the studio building bore plenty of scars of the recent conflict.

FBS Benghazi had three German POWs working for them while they waited for repatriation. One was the unit driver, another spent long hours manning the control room. The third was the chief clerk.

As the troops left the Mediterranean for demobilisation, the Middle East Broadcasting Network lost its desert outposts. Headquarters of FBS MELF moved to part of a commandeered civilian office in St. Julian's Way (now renamed King David Street, after its hotel), in Jerusalem. Studios for South Palestine were in the Hospice of the Church of St. Pierre en Gallicantu, on Mount Zion, linked by landline to transmitters at Beit Jala, some seven miles south. Studios, transmitter and accommodation were all on one site on Mount Carmel, served North Palestine. Haifa, with by far the greatest bulk of troops in the Middle East, was within earshot of the desert station at Kabrit at the southern end of the Great Bitter Lake. Further westwards, along the coast of North Africa, Benghazi was already on the air and, in Kenya, the FBS station in Nairobi broadcast on time borrowed from Cable and Wireless.

An aerial view of FBS Kabrit – 1947.   (© *Crown Copyright: FBS 768*)

At night, the terrorists were beginning to be active but the young servicemen were unwilling to acknowledge any danger that threatened their freedom. With the sound of gunfire all around them, they would try to locate its source from the roof of St. Pierre and then go down to the bars and cinemas in the city centre. This was strictly prohibited, but discipline in Forces Broadcasting had always been easy and charges by the Military Police tended to be dismissed when the offenders appeared before the Chief Technical Officer, Major Desmond Mansell.

But the situation in Palestine was worsening daily. Guns were important and to lose one was a heinous crime. Rifles were fetching £100 and though the idea of selling one to a terrorist was abhorrent to every soldier, it was automatically presumed that if a soldier lost his gun, he had sold it.

Johnny Goodman had his revolver stolen from his Haifa billet and was given 40 days in a detention camp run by the Parachute Regiment..."not exactly Butlins," he remembers.

In Jerusalem, where announcer Johnny Watson and Arthur Appleton were serving, there was a panic when it was discovered that Watson's rifle had been stolen. The RAF Police came for him when he was on the air presenting his

Major Ken Ellis and Sergeant Tim Heffernan working in the Control Room of Station JCPA
– 1946.   *(© Crown Copyright: FBS 721)*

classical concert programme. Arthur Appleton pleaded with them to let him
finish, but the police would not wait. Johnny Watson left between records and
another announcer took over as the detention party led him out.

At Beit Jala, the engineers, on returning to their Nissen hut, discovered that all
their rifles and pistols had been stolen. They were found guilty of neglect, but
Harry Salisbury, one of the engineers, put forward a joint defence for the
soldiers that, since there was an armed Arab Legion sentry within 50 yards of
the hut, it should be regarded as an arsenal under British military guard. This bit
of service law prevailed with the Administrative Officer, Captain Jack Butler (not
happy to see half his transmitter staff carted off to detention) so the soldiers
were let off with a fine of £9 for each weapon lost. Standing orders for the RAF
were different and one luckless airman spent 28 days at Moascar Military Prison
in Egypt.

In May 1947, a fundamental change in the role of Forces Broadcasting
occurred. Leslie Knight was forced to broadcast hourly IS (internal security)
messages from the Hospice on Mount Zion to keep the troops informed. He

protested that Forces Broadcasting existed solely for entertainment and welfare purposes. "The effect of this ruling would be to make FBS an operational unit subject to terrorist activity," he claimed. But his objections were overruled by the GOC and the Army quickly installed a direct line between the operational headquarters in Palestine and the Studio Controller's desk in St. Pierre. So began the operation code-named "Beetle". In later years, this system was used on occasions in North Africa, Cyprus and Aden when the Forces Stations kept civilians as well as the military in touch with the Command.

Neither Forces Broadcasting nor Army Welfare were happy and on May 14th, Lt. Colonel S.T. James wrote on behalf of the Director of Army Welfare Services:

"...I feel that I should point out that, if the installations were attacked, damage might result which might cause a prolonged break in transmission. If this were to happen, not only would the IS broadcasts automatically cease, but the troops would be deprived of broadcast entertainment which, under present conditions, is believed to be of considerable importance in maintaining moral."

In practice, even at the height of the emergency, the most frequent hourly message was "Beetle... nothing to report," and the broadcasters objected only on the grounds that it interrupted their programmes.

The hurried exodus from Palestine meant a pause for Forces Broadcasting in the Middle East, though the Station at Kabrit was building fast. In Cyprus, the advance party from Haifa was ready for test transmissions by the early part of June.

Against this background, Leslie Knight drew up plans for the withdrawal and regrouping of Forces Broadcasting to Malta. But there were two prime difficulties in the fulfilment of Leslie Knight's dream of a Broadcasting Network based on the island. While the studio centre at St. Francis Ravelin would pose no problems, the Royal Artillery had snatched back the first site earmarked for the 7½ kw short-wave transmitters.

Further east, Cyprus had been involved in test transmissions since June, perpetuating the old FBS 4 of Haifa. Ahead of the last parties out of Palestine, Sergeant Arthur Haywood had arrived on May 3rd to prepare the disused airfield near the village of Kato Lakatamia for its new life as a radio station. Ten days later, he returned to Haifa and he and Ray Joyce brought over the first lorry-load of equipment and began to install the generators. When Alan Langford flew in from Kabrit, they became a three-man team of navvies-cum-radio mechanics-cum aerial riggers to unload the huge crates, install the transmitter and set up 100 ft aerial masts. Within a month of Arthur Haywood's arrival in Cyprus, they had done it.

Meanwhile, the REME descended on the olive groves at Lakatamia to continue the transformation. Apart from Nissen huts, the remains of a primitive swimming pool and a large hall that became the library, most of the derelict outhouses and barns had been a farm.

But the equipment in Cyprus had suffered during its journey from the desert via the wharves and quays of Haifa and Port Said. Despite desperate efforts by the technicians, the inevitable happened and the battered transmitter gave up. FBS 4 at Lakatamia was off the air before they had reached full broadcasting.

The Cyprus staff, suffering from the July temperatures which regularly topped 100 degrees, were almost as tired as the exhausted transmitter. Their spirits rose when the record library from Sarafand arrived at Lakatamia, yet opening it was heartbreak. The cases were battered on the outside and inside they could not believe the devastation. Worse still, the files were missing and, for the first few weeks, everyone who was not actually on the air or working on the equipment joined Kay Donnelly, the new librarian, for a massive re-cataloguing.

On Sunday, July 18th 1948, Constant Harker wrote in the Cyprus Sunday Mail: "Rumours were flying when the disused airfield at Lakatamia recently became again the scene of much activity. Convoys of heavy lorries were seen heading from Famagusta via Nicosia to this remote spot, laden with crates of many shapes and sizes. Carpenters, bricklayers, plumbers and electricians attacked the dilapidated buildings with unwonted frenzy. Tall masts appeared towering above the squat olive trees and – the secret was out – Cyprus was to have its own radio station."

The Sunday Mail's leader column announced: "To our readers. Cyprus has now its own broadcasting station which, although primarily intended for men and women of the Forces, will certainly have many thousands of civilians, both in Cyprus and abroad, among the listeners to its programmes." It went on to highlight one of the Forces Broadcasting Service's most popular programmes 'Letters From Home'. "Among the interesting new features shortly being introduced in to the programmes from the Forces Broadcasting Station is a weekly hour of 'Letters From Home'. Your relatives and friends in the UK can choose a request item and dedicate it to you with their own special message, which will be read out for you over the air. You will be notified in advance by the announcer concerned as to when your request and message can be heard."

By today's standards, the station was very primitive and had a few peculiarities, which caused problems for the new team. According to Kay Donnelly, when it rained on the corrugated roof the drops sounded like falling rocks, so they had to stop the continuity and just play continuous music.

In the summer, the windows and doors had to be left open to make the temperature in the Studios bearable, but this often resulted in some strange noises 'off mike'. As Kay recalled: "On one occasion the continuity announcer was accompanied by the lowing of a cow and another of our announcers was interrupted while reading the weather forecast by the local priest, who put his head through the window and started talking in Greek. He had no idea his enquiries were being broadcast over the entire island. Apparently he was asking about a missing chicken." Also, there were several complaints about Kato Lakatamia's church bells ringing at precisely the same time as the local news was being broadcast. Suggestions by listeners that the church should delay its bell ringing were not followed up!

Despite its noisy shortcomings, the Station was a success and the local papers were full of praise. The contribution made to the island by FBS Cyprus was best summed up by an article in 'Soldier Magazine': "This station has done a great deal to build up goodwill for the Army in Cyprus in its efforts to entertain, not only the Army but the Greek, Turkish and Armenian population as well."

A publicity photograph of the announcers at FBS Lakatamia, Cyprus – 1949

(© Crown Copyright: FBS 962)

By the start of 1949, No 4 FBS Cyprus was opening up at 6.30 a.m. with 'Musical Clock' and, apart from a station closedown from 8.30 a.m. until 11.30 a.m., continued broadcasting until 11.00 p.m. By now the Station had settled into a normal FBS routine. Ziona Caspi, ex-FBS Jerusalem, was presenting a one-hour nightly show called 'Ask For Another'. Esther Lendner, who, like Ziona, had been smuggled out of Palestine by their colleagues at FBS, was introducing the hospital request programme 'Personal Touch' and the popular 'Letters From Home'. A programme in Greek called 'The Cypriot Half Hour' was for Greek Cypriot members of the Cyprus Regiment. However, before the year was out, firstly Leslie Diamond and later M.K. Touman presented a weekly edition for the Turkish Cypriot members of the regiment.

As 1949 drew to a close, Angus Bentley, writing in the Sunday Mail, highlighted one of the programmes, which was to become a tradition with FBS World-wide (Wireless For the Blind). "We do not need to be blind to realise the extent of suffering that the blind have to bear. A Christmas appeal is being launched by the FBS Stations World-wide to provide wireless sets for the blind. We feel sure that civilians in Cyprus will eagerly welcome the appeal launched by FBS Cyprus for the Wireless For The Blind Fund. FBS has created a solid and welcome common ground in Cyprus between servicemen and civilians and a general contribution towards the Fund will help to further establish and reaffirm the bonds of friendship."

In Malta in 1948, Leslie Knight began to implement his plans. His aim was to transmit the bulk of programmes on short wave from Malta, with Cyprus, Kabrit, Benghazi and Tripoli acting as little more than relay stations with only a minor input of their own. The studio complex to cope with it would require a scope and size that none of them had seen before and which only the BFN Studios in Hamburg could surpass. The plan was for two continuity studios, one talks and one live productions studio, plus a control room and recording channel. Also, he hoped to replace the hotchpotch of equipment remaining from the days when the Stations had been Mobile Units with new and better equipment.

In October, Leslie Knight visited FBS Tripoli, which since July had been relaying largely the BBC General Overseas Service and which was proving popular, despite reception difficulties.

At the insistence of the local Foreign Office representative, he agreed reluctantly to devote a certain period each day to broadcasting in Arabic and Italian for the local population. It was, Leslie Knight claimed, bad broadcasting policy to break into hours of transmission with material in a language which was

A group photograph of the staff of FBS Malta. Left to right: Jean Spooner, Tom Singleton, Jill Brazier, Eric Wood, Wendy Barnes and Peter Dabbs – 1949.   *(© Private Photograph)*

incomprehensible to the regular listeners, but, eventually, Benghazi and Tripoli provided a service of both information and entertainment, staffed by local Arabs.

However, Leslie Knight's dream of a single voice for the Middle East was running into difficulties. The rainy season at the end of 1948 had held up work on the transmitter site and the same thing happened at the end of 1949. With the continual delay in delivery of vital equipment, the short-wave service was still not operational.

Meanwhile, the various outstations were compiling their own programmes and developing individual styles. By the time short-wave transmission opened in 1950, there was already some opposition within the Commands, particularly Cyprus, to a programme policy, devised centrally, that was not specifically tailored for their own needs.

Leslie Knight fought hard to save his network and there was a suggestion at one time that the BBC might take over. However, early in 1951, after a great deal of discussion and controversy, and against Leslie Knight's advice, the military authorities decided to close down the Malta Station and move the headquarters of Forces Broadcasting to Fayid in the Canal Zone.

The Times of Malta for Saturday, March 17th 1951 carried the following story: "In the interest of economy, the Forces Broadcasting Service in Malta will close down at 22.00 hours tonight. The red light over the studio door will flicker out for the last time and the seven transmitters at Zonkor Point will cease to relay music and entertainment to the British Forces in the Middle East. It may be too late to secure a reversal of this policy decision to maintain, at the very least, a rudimentary service within the island. So at 10.00 tonight, Malta's name is expunged from the broadcasting map."

There was precious little peace and goodwill in Jerusalem during Christmas 1947. A favourite terrorist trick was to blow up the landline between Mount Zion and the transmitter at Beit Jala. The broadcasters joked that they did not know whether it was a calculated act of terrorism or simply an extreme criticism of the programme. To keep on the air when this happened, the engineers had fitted a small hut at the base of the mast at Beit Jala with a couple of turntables. When the landline went dead, a duty announcer jumped into the 15-cwt truck with a load of records and played them until someone restored the service.

Time was running out for the British and the broadcasters in Palestine. Many were returning home and among them was Gordon Rollings. The day before he was due to leave, he defied Standing Orders by going downtown to collect a suit that he had ordered for his new civilian life. As he had gone with two colleagues, he was deemed to be safe, but on the spur of the moment he left his companions to buy an item from a nearby art shop. As he was making his purchase, a look of horror came over the shopkeeper's face. Silhouetted in the doorway were two terrorists. As Rollings swung round with his Sten gun in his hand, one of the terrorists shot him in the legs and stomach from close range. He was to spend the next two months in hospital near Kabrit.

Leslie Knight issued a Part 1 Order on February 6th 1948: "With the recent increase in local acts of violence, marked by the blowing up of the Palestine Post building, it has become apparent that the usual hooligan reaction can be expected from the usual hooligan sources. The shooting of Trooper Rollings in a crowded shopping area was a typical example of this and the fact that the assailants escaped indicates that the local population can be assumed to encourage and condone such hooligan activities. Similar incidents must be expected in the name of reprisals for all manner of obscure and imaginary incidents.

W.e.f. today, no vehicle of Forces Broadcasting will move after dark without the authority of an officer or NCO.

Vehicles that have to be on duty will move in pairs, at least 150 yards apart. If the first vehicle halts, the rear one will, on no account, close up. The driver will pull into the side of the road and the crew will dismount and prepare to cover the leading vehicle with fire if necessary. The reason for this is that no Jew or Arab can hit anything over 50 yards away at night, unless he is very lucky indeed.

Movement on foot in Jerusalem out of the zones is highly dangerous. If you must move in the town, move with as many other people as possible – don't bunch – don't let any member of the party out of your sight for a single moment. You must carry arms at all times, in or out of the billets and you must be prepared to shoot at a moment's notice. In crowded conditions, you will only have a matter of seconds from the time you see that a man is armed to the time he shoots at you."

The members of FBS were often confronted by the Irgun Zvai Leumi propaganda posters, which were designed to undermine their morale:

"To every British soldier:

Here's the best way for you to stay in this country forever.

1. Get mixed into every trouble with this country's men when you are on or off duty.
2. Be tough. This will keep the fighting going and keep you here. If you are not very enthusiastic but your pal is, never mind; someone will pay for it. It may be you, but maybe it's worth it.
3. No doubt you enjoy life in tents, in a friendly camp atmosphere; keep the struggle on to make your camp life last.
4. The Government is shedding so much of its blood for you that you will be grateful to do your part to make the political decisions for them. Risk your life every day so that the Government may have ten more years to make up its mind and clear out of Palestine.

But... The best way to shorten your Conscription period and force the Government to a decision and to avoid risks is:

1. Avoid getting mixed into trouble with this country's men.
2. Remember there is a sick parade every morning.
3. If you must go on patrol, go slow.
4. Keep an eye on your pal because you may be in a mess as a result of his enthusiasm.
5. Be as passive as possible.

Only your reluctance to be killed for their faults will teach the Government that it is up to them to clear the position."

Against this background, Leslie Knight drew up plans for the withdrawal and regrouping of Forces Broadcasting. His first priority was to make sure that the troops in Palestine had a broadcasting service right to the end.

Basically, the idea was that the few who were left in Jerusalem should withdraw to the big military base at Sarafand to provide a service for the south of Palestine until the time came to draw back to Kabrit and Port Said.

Further north, No 4 FBS would continue within the enlarged Haifa enclave. This would be the final toehold of Forces Broadcasting in Palestine.

On 2nd March, 1948, an advance party arrived at Sarafand to set up a Mobile Studio designated No 1 FBS in a 15 cwt van with an area some 10ft by 6 ft.6 in. which they could also use for OBs. The Station was equipped with two BC 610 transmitters and three AR 88 re-broadcasting receivers. The van was parked between bungalows that had been married quarters and the perimeter fence. This huge isolated garrison camp with neat office blocks, married quarters and a NAAFI shop, was a little Aldershot in the sand, but it was not necessarily so pleasant. A booklet issued to families (long since departed) listed under 'Health and Hygiene' advice on heat stroke and heat exhaustion, sunburn, malaria, dysentery and smallpox.

Even before Sarafand opened, formal control in this confused war had virtually disappeared. British troops and police were concentrating on maintaining the status quo and trying not to appear to favour either community. For months,

Packing up of the Record Library of FBS Sarafand – 1948.   *(© Crown Copyright: FBS 806)*

illegal barriers or roadblocks had been the bane of everyday life and in February 1948, Leslie Knight warned his fellow broadcasters:

"Higher authorities have directed that in future after dark all vehicles challenged by police or other people playing at police will halt and identify themselves. That this is extremely annoying and degrading and that no courtesy can be anticipated from these people is an unpleasant fact that must be accepted for your own personal safety."

Ivor Wynne-Jones, who later became a well-known author, kept a diary which gave a stark account of the last few days of FBS in Palestine:

April 10: Went to Jerusalem. Got involved in the battle for Quastel. On the way back, got mixed up with a Jewish convoy, which came under Arab attack.

April 14: Left Sarafand for Jerusalem 1530 hrs. in 7-ton (AEC Matador). Thrown out of convoy and continued alone, taking the Ramallah road. Came under fire in Sheik Jarrah and near Zion Gate. Arrived FBS 1800.

April 15: FBS Jerusalem evacuated. Thrown out of the convoy because we were towing an engine-less truck laden with equipment. A brigadier said we would endanger his convoy in which the FBS Chevrolet mini-bus (Chevrolet C8A personnel carrier) was being used to carry senior officers' wives. We left alone and we arrived in Haifa at 1800 hrs.

April 21: Up to Ramallah. Stopped by a roadblock and armed thieves at km 33, but drove them off and demolished the roadblock with our hands.

April 25: Finally left Sarafand for Haifa.

As Sarafand ran down, the NAAFI shop closed and the broadcasters were in danger of going hungry. Although the broadcasters had ration cards, they were not officially entitled to use the cookhouse. However, Gordon Cox, one of the FBS engineers, came up with the idea of playing records for the cookhouse and bakery staff in exchange for bread. He was staggered by the amount of bread, packed in unmarked sacks to avoid interception by the Military Police, that turned up after a record had been played. He also managed to obtain tins of meat from the local shops, whilst the local people provided the broadcasters with bags of oranges.

By the third week in May, the remaining FBS staff were down at the harbour, stripped to the waist, stacking equipment on lorries and the quayside ready for the tank landing craft that would carry it to Cyprus. As Leslie Knight, who had returned briefly, was working alongside his staff, an officious military policeman came up shouting:

"You're improperly dressed," demanding Major Knight's name and company, but omitting to ask for his rank. When the MP turned up at the Station and demanded to see the Commanding Officer, his chagrin was complete when he found himself saluting the same, though now fully-clothed, person.

The British Mandate for Palestine ran out on May 14th, 1948 and the last British High Commissioner, General Sir Alan Cunningham, visited Haifa to tell the broadcasters that they had done a good job maintaining morale.

At the other end of the Mediterranean, the Forces station in Gibraltar had been providing a service for the Forces for several years.

The first radio organisation to operate in Gibraltar was a Rediffusion Line System, established in 1934. In 1940, the station was requisitioned by the Governor for Command entertainment and was jointly controlled by the Chief Signals Officer and the Command Welfare Officer. Three years later, the company, RLS, was liquidated and the War Office, which continued to operate the service well into the Sixties, bought the equipment.

In May 1943, the Ministry of Information brought a medium wave transmitter into operation and it became known as 'Radio Gibraltar', which broadcast in English, Spanish and Arabic.

At the end of the war, Radio Gibraltar closed down, except for occasional official broadcasts such as addresses by the Governor, the relaying of public ceremonies and the announcement of the winning numbers in the weekly government lottery draws.

This left the Forces Radio Station on its cable system as the only source of local broadcast entertainment. However, most of the residents of Gibraltar, both service and civilian, managed to listen to the station, which was then known as 'Radio Distribution'.

In 1948, Marjorie Hoare joined Radio Distribution, which was still run by the Royal Signals and Command Welfare. Although the Royal Signals provided the extensive line maintenance, all the broadcasters were recruited locally.

Years later, Marjorie recalled her audition before a board of Army officers. The chairman said: "Just remember that you are employed to link together programmes competently and unobtrusively, and you must always remember your manners." For the privilege of joining the station, she was paid £3. 10s. per week as an announcer/librarian.

Not long after she had joined the station, she was asked to present Elgar's 'Dream of Gerontius', which she approached with some trepidation. "If I remember rightly, the work ran to 24 sides of the 78 rpm records and my major concern was to get the numerical sequence right! Often I was on my own in the studios and I can recall listening to Valentine Dyall's spine-chilling 'The Man in Black' and thinking about my walk home in the dark."

There were problems for the station and its staff in the late Forties when heavy rainstorms flooded the antiquated storm drains. Water poured in through vents under the floorboards and regularly flooded the rooms on the lower levels of the building. Marjorie recalled positioning herself in front of the microphone to avoid sitting ankle-deep in water when she was broadcasting.

At approximately 10 p.m. in April 1951, the Naval Armament vessel 'Bedenham', together with an ammunition lighter, blew up in the harbour almost opposite Wellington Front, where the Rediffusion studios were situated. The force of the explosion was felt all over the Rock, 12 people were killed and more than 40 injured, whilst damage to the buildings and property was widespread. But, although there was considerable damage in the areas around Wellington Front, the studios appeared to have suffered little. They were protected from the blast by the thickness of the walls of the massive stone bastions, built in 1850, which housed them.

Inside the studios the picture was very different. Almost every window in the corridor had been shattered. Panels of hardboard that had been used to line the interior of the studios were torn revealing great gaps in false ceilings and walls through which poured a steady stream of sawdust, which was used for acoustic purposes. Fortunately, there was little damage to the vital equipment and the staff, working through the dirt and the debris, had the station on the air very quickly. However, in the library, they were confronted with a sea of broken gramophone

A Programme Meeting of the Forces Broadcasting Service in Delhi – 1944, seated behind the desk is Major Bryan Cave-Browne-Cave, others in the group – Roy Spear, Sue Stevens, Ross Parker, Edgar Hunt, Arthur Smith and Ricky Caruncho.   (© Crown Copyright: FBS 632)

records. Apparently, the blast from the explosion had blown in a wooden partition, which supported one of the largest record racks. The record librarian was not happy because she had spent the previous day indexing all the latest records!

In India, as in most other theatres where Forces Broadcasting started, short periods of time each week were rented or loaned from All India Radio at a number of their stations including Delhi, Bombay, Calcutta, Madras, Lahore and Lucknow.

The officer who put forward the plan for centralising this combined effort and producing one main programme from Delhi was Major Jack Frost, who had once been with BBC's Children's Hour. He later persuaded the authorities to transfer Lieutenant Colonel Bryan Cave-Browne-Cave from Lucknow, where he was running the 30 minutes a week of Forces Broadcasting to Delhi.

India, as it is easy to understand, had daunting problems of its own. Nonetheless, the service operated by a small but dedicated company of Forces broadcasters from their headquarters in Delhi must rank as one of the most impressive achievements in the story of Forces Broadcasting.

British troops, serving first in India and later in the battle areas of Burma, were indeed far from home. For this reason, and because their exploits were less publicised than those of the men fighting in Europe, at times they felt both isolated and depressed.

Jack Frost had pioneered the famous 'Calling Blighty' programme and these involved long journeys throughout India. It was on one of these journeys that he visited Lucknow. The difficult negotiations, which eventually led to the establishment of the vitally important All Forces Radio Programme, was carried out by Bryan Cave-Browne-Cave. India, South Eastern Asia Command and the American army were all involved and studios and transmitters were secured only after a running battle of memoranda and counter-memoranda.

At last, the situation was resolved and in February 1944 the All Forces Radio Programme started with 50 programme hours each week.

The original accommodation for the Forces Broadcasting pioneers in India was in the G.H.Q. Delhi, but the unit soon moved to some old Indian army buildings, which were just outside the military belt. Conditions were primitive. When desk drawers were opened, rats jumped out. When field-telephones were rigged in the beam of the huts, the same inquisitive beasts would climb down the wires and drink the ink from the inkwells. Snakes and monkeys were encountered daily by the men in the Matapan Lines as they made their way to the studio.

Reception in the theatre was often erratic and limited and it was clear that one of the most valuable services radio could contribute was an exchange of personal messages – using both records and film – between the fighting man and his family at home. Initiative, organisation and a disregard for leave and leisure on the part of the message gatherers had remarkable results.

However, it was the special service 'Calling Blighty' which caught the imagination of soldier and civilian alike. This was a system of sending messages home from servicemen and women to their families, either as recordings or on film.

The possibilities were underlined when the War Office in London sent a message that the wife of a soldier serving at the front was seriously ill. Doctors, the cable added, believed her only hope of recovery was a personal message from her husband.

A high priority instruction was sent to the All-India Radio studios in Calcutta. At the same time, a 'Stand-to' order was sent to a radio-beam station directly in contact with England. At one moment, a private soldier was facing the Japanese in a forward position: in the next, he had been snatched out of the battle area and driven by staff car to an airfield nearby. He then flew to Calcutta and recorded

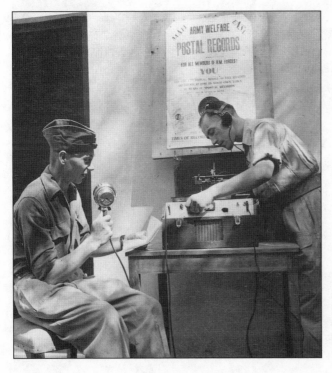

Recording messages, via the Postal Records system for the families back home, organised by FBS in India – 1945.
(© Crown Copyright: FBS 612)

comforting words for his sick wife. The disc was flown to the beam station and several hours later the message was in London, ready for transmission to the hospital. Next day, a War Office signal arrived: "Inform Private ––––––––– wife now out of danger thanks to message."

This compassionate message was only one of more than 11,000 greetings dealt with each year by the 'Calling Blighty' team organised by FBS in India.

At the same time, another team continued to operate what was called the Postal Record Scheme. An officer and a number of sergeants travelled constantly up and down India recording messages on small metal discs for transmission to relatives of servicemen and women. For some children, it would be the first time they had ever heard their father's voices.

Radio SEAC (South Eastern Asia Command) was officially opened in May 1946. It was the brainchild of Bryan Cave-Browne-Cave with total support from Lord Mountbatten. The station itself, the most ambitious Forces Station in the world,

The Headquarters of the Forces Broadcasting Service Radio SEAC, Ceylon – 1946.

(© Private Photograph)

was in a palm grove, 15 miles from Colombo. It had an immense coverage, taking in India, East Africa, Australia, New Zealand, Indo-China, Japan, The Pacific Area and even the West Coast of America. Specially directed transmissions to the UK were beamed on the 19-metre band between 6.30 p.m. and 8.00 p.m. on Sunday: reception in all parts of the country was excellent and it was an invaluable link between the men in the Far East and their families at home.

Just before he left, Cave-Browne-Cave arranged for the entire record library in Delhi to be sent to SEAC together with every record programme it had retained. Broadcasting to the Forces was now in the hands of David Jacobs, McDonald Hobley, Desmond Carrington, Charles Chilton and Alexander Moyes. In April 1949, this magnificently equipped station was transferred to the Ceylon Government and began operating as Radio Ceylon.

When the Allies landed in France in June 1944, no one now questioned the fact that broadcasting had a vital, not to say indispensable, role. Mobile Broadcasting Units were ready to follow the fighting Forces.

The Army's broadcasters had begun their war after their American colleagues, but this time the position was very different. Credit should be given to 21 Army Group and Forces Broadcasting as they left the Americans standing. Long before D-Day, technicians were working on No.1 Field Broadcasting Unit. This consisted of four mobile transmitters and studios, each a self-contained and independent sub-unit. Their specifications owed much to the meticulously reported trials, errors and successes of the Army broadcasters in North Africa and Italy.

Major John McMillan was given command of No.1 Field Broadcasting Unit and he operated directly under the command of 21 Army Group. It had become clear that the ambitious Allied Expeditionary Forces programme was becoming less effective as the Army advanced out of BBC transmitter range through Belgium and Holland. This was where the Mobile Units came into their own.

They could be sited in such a way as to cover the entire fighting front and were equipped with superb communications receivers, with the result that the soldiers could pick up the A.E.F. programmes beyond the BBC's existing medium wave transmissions.

These small units adopted the call signs BLA 1, 2, 3 and 4. From the welfare point of view, the troops now had an excellent link with home and broadcasting was accepted in North West Europe as an important part of service life.

The Field Broadcasting Unit halted in Hamburg and Lieutenant Colonel Eric Maschwitz, who had helped bring Army Broadcasting into being, had pinpointed the Musikhalle in Hamburg as a most desirable headquarters for Forces Broadcasting in Germany.

Four members of BLA 3 under canvas in Holland. Left to right: Corporal Bob Christie, Sergeant Jack Deragon, Lance Corporal Andy Hinchcliffe and Captain Bob Keston – 1945.

(© *Crown Copyright: FBS 1345*)

One night he and John McMillan approached the apparently deserted building and hammered on the door hoping to gain entrance. Suddenly, a rather frightened individual emerged and opened up. Maschwitz and McMillan duly announced that the Musikhalle was to be taken over by the British Army, and since no official paper was available for the purpose, wrote the words: "Requisitioned by Army Broadcasting" on an old envelope and stuck it on the imposing front door.

Having secured a "Broadcasting House", their next objective was to acquire a transmitter powerful enough to cover the whole of the British Zone. The ideal station was at Norden, said to be the most modern in Europe and already in use by BLA 2. A small detachment from No.1 FBU HQ drove through the remnants of the defeated German Army and arrived at the site. The German staff were ordered to rearrange the aerial array to give less coverage to the north and west and more to the south and east, which they did with remarkable speed, and the station remained on air until the Musikhalle was ready to broadcast.

Major John McMillan and Captain Frank Rogers, BFN's Admin Officer explaining the technical equipment at BFN Hamburg to Maurice Gorham of the BBC General Overseas Service.

(© Crown Copyright: FBS 1339)

John McMillan decided that the listeners should be kept informed about the progress of BFN, and on 2nd June he made the following announcement: "Next Tuesday, 5th June, a radio service known as the British Forces Network will come on air for the first time." However, McMillan had jumped the gun and the service still retained the name of BLA 1. The title British Forces Network had been reserved for the official opening in July but the Musikhalle was referred to as British Forces Network House.

The need to get the Musikhalle on air as quickly as possible meant that, while the engineers were working on studio conversions, craftsmen with particular skills were sought from the Forces in and around Hamburg to deal with such problems as old-fashioned electrical wiring etc. At the same time, programme staff drawn from the BLAs started to work on programme schedules, with fierce competition between the various departments for the prime slots.

In the meantime, the Royal Signals, REME and Royal Engineers were working non-stop to repair hundreds of miles of broadcasting cables. In exactly

46 days and nights, the task was completed with just four minutes to spare. At 07.00am on 29th July Sergeant Gordon Crier announced: "This is the British Forces Network in Germany", followed by the News and the first edition of 'Sunrise Serenade'.

John McMillan was aware that many of the men who had travelled across Europe with the BLAs would soon be demobilised. So he set in motion a system for finding replacements. Notices were sent to all units informing them of their requirements. The would-be applicants would need to have a sound educational standard, good voice, clear diction, intelligence, initiative and a capacity for work. Knowledge of music would be an advantage.

One of those who applied was Private Nigel Davenport of the Royal Army Service Corps. He had seen the notice and, with a certain amount of trepidation, approached his less than enthusiastic CO for permission to go to Hamburg for an audition. When he arrived in BFN Hamburg, Raymond Baxter auditioned him and informed him he had passed. He started life as a continuity announcer, then moved on to become a record programme presenter and finally "a bit of a star". "Sergeant Trevor Hill, our Head of Features and Drama, had written, with his future wife Maggie Potter, an excellent children's serial called 'The Adventures of Robin Hood,' he said. "In the cast were Cliff Michelmore, Raymond Baxter, Geraint Evans, Brian Mathew, Bryan Forbes and Roger Moore. I played the part of Robin. Years later, Trevor told me that a group of school children came to the Musikhalle for the express purpose of meeting Robin Hood. He told me that I looked so awful that he had me smuggled out of the building by the back door – I think he had a point as I was a rather spotty youth at the time."

In November 1945, the BBC and BFN extended their joint productions beyond 'Family Favourites'. On Saturday, 24th November, listeners to 'In Town Tonight' heard a rather patriotic introduction: "We stop the roar of London's traffic to bring to the microphone some of the interesting people who are 'In Town Tonight', and we take you over to BFN Hamburg to hear from the men of the victorious British Army of the Rhine telling you about their experiences." Later that same evening, Roy Plomley's 'Desert Island Discs' came live from the island of Norderney in the North Sea. The castaway was Able Seaman Henry Wheeler and BFN provided the engineering support.

Three weeks later, Field Marshal Montgomery recorded his Christmas message to the troops in BAOR from a Combined Services' Carol Concert.

Listeners to BFN were able in June 1948 to follow the build-up to the Berlin Airlift. Nigel Davenport, now BFN's chief announcer, was informed that he had to do the next early morning shift, even though he was just finishing his third consecutive night shift. The reason: he was to make the announcement about the

Peter Aldersley, Nina Stone, Oliver Barnes, Brian Sharpe and Ron Icke rehearsing in the studios of B 7 ABS Graz – 1946. *(© Crown Copyright: FBS 1568)*

start of the airlift. Trevor Hill decided it had to be covered and, with Cliff Michelmore and Raymond Baxter as his reporters, produced a feature which was carried that night by the BBC.

In July 1948, a conference was held in the Musikhalle to set up a BFN Advisory Committee. Its aim was to examine the output of BFN and make suggestions for its improvement and was chaired by Charles Max-Muller of the BBC. Among the suggestions was that BFN's schedules should be submitted to the committee for approval, but the chairman quickly rejected this. The RAF representatives felt that BFN should be broadcasting more cultural, educational and moral items as well as extolling the pride and interest in the service. They wanted space made for these items at the expense of some of the 'swing and jive' programmes. They also suggested that BFN's request programmes should be cut by 50 per cent and replaced by planned music programmes. It was pointed out by Alec Sutherland, the Station Director, that request programmes such as 'The 1700 Club' were the most popular programmes on BFN, and that if cuts had to be made, they should be in other areas. The RAF representative believed only a minority of listeners kept these shows going and wanted a compromise made between providing what the troops wanted and what the Commander felt was good for them. Alec Sutherland rejected this idea but he welcomed the concept of an advisory committee.

In 1945, the Adjutant General Sir Ronald Adam wrote to the BBC to ask if they would be prepared to take over the Forces Broadcasting Service in overseas Commands. Sir Ronald was concerned that the demobilisation process would soon make a Forces Broadcasting Service difficult to sustain. The BBC accepted the responsibility in principle, but agreed a two-year moratorium.

In 1947, following an intensive examination of the costs involved, the Corporation decided that £590,000 would be required to run the FBS in the first year of its operation. The BBC assumed that this expenditure would come in the form of a "grant-in-aid" from the Treasury. The estimate did not include capital expenditure for accommodation or technical equipment.

However, the BBC saw problems in staffing and technical support. More significantly, there would be rights problems as separate contracts would have to be issued to artists and musicians as Forces Broadcasting would not be able to obtain Transcription Services under its existing authority.

When the BBC originally undertook to consider the takeover of Forces Broadcasting, it was hoped that the War Office would be able to provide them with a disposition of the Forces and their locations. However, by the end of 1947, the Services had not been able to forward this information and so the BBC recommended that the proposals should be put on hold.

Another problem facing the BBC and the War Office was: would a Forces Broadcasting Service be necessary in any future emergency or future war and by whom should it be administered and what should be its organisation?

In February 1949, Adjutant General Sir James Steele wrote to Sir William Haley, the Director General of the BBC, about the ongoing debate between the War Office and the BBC: "There are several reasons why we should surrender control of our broadcasting service in the near future. With our small regular Army, it is impossible to provide specialists for broadcasting duties only, and it is obviously inadvisable to employ National Servicemen in this kind of work. The equipment required is not a normal service issue and we have no experts to advise us on its provision. The linking of the British Forces Network in Germany with the BBC Light Programme in 1950 (due to the Copenhagen Plan) will entail an even closer liaison with the BBC. Taking all these factors into consideration, I feel that the question should be considered and a firm date of handover fixed. I suggest 1st April, 1950 would be the most convenient date."

In June 1949, a committee was formed to re-examine the question and its terms of reference were "to advise the War Department and the BBC on the steps which will be necessary should the War Department decide and the BBC agree to the Forces Broadcasting Service being transferred to the Corporation". The committee examined the relevant data assembled by a small sub-committee of BBC and War Department representatives, the latter also representing the Air Ministry. The Admiralty representative informed the committee that his Service did not wish to be associated with the organisation of Forces broadcasting in peacetime.

In September 1949, the BBC proposed that it should not be asked to accept responsibility for all the operations at present carried out by the Forces Broadcasting Service. The BBC would accept programme and technical responsibility for Hamburg, Graz, Trieste and Malta, but it suggested that the existing FBS subsidiary stations in Austria, Klagenfurt and Vienna and in the Middle East - Kabrit, Benghazi, Battisti, Cyprus and Tripoli - should be operated by the Army simply as relay stations with no local origination, except for brief operational periods for local announcements not involving the use of specialist broadcasting personnel.

In 1950, the Director of Personnel Services at the War Office, Major General Blomfield, asked Sir Ian Jacob whether a decision could be reached on the take-over within the next few months because the FBS staff were becoming disturbed about their future. He was also concerned as to whether they had allowed enough money in the 1950/51 estimates for charges that the BBC may raise for operating the service.

However, in September 1950, after much discussion about the BBC proposals, the War Office finally decided not to ask the BBC to take over Forces Broadcasting.

In retrospect, the BBC were not prepared to make concessions on either programme content or standards of the staff involved. They were also aware that the War Office, in running Forces Broadcasting, had one outstanding advantage, and that was the ability to hide costs in other people's budgets i.e. transport, accommodation, food and telephones.

In the Forties, Forces Broadcasting opened 38 radio stations stretching from Algiers to Vienna, Baghdad to Khartoum. By the end of the decade, 27 of these stations had closed due to the ending of the war and the demobilisation of the British Forces.

The future of Forces Broadcasting was by no means secure.

A Radio SEAC production – 1945

(© Private Photograph)

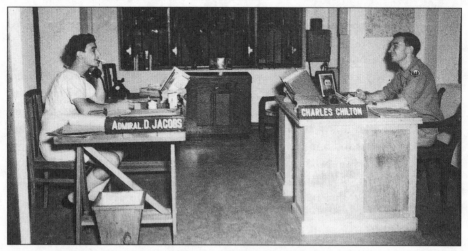

David Jacobs and Charles Chiltern shared an office at Radio SEAC. It appears that both made good use of the local sign writer. David's rapid promotion to Admiral was commented upon by Admiral Mountbatten when he was visiting the radio station. He asked whether he should be saluting 'Admiral' Jacobs or should it be the other way round! *(© Private Photograph)*

CHAPTER TWO

The Fifties
Broadcasting in Interesting Times

The Chinese have a saying when they are wishing bad luck on a competitor: "May you live in interesting times." This could have been the motto of the young National Service broadcasters and their civilian counterparts in Forces Broadcasting. Not for them the splendour of BBC Broadcasting House in Portland Place; their studios ranged from the elegant Musikhalle in Hamburg to a former Gestapo Headquarters in Trieste.

In early Fifties Britain, rationing still applied to meat, bacon, tea, sugar, butter, cheese and sweets and, if anything, it was more austere than it had been in 1945. Income Tax was 9s. 6d. in the pound and the chance for a young would-be broadcaster to get away from it all and join the Forces Broadcasting Service was very appealing. He was guaranteed an overseas posting to either Germany, Austria, the Canal Zone in Egypt, Nairobi, Trieste, Benghazi, Tripoli, or Cyprus.

One such enthusiast was Gunner Alan Kumm who had been posted to the Royal Artillery at El Ballah, Egypt, in 1950. After months of wondering whether his application to join the Forces Broadcasting Service had been successful, he received the news he was being posted to FBS Fayid, serving the Canal Zone.

FBS Fayid was on the desert side of the military hospital in a scorching four acres of sand, barbed wire and flies. It was made up of a central block of studios, library and transmitter hall with a corrugated iron roof; a row of tents where the single men lived; another for the Arab cleaners, night watchmen and ghaffirs; and a clump of tents round the studio building for use as offices and stores.

The ridge tents had concrete or wooden floors and sides that rolled up. They held up to six people. These tattered Desert War relics had seen more active service than most in the Canal Zone. They were as dry as a bone, but at night they came alive with bed bugs and during the day the heat inside rose to a furnace, particularly when the Khamsin blew. This hot, dry wind carried clouds of sharp, gritty sand and had been known to scour the paint from a lorry.

Captain Dennis Garbutt, of the Royal Signals, was in charge of FBS Fayid. He explained to Gunner Kumm that he would have a meal allowance so he could eat at the Church of Scotland canteen. This was because there were no facilities for cooking in the camp and, as announcers worked odd hours, it would be impossible to fit them into a barrack's cookhouse routine. Alan Kumm recalled: "When times got a bit hard, we would drift into any nearby camp and eat whatever food was available in their cookhouse. Most of it was so awful it was hard to imagine how people could turn reasonable raw material into such culinary disasters. Even the local fruit and vegetables could cause trouble with the possibility of a 'gyppy tummy' with every bite."

Alan Kumm had just two weeks training before he was launched as a fully-fledged announcer. His mentor was RAF Corporal Bill Mitchell, who was the Forces Broadcasting Service's longest serving announcer in the Middle East, having joined FBS in 1946. Alan's first task of the day was to obtain a copy of the programme schedule, find out which programmes were his responsibility and which records had been agreed by the Central Programme Office in Malta for playing on the early morning record programme.

Because so many programmes were based on 78-rpm records, steel gramophone needles were very important and had to be changed frequently. It was a disaster when on one occasion they ran out and GHQ Stores could not help. The audience never realised that, for one week, the team kept the station on the air using thorns from the cacti outside the studio window.

Virtually all the news carried by FBS Fayid came from the BBC's General Overseas Service and this was a major headache for the duty announcer. Reception varied with the weather conditions, and could deteriorate completely in the event of sunspots. At night it was impossible to pick up the signal and so FBS came into its own and broadcast record programmes, introduced either by the duty announcer or by visiting personalities i.e. Combined Services Entertainment (CSE) artistes such as Ivy Benson and her All Girls Band.

At the time, Alan Kumm was paid 28 shillings a week with 4s 1d deducted for his insurance stamp. There was no promotion for the servicemen in FBS and no extra allowances. In Fayid, his food allowance was handed over to the manager of the Church of Scotland canteen. In the beginning the food was good, but it rapidly deteriorated and it came as no surprise when the manager of the establishment disappeared with all the money.

Social life was extremely limited locally and the role of the AKC and Astra cinemas loomed very large. As soon as a film starring someone like Doris Day appeared, FBS would be inundated with requests for the songs from the film and the staff were often given free tickets to the cinemas.

When King Farouk abrogated the treaty by which the troops held the strip along the Canal, the Egyptians blockaded the zone for five months. As well as a shortage of food, there was an increase in terrorist activity and a visit to the

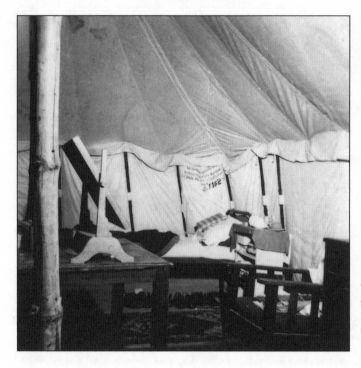

The accommodation for the members of FBS Fayid, comfortable until the sandstorms – 1950.
(© Private Photograph)

cinema usually required a party of two or three, with at least one of the FBS staff carrying a Sten gun.

There were around 100 girls in the Canal Zone and 100,000 troops: the prospect of taking one out was so remote that no one really bothered. However, the FBS broadcasters were considered "personalities". When either Alan Kumm or his colleague David Wilmott took out one of the girls, they had to sign the Army form for taking "Stores on Charge" and they had to get a receipt for the girls when they took them back to camp!

As Alan Kumm recalls: "We were luckier than most of our service colleagues, who had to endure massive boredom. We could always go into the radio station and listen to the latest records or BBC Transcriptions. At the same time, we wondered why the American forces at the Wheelus Airbase in Libya had their own base TV service, whilst we had to make do with our limited radio service."

In 1951, shortly after the arrival of Forces Broadcasting headquarters from Malta, it was decided to move the Station into a newly equipped studio block in a large Nissen hut beside the GHQ office.

At the new studios there were still no tape machines or long-playing records and a classical concert meant a pile of discs some 18 in high. The announcer's

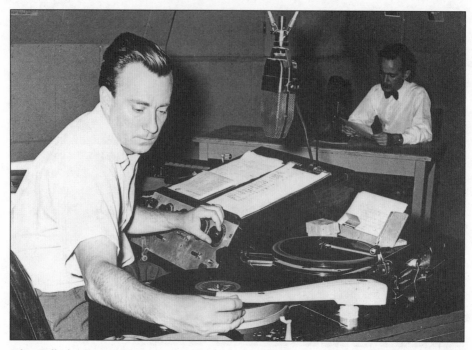

John Bull, the Senior Engineer of FBS Fayid and later Station Controller of FBS El Ballah, recording the NAAFI Newsletter with Ronald Walker – 1955.

(© Crown Copyright: FBS 883)

prime technical skill was to synchronise the overlap from one disc to the next so that the join was imperceptible. Today, it is a lost art.

For the Coronation of HM the Queen in 1953, Neville Powley put out a live broadcast of the Fayid Coronation Parade and, on the same evening, Leslie Knight returned to the studio to produce a celebratory 'Songs of Britain', which featured bands and choirs from the Canal Zone.

By then, it became clear that time was running out for the British in Egypt, following the Egyptian coup in which Colonel Nasser replaced General Neguib.

The last Fayid Station Commander was John Bull. Although John was a qualified radio engineer, he took part in many of the plays produced for Forces Broadcasting and wrote and produced his own programmes. His biggest success in this field was a series of programmes he wrote and produced for 'Children's Hour' while in Benghazi. Although written specifically for children, 'The Adventures of Captain Steele', written before the days of 'Dan Dare', was such a success with the men – and the officers – of the Command that it was syndicated for all FBS Stations in the Middle East.

This series was followed, with equal success, by 'Jack Steele - Fighting Marshal'. This second series so captured the imaginations of the service children that they invariably played out each instalment in their playgrounds after the broadcasts. "Walking home from the studios one evening," John recalled, "shortly after a programme in which I had made use of Steele's prowess with the lariat, I found one half of the children of Benghazi lassoing the other half and dragging them around the playgrounds. I dashed home and rewrote the next chapter in which there was a lynching scene. I'd had a vision of hundreds of little bodies swaying in the breeze among the trees in the playground. Even the grown-ups taking part in the programme were often carried away in their enthusiasm and it was nothing for a chair to sail through the studio window during a saloon fight. As for the fighting marshal himself, he took to riding to the studios on a horse, much to the delight of the children."

Although the programmes were very popular with the service audience, few listeners appreciated how much effort they took. As Fayid had limited sound effects discs, John and his staff spent many hours experimenting to find just the right noise for a spaceship taking off, a window breaking, a shirt tearing, a depth charge exploding and an aeroplane crashing.

Actor SAC Anton Rodgers and David 'Dad' Davis began to write a series of plays and quite happily sat up all night writing in sound effects which meant that, after closedown, everyone could have great fun breaking plates and stirring water while they recorded the plays on discs. One mistake and they had to start the whole thing again.

As always, the aim of Forces Broadcasting was to give a service to the end, and the evacuation that followed the Egyptian Coup was planned in two stages. With the help of REME, the engineers converted two teleprinter vehicles. One housed a continuity studio and control room, and the other held two small transmitters. Once more they were back to the, by now familiar, routine of stripping the equipment and packing. The route out of Egypt gave rise to one notorious BFBS story of how Bill Mitchell, in one of the lorries, managed to add one-third of the record library to the garbage in the Sweetwater Canal.

In August 1955, John Bull published his plans for the redeployment of No 3 FBS from Fayid to the Omar Camp at El Ballah. The move began on October 11th when Bill Mitchell, the programme organiser, and Phil Harding, the senior engineer, left with the librarian to set up the Mobile Unit. With many of the civilian announcers already posted to other stations, No 3 FBS recruited National Servicemen to help them stay on air until the final closedown. Among the announcers were Lance Corporal Mike Danvers-Walker who presented 'Ask For Another', the evening request programme, and David Griffiths, another Lance Corporal, who specialised in serious music and magazine programmes. Phil

Harding, who had already presented a series of evening programmes called 'Rendezvous', was in charge of both the programme and engineering side of the new Mobile Station. While all this was going on, back in Fayid the team was dismantling the old studio system and preparing for equipment to be packed and despatched to other FBS stations.

FBS Fayid finally closed in 1955 and the Mobile Unit at El Ballah took over, ending its operation at Port Said in March 1956. When the Mobile Station's studio trucks were shipped to Cyprus, Fayid had become part of FBS history.

Three thousand miles away from the hot sun of Egypt, BFN Hamburg's Musikhalle was the jewel in the Forces Broadcasting crown. However, things were about to change for the members of BFN Hamburg and their audience in Germany. On 12th March, 1950 Leslie Perowne, Station Director of BFN Hamburg, wrote the following for the front cover of the BFN Bulletin:

"BFN has not packed up, nor is it going to pack up, but it has altered its face a bit. Why? Because of the Copenhagen Plan. The Copenhagen Plan is an international allotment of wavelengths to broadcasting stations throughout Europe. At the conference at which the plan was formulated it was decided that BFN would have to share the same wavelength as the BBC Light Programme.

"This, in effect, means that BFN will radiate its own originated programmes from 06.30 until approximately one hour before sunset in Germany; then it will rebroadcast the BBC Light Programme until summertime is introduced in England.

Because of BFN being unable to originate any of its own programmes during the evening hours, many of your favourite programmes have had to be moved to new times during the day.

"Nobody regrets these changes more than we do but we feel sure you appreciate their inevitability. We know, however, that we can count on you for your loyal support and that you will continue to listen to BFN, your radio service."

The BFN schedules now had to absorb the BBC's Light Programme output. In winter, the BBC relay began at 3.00 p.m. The first casualty of this move was BFN Hamburg's most popular request programme 'The 1700 Club', which had started in 1946 and had now disappeared from the programme schedule. In its place was the BBC's long running radio serial 'Mrs Dale's Diary'. It was not long before the complaints arrived on Leslie Perowne's desk, including one letter which asked the question: "When is this woman going to die?" There was relief when the summer months saw a curtailing of the time given over to the BBC

Light Programme (the join was now 6.00 p.m.). One BFN announcer was heard to remark when he opened up the '1700 Club': "The body of Mrs. Dale now lies in peace."

Demobilisation was beginning to cause another major problem for BFN. No sooner had a serviceman settled in, than it was time for him to return to the UK. As a result, advertisements inviting servicemen and women to apply for an audition were being distributed in Germany and the UK. Many applied and among those chosen were Tim Gudgin and Bill Utting.

Working for BFN in the early Fifties meant putting in a six-and-a-half day week and Gunner Bill Utting recorded in his diary that in one month he did 16 continuity shifts, produced and presented three 'Services Cinema' programmes, introduced two military band concerts, took part in four feature programmes, two plays, presented two 'Early Bird' record programmes and continued to write and record 'Morning Story'.

In the autumn of 1950, Leslie Perowne came under considerable pressure from the listeners, who still did not understand why BFN had to relay the BBC Light Programme from one hour before sunset to closedown. Once more he chose to write an editorial for the BFN Bulletin: "When once we have gone over to the Light programme, we are unable even so much as to make an announcement at our own microphones, let alone (as some people suggest) relay the Home Service or the Third Programme. So please don't ring us up to complain that we are not broadcasting a rugby international from the Home Service at 16.15 hours on a Saturday afternoon or ask why you have to endure 'Woman's Hour'. It's all part of the Copenhagen Plan and once again we assure you there is nothing we can do about it."

As well as dealing with listeners' complaints over this issue, Leslie Perowne became enmeshed in a battle with the Security Services of BAOR.

On 19th May, 1950, the Daily Telegraph carried a small item about the Duke of Gloucester taking the salute at a parade of 10th Hussars in Iserlohn. BFN were invited to cover the parade and were due to broadcast the edited highlights the following day. However, they were instructed by the Security Services that on no account should mention be made of the Duke of Gloucester's presence in Iserlohn.

Perowne immediately sent a letter to the Adjutant General's Office asking why, when PR Rhine Army had given a press handout with all the details of the regiment and its location to the BBC, Nord West Deutchse Rundfunk (NWDR) and the local press, was BFN to be excluded? "As a result, we have a state of affairs where the Press, the BBC and the German Radio may say (and probably have said) the location of this parade and yet the Services own radio station may not mention it."

Inside the studio of FBS Klagenfurt with Corporal Strawford in the studio and 2nd Lieutenant Peter Bulmer and Corporal Crowest in the control room.   *(© Private Photograph)*

This was not the first time that the Security Services had clashed with Leslie Perowne over what they saw as lack of security in broadcasting by BFN. They were unhappy that requests were played for servicemen which gave away their unit and sometimes location. Their suggestion was that BFN should limit the information to "Private Snooks of the RASC serving in Germany".

Perowne pointed out that, as every unit had outside its barrack gates a large regimental sign, usually embellished with battle honours, he had no doubt that the Russians knew exactly who was where.

Further pressure was applied to Leslie Perowne on 19th December, 1950 when he received a letter from a Colonel Fraser, saying BAFO (British Air Forces of Occupation) had complained to the Air Ministry over the extravagant staffing of BFN and that they were proposing to take away BFN's only RAF officer, Flight Lieutenant Don East. Perowne wrote to Colonel John Pemberton of Army Welfare saying that the complaint had originated in a report from Squadron Leader Roy, Command Welfare Officer, BAFO, who had said publicly that: (a) he never listened to BFN; (b) he disliked BFN and all that it stands for; and (c) he had never visited BFN.

Years later, Leslie Perowne was still of the opinion that the RAF, having lost their battle in 1948 to turn BFN Hamburg into a local form of the BBC's Third Programme, had decided to add to the delicate situation.

The effect of the Copenhagen Plan was demoralizing the staff, especially as BFN was not broadcasting during peak time and the talk of redundancies made many of the German staff very worried.

It was no secret that Army Welfare in BAOR (British Army of the Rhine) was already looking at ways of saving money by reducing BFN to nothing more than a BBC Light Programme Relay Station broadcasting local news and weather, directly responsible to the Command in an emergency.

The number of staff at BFN Hamburg was to be reduced to 32, both British and German, and several of the broadcasters felt it was time to move on. Chris Howland left to pursue a career with German radio and television, Neville Powley, Hedley Chambers and Jack Pickering joined FBS stations in the Middle East, Don Moss moved on to Austria, whilst Alastair McDougall, Tim Gudgin and Ron Balaam began their association with FBS Trieste.

When Don Moss arrived in Austria, he discovered that many of his fellow broadcasters, instead of eating in their official military quarters, had gone native. They had discovered the food from the Gasthaus on the bottom floor of their studio block was excellent, but it led one day to Don Moss's downfall. He was late on shift and rushed into the studio carrying a bottle of beer and the largest ham roll that the Gasthaus could provide. He was presenting a record request show and, while the music was going out, he had time to snatch a mouthful of food. Unfortunately, one disc ended rather abruptly and he tried to read out the next request through a mouthful of ham and bread. His muffled performance was overheard by the local Commander who complained to Ron Icke, the Station Commander of BFN Austria. Don was banished from the airwaves for the next two weeks.

In the early Fifties, BFN Austria opened a small station at RAF Zeltweg just outside Vienna. The organisation's representative was a most unsoldierly-like character, Dick Geilgud, a shy, ungainly young man, who was overshadowed by his father Val Geilgud, Head of BBC Drama, and his even more distinguished uncle Sir John, the actor. On reporting to the Commanding Officer, Dick carried out a guards-like halt and, as he went to salute, his feet slipped from under him and he slid straight under the CO's desk.

The Austrian network in 1953 was grossly understaffed. For one whole summer, Pat Pachebat, Willis Toogood and Gerald Sinstadt were the entire broadcasting staff of BFN Graz and, on more than one occasion, they slept behind the record racks in the library and opened the station in the morning and closed it down at night.

Gerald Sinstadt found Austria gave him a chance to indulge his love of opera and, as the Opera House was just across the road from the studio and the broadcasters were given a special half-price concession for the performances, he spent many a happy hour listening to some of Europe's finest opera stars. He became so friendly with the opera company that on one occasion he was allowed to take part as a soldier in 'Aida'. Leaning his spear against a piece of scenery to get a better view, Gerald was so fascinated by what was happening on stage, he forgot to reclaim it. As the soldiers marched off, the audience could see, quite clearly, one spear leaning against the set. Gerald was not invited to take part again!

The staff of BFN Austria received a crate of new records every two months. This was a great event in their lives and all the programme staff would sit up late into the night playing every side of every disc and deciding which programmes they should appear in. It gave the young announcers an almost encyclopaedic knowledge of the record library.

PRE-ELECTION BROADCAST

RELAYED BY FORCES BROADCASTING SERVICE AUSTRIA

TUNE IN AT THE FOLLOWING TIMES

DAY	DATE	TIME From	TIME To	SPEAKER	PARTY
SUNDAY	OCT. 7th	1745	1815	RT: HON: HERBERT MORRISON	LABOUR
TUESDAY	" 9th	1745	1815	" " WINSTON CHURCHILL	CONSERVATIVE
WEDNESDAY	" 10th	1345	1355	MR DINGLE FOOT	LIBERAL
THURSDAY	" 11th	1745	1805	MR JAMES GRIFFITH	LABOUR
FRIDAY	" 12th	1745	1805	MISS HORNSBY SMITH	CONSERVATIVE
SATURDAY	" 13th	1345	1355	MR JOSEPH GRIMOND	LIBERAL
SUNDAY	" 14th	1745	1805	LORD WOOLTON	CONSERVATIVE
TUESDAY	" 16th	1745	1805	MR RICHARD STOKES	LABOUR
WEDNESDAY	" 17th	1745	1805	A CONSERVATIVE SPEAKER	
THURSDAY	" 18th	1745	1805	MISS MARGARET HERBISON	LABOUR
FRIDAY	" 19th	1745	1805	MR FRANK BYERS	LIBERAL
SATURDAY	" 20th	1745	1815	A CONSERVATIVE SPEAKER	-
SUNDAY	" 21st	1745	1815	RT: HON: CLEMENT ATLEE P.M.	LABOUR

KEEP THIS HANDY BY YOUR RADIO

A pre-election broadcast schedule of FBS Austria – 1951.

(© BFBS Archive)

The announcers often slept on the station. Pat Pachebat recalls the time when Gerald Sinstadt failed to turn up for the breakfast programme and Pat, still in his pyjamas, managed to get the station on air on time. Unfortunately, he made reference to his attire and this was overheard by the Chief of Staff. "Looking back, I think I was very lucky to be given another chance," he said. Pat was more fortunate than Lance Corporal Eddie Barnes, who later became the Head of BBC TV's Children's programmes. He too had overslept and greeted the Padre, unwashed, unshaven and in his dressing gown. The Padre complained and Eddie was so annoyed that, when the Padre's five-minute slot under-ran by almost two minutes, he filled in with 'Jiving with Jarvis' by the King Cole Trio. He was immediately posted back to his unit.

By now it was becoming clear that the Four Power Control of Austria was coming to an end and that the British troops would be withdrawn. Many outsiders, including members of the Queen Alexandra's Nursing Corps, took part in programmes including a studio version of Ivor Novello's 'Kings Rhapsody' - using discs for the songs with the broadcasters and volunteers speaking the dialogue.

In 1954, Tony Wheatley was moved from Trieste to supervise the eventual closedown of BFN Austria. As the British troops left, with only the Middlesex Regiment remaining to tour every Austrian village and town where the British had built up good relations, the nucleus of Forces Broadcasting moved back to Klagenfurt, setting up headquarters in Mobile Studios. In 1955, the Russians finally withdrew from Eastern Austria and on 25 September, BFN Austria made its last broadcast. Then the records were packed and the equipment crated for BFN in Germany. For the staff of BFN Austria, it was time to move on.

In 1950, Guy Thomas was called up for his National Service with the Royal Corps of Signals. Having worked at the BBC for a few months after leaving school, he had heard about Forces Radio and decided when he went to sign on that he would ask to be posted to an FBS station. The major, who was conducting the interview, said: "Ah, yes, but I'm afraid broadcasting is for officers and gentlemen." Yet when Guy applied for a position at the BBC after two years at FBS, the personnel officer dismissed his experience in Trieste: "Forces Broadcasting? Enthusiastic amateurs."

Like most Forces stations of the period, equipment was primitive. Trieste had a combined studio/control room trailer parked in the magnificent gardens of Villa Triste so that you stepped out of the French windows into the van. This was the original B6/B4 that had slogged through Italy. A big drama and music studio known as Studio A was set up in the old ballroom and a tiny one-man emergency studio, 'D', was built on the attic floor. The latter was designed to provide a service in times of trouble, but was used mainly as an early morning and late-night studio. Though nobody realised it at the time, this was a predecessor of the present-day self-operated studio.

The military intention was that, in the event of a riot, one or two broadcasters would take refuge in the attic studio with a pile of records and access to the BBC General Overseas Service. There, completely independent of the main control room, they would continue a service to the British Forces in Trieste while the remaining broadcasters put up a gallant fight below, making use of the rifles that most had not seen since they arrived in the city.

For many, it was their first taste of an opulent way of life that was non-existent in Britain. In Trieste's trattorias, ristorantes and nightclubs, with their plentiful food and drink, it was hard to realise that, technically, the Italians were the defeated nation.

Usually, there was not much time for nightlife. Whatever the establishment on paper, numbers were constantly below strength and, at one period, the station was run by Ian Woolf with a station sergeant and four other ranks, plus Italian technicians covering around 18 hours daily. A typical day might begin with 'Early Call' at 6.30 a.m. followed by a journey into town to proof read 'The Announcer', (The Trieste Radio Times). This was remembered as a tough job. Especially if the proof-reader had limited knowledge of the printing trade and not much Italian with which to communicate with the local type-setters. Then it was back for the lunchtime continuity shift followed by an afternoon trip to the Field Hospital to collect record requests for the 'Hospital Special' show. This then led to another continuity shift around 8.00 p.m. In the late evening, the studio would still be going strong with a phone-in request programme until midnight, or a musical miscellany played by the Venezia Guilia Police Band, or a visit to the Opera, or a nightclub.

The Trieste service had almost no money, few experienced broadcasters, and little equipment: the entire OB microphone stock was one BBC ribbon mike with 85 ft of cable and one Ferrograph tape recorder. What the Station did have was cohesion - because in its relatively short life span most of the staff knew each other. They overlapped because many did both a National Service and a civilian tour. It also had talent!

The staff argued programme ideas at weekly or quarterly programme meetings. "We had one meeting that went on for two days," Ian Woolf remembered. His policy was to encourage everyone to submit their own ideas and produce their own programmes.

"We made it up as we went along," was Brian Tesler's description. "Ian let us do anything as long as it worked out reasonably well." It may appear very unlike

Guy Thomas, FBS Trieste – 1950. *(© Crown Copyright: FBS 1059)*

The weekly programme meeting in the Villa Triste at FBS Trieste. This was to be one of Ian Woolf's last meetings before he moved to Nairobi, among those attending were Alan Parfrey, John Dienn, Ian Fenner, and Ronald Balaam, immediately to Ian Woolf's right is his successor, Tony Wheatley – 1954. *(© Crown Copyright: FBS 1060)*

a professional programme policy, but in fact the station was giving the British troops their first taste of 'free' radio, a format that was later adopted by the pirate and local stations.

To an extent, the broadcasters were 'doing their own thing', making the sort of programmes that they wanted to make. No one knew whether the average soldier appreciated a poetry programme, but they had one. More certain was the success of the comedy series 'Laugh with your Luncheon', which the station wrote as a team. It was performed by Michael Baguley, John Jacob, Ian Fenner, Brian Tesler and Richard Fraser-Harris.

Among the more outrageous exploits were the stunts brewed by Brian Tesler, John Jacob and engineer, Johnny Rothwell. On one occasion, Tesler and Rothwell hid with a transmitter in a hillside cave overlooking the city and challenged listeners to find them before the records ran out. A contingent of Military Police found the pair, as though on cue, about seven minutes before the end of the hour-long programme. That particular scheme was not repeated. The military were not amused because every spare jeep in Trieste had been commandeered to scour the hillside.

In another stunt, the Tesler, Jacob, Rothwell team dreamed up the idea of a fake parachute drop scripted and compiled in a studio. As Brian Tesler gave his airborne commentary, Johnny Rothwell inadvertently cut the engine effects. Amid the ensuing panic, Brian Tesler said: "There's only one thing to do, climb out on the wing and drop into the harbour." He completed the 'drop' with commentary and an authentic splash then, as John Jacob prepared to fade the programme, the studio phone rang. At the other end was a crisp voice: "Captain Roberts here. I've a launch in the harbour. Can we be of any help?" The station had been certain that everyone would know that the stunt had been a jape but the episode illustrates the involvement of the listeners, and the broadcasters fostered the idea for servicemen and families that it was 'their' radio service.

They initiated a phone-in request programme and a phone-in crossword when anything of the sort was completely foreign to the BBC and around 20 years before local radio thought of the idea. In the attic studio before midnight, calls to Trieste 95908 jammed the lines.

At the time, the wartime tradition of top artistes giving their services to the forces was still much alive and many of them came out under arrangements with Combined Services Entertainment. All of them were invited to FBS and appeared to enjoy the experience. Gracie Fields was one of the those who came to be interviewed in studio A, the onetime ballroom at Villa Triste, as well as Music Hall stars Ethel Revnell and Joan Turner. The Old Vic Theatre sent out their first post war European tour with a production of 'Twelfth Night', which

John Jacob, Brian Tesler and Johnny Rothwell, FBS Trieste – 1952.

(© Crown Copyright: FBS 1076)

included performances at Trieste's Opera House, the Teatro Communale Guiseppe Verdi. The stars were Celia Johnson, Roger Livesey and Ursula Jeans, all of whom gave up a planned summer visit to the beach so that they could recall some hilarious memories of the Theatre and Films. Joining them on this tour was the Shakespearian actor Ernest Milton, who stayed even longer at the Station, revelling in recording some of the speeches from the great plays. However, best remembered was Tessie O'Shea who arrived with a large entourage. Too late, the staff discovered that when they had departed so too had all the station ashtrays, borne away as souvenirs. Even Maria Callas visited the villa after her historic first performance in the Verdi Opera House in the city. It is a measure of the War Office parsimony that it carped at the cost of recording her, claiming that she could have easily been broadcast 'from a record'.

There had always been a history of politics by riot in Trieste, brought about by the city's origins. It had been part of the Austro-Hungarian Empire until the end of the First World War when it was ceded to Italy and some of that empire had become the new state of Yugoslavia so the Yugoslavs continued to make claims to the city. As the war in Southern Europe drew to a close, the German Commander in Trieste, with limited forces, had two choices. He could defend it against British and American troops or fight the Yugoslavs. He chose the latter but the Yugoslav partisans attacked, gaining two-thirds of the city through house-to-house fighting and paying dearly in blood. The Germans surrendered to the British and Americans, but both Italians and Yugoslavs believed that they owned Trieste.

This led to periods of acute political tension in the early days of 1946 and 1947 and later in 1952.

In a curious way, the station found itself isolated from the strife and many of the staff wondered why they were learning more about the troubles in the city only half a mile below them from the BBC than at first hand. But in October 1953, there was no ignoring the political reality. Sir Anthony Eden announced that the 'running sore' of Trieste had to be cured and the British Military must pull out of Zone A. In March 1954 the GOC, Sir John Winterton, decreed that the British troops would evacuate within five days and the families would go immediately. The broadcasters disconnected the trailer, stripped studio A, waved goodbye to their families, shipped off some of the record library (the Americans were not so far-sighted and tipped theirs into the sea) and relied solely on the self-operated studio D in the attic.

The evacuation plans were short-lived. Both Italians and Yugoslavs were making warlike noises, moving troops up on either side and the British and Americans realised that war would break out if they departed. The troops remained and the broadcasting station climbed back to full production.

But the heart had gone out of it. Wives and families had left and the tension heightened a sense of insecurity in the civilian staff, already working on contracts that gave all the advantages to the Crown. Morale was bad, but the War Office had told Ian Woolf to keep the station going as long as it was needed.

On the working side, they devised time-consuming exercises such as a series on 'Trieste by Night', looking at the sort of street cleaning, bakery and printing jobs that filled the dark hours. Using their Ferrograph recorder, the project occupied many weeks, while Guy Thomas and Geoffrey Noakes embarked on a history of the city.

Totally apolitical, it attempted to give the servicemen something of the background and history of the place in which they were serving.

In October, 1954, after a political agreement had been reached for Trieste, evacuation became a reality. Everything had to go and at 9 p.m. the BBC news was heard for the last time. Three minutes later, Ian Fenner shinned up the mast and cut the aerials and the staff spent most of the night shuttling equipment between the transmitter and the villa.

Next morning Trieste was at its most beautiful. Ronald Balaam had saved a little grappa from a holiday in Yugoslavia. As the sun came up, he stood at his bedroom window and then poured the last of the fiery liquid into a tiny glass. "I drank to the sunrise, I drank to the station, I drank to Trieste and then I flung the glass out of the window."

There are no reports of engineers or programme staff cutting the aerials at BFN Hamburg or of staff taking one last glass of schnapps as a toast to the old station when it closed. However, BFN's move to its new location was planned with all the precision of a military exercise.

Dennis Scuse, who replaced David Porter as Station Director, had realized that BFN's Hamburg days were numbered. "Plans were being discussed to move the British Headquarters administration to the other side of the Rhine. As it looked as though we would have to move, I suggested that BFN should take advantage of the new German radio system called VHF: instead of getting rid of all our staff, we could continue to fulfil our role and provide a better service. Once we had

Dennis Scuse and Bill Crozier on stage for a concert in Rheindhalen – 1956.

(© Crown Copyright: FBS 487)

decided to move from Hamburg, the problem was where? In the end, the solution was literally under our nose. When our Technical Officer, Pip Duke, and I went to Cologne, we stayed in the Civilian Officers' Mess in Parkstrasse. It suddenly dawned on me that this splendid house would make an excellent studio centre and it would give us all the broadcasting facilities we required. The main drawback was that, by itself, it wasn't large enough to provide all the necessary offices and storage accommodation that we needed. However, luck was on our side because at the bottom of the garden there was a similar large house which had been used as an Officers' Mess and, if we could have the two, we would have exactly the right amount of accommodation. After a few enquiries, and a certain amount of discussion, it was agreed we could have both buildings."

Several months before the move, new staff were employed in Cologne and sent to Hamburg for training. The Military suggested BFN Hamburg should close down on 31 December 1953 and reopen the following day in Cologne. The idea was rejected by Dennis Scuse because his small staff would be working non-stop over the Christmas period and he felt it would be unfair to ask them to undertake a major move as well.

With exactly one month to go before BFN Cologne came on air, Alastair McDougall and Eric Hamer were sent to the new studios to begin the programme integration. They found they had one chair, one desk and one telephone. The idea was that Alastair would introduce the housewives' programme called 'For You At Home' 'live' from the Cologne studio, but without making reference to its new location. The requests were still going to Hamburg and were being sent by express post to Cologne. In order to cope with any last-minute delays, the programme, which was normally on air from 9.10 to 10 a.m., was now going out one hour later.

The last programme to come from BFN Hamburg was introduced by Bill Crozier, but Dennis Scuse made the closing announcement. The next day, the rest of the team set off for the new station in Cologne leaving behind a host of memories.

On 26 February, 1954, BFN Cologne opened its new studios in Marienburg with the same announcement BFN Hamburg had used eight and a half years earlier, "This is the British Forces Network". The honour of making the official opening announcement fell, not to Sgt Gordon Crier, who had long since returned to the BBC, but to John Mead. As Dennis Scuse, the Station Controller of BFN Cologne, remarked: "In Hamburg, the opening announcement came from a studio which had once been a dressing room used by world famous conductors in the Musikhalle; now we were using a room which, up until six months ago, had been a bedroom in a beautiful house on the outskirts of Cologne."

Ingrid Lloyd and Gunter Meyer-Goldenstadt in the recording cubicle of a studio, BFN Cologne – 1955. *(© Crown Copyright: FBS 398)*

The last BFN Bulletin of 1955 announced the arrival of VHF. For several years BFN had been broadcasting on 247 metres in the medium waveband but from January 1st, 1956, it would be heard only on VHF. The editorial explained: "The biggest argument against VHF is that some initial financial outlay is required on the part of the individual in equipping himself with a set capable of receiving these broadcasts. To offset this, official sets have already been issued and the majority of our listeners who live in barracks should be able to receive us. For those of you who do not live in barracks, a special scheme has been arranged by Headquarters Northern Army Group whereby you can purchase a very good model for a very reasonable price. There is no doubt at all that VHF broadcasting has come to stay and the BBC is already broadcasting on VHF in the London area and soon this coverage will spread through all England. For these reasons, by equipping yourself with a receiver capable of receiving VHF, you will in fact be ahead of the majority of people in the United Kingdom."

Dennis Scuse remained with BFN until December 1957 when he was succeeded by Ian Woolf, whose previous Forces Broadcasting experience had been in Italy and Kenya. He said: "When I took over on January 1st, 1958, I visualized that my contribution to BFN would include improving its programme-gathering reach, improving reception of the BBC on which we depended totally for world news and comment, improving the lot of the German staff, whom I felt to be rather left out of things, and setting up audience research. The latter proved a tall order because it called for extra money and effort. Naturally, neither was available and there were doubters who argued that audience research was a frill BFN could do without." As Ian quickly found out, there were many who felt that BFN's role should be to educate the troops. He explained that BFN's mission required them first to entertain, second to inform and third to educate. "As I repeatedly pointed out, unless we first capture the audience (by entertaining it) we could hardly hope to be able to inform or educate it." Ian argued that a second reason for mounting good audience research was that it provided first class ammunition with which to convince BFN's backers – the War Office, Treasury and its agencies – that money spent on broadcasting was money well spent.

On February 20th, 1958, Headquarters BAOR re-issued the 1955 BFN Peacetime Charter. Ian Woolf was informed that BFN had to provide a satisfactory news service to include, wherever possible, a direct relay of the BBC News and items of local news. It was required to broadcast local weather reports and provide servicemen with spiritual and general education. BFN's role was also to provide its listeners with entertainment, making full use of a simultaneous

David Hamilton in A studio BFN Cologne – 1959.   (© *Crown Copyright: FBS 400*)

re-broadcast of the BBC programme and BBC Transcription Service recordings. Finally, it was to originate only such other programmes, at no additional expense, as could be accomplished by the minimum staff necessary for the above tasks and the functions required in an emergency.

At the time, BFN staff was too small to meet any extra programme commitments. In 1958 there was a total of 12 civilians and two RAF attachments. They were expected to broadcast for 120 hours a week. This left little manpower to dream up, compile, script, produce and present the 60 odd hours which had to be provided from BFN's own resources.

In 1951, the broadcasting service had been split, on the orders of the Army Council, with the Director of Signals responsible for the technical side while the Adjutant General looked after programmes and staff recruitment. In 1958, a paper from the Executive Committee of the Army Council accepted that Forces Broadcasting needed to be controlled by one department and in 1960, Jack Knott was seconded from the BBC to produce a report, which would later become the foundation of the British Forces Broadcasting Service.

If BFN Cologne felt it had staffing problems, they was nothing compared to the difficulties faced by the men trying to run broadcasting in North Africa.

Towards the end of 1954, the run-down of British Forces in Tripoli itself and, to use a well-worn army cliché, the exigencies of the service, decreed that FBS in Tripoli should close down. Tripoli's Station Commander and his staff were all at an air show when word came: "You've got to pull out by the end of the week." Steps were taken and plans were made for the posting of personnel and the dismantling of the equipment. When news of this reached the Libyan authorities, and it was realised that the closing of FBS meant also the closedown of the Libyan Broadcasting Service provided by FBS, consternation reigned and is understood to have reached as high as the King himself. Sufficient to say, FBS Tripoli was reprieved for a further three months. This respite, together with changed conditions, allowed for a reappraisal of the closedown and it was decided that FBS Tripoli should stay.

During those three months of doubt and uncertainty, many FBS staff went to fresh appointments, local employees found more certain occupations and the staff shortage became acute. Peter Holwill and Gordon Mills came from FBS Fayid to keep the station on air.

Things ran smoothly until the Suez Canal crisis in October 1956, when families were evacuated. FBS Tripoli maintained a 24-hour short wave link with District Headquarters, which enabled them to reach all families in their homes prior to their evacuation. Though the service had been involved in the 'Beetle

Internal Security Exercise' in Palestine in 1948, this was the first time they had broadcast instructions to British and other expatriate civilians to come into the barracks and their value under such circumstances was clearly demonstrated.

Although British troops from Libya were not deployed in the invasion, they were, after all, in the country next-door and there was a great deal of local ill-will. Pat Pachebat, who was running FBS Benghazi at the time, remembers a particular incident: "One evening I was on late shift and when I arrived at the station the next morning I found incredible activity all around FBS. In the early hours, a bomb had been detonated at the transmitter site. We had no home telephones in those days so, although I was in charge, I was actually the last to know about it. Luckily, most of the blast went outwards and there was very little internal damage, certainly not enough to put us off the air."

The local insect population caused a number of problems for those who served in North Africa in the Fifties. When Peter Kirby was living in Tripoli he became fascinated by some little 'lobster-like' creatures, which he fed with breadcrumbs and which were becoming quite tame. When he mentioned this to some of the old hands, they pointed out that he had been helping to nurture a brood of scorpions. If the staff went to the local AKC cinema, there was a ritual stop in the foyer after the film while they removed the bugs, which had been hiding under the cinema seats, from each other's arms.

Back in Benghazi, the problem turned out to be bees! At first, the announcer heard just an occasional buzz when the microphone was 'live', as a bee zipped by. But, after several days of increasing activity, it was actually quite dangerous to be on duty in the studio with dozens of them flying around. Pat Pachebat called for help and recruited an amateur beekeeper who knocked down part of the studio wall and captured the hive and most of the bees in a huge sack. "I was then tasked with putting this sack of angrily buzzing bees in the boot of my little Morris Minor and driving to the outskirts of Benghazi where I handed the sack over to a commercial beekeeper. It was not a pleasant experience driving for some 15 minutes with hundreds of bees buzzing like crazy just four feet away."

For the engineers in Tripoli, trying to keep the station on air could be a daunting task. Much of the equipment was very old. In his report in 1956, Leslie Knight noted: "In both Tripoli and Benghazi, up-to-date gramophone records and transcriptions cannot be broadcast owing to the fact that there is no long-playing equipment available."

The recording studio had the worst acoustic that Harry Deadman, a recently arrived engineer from Britain, had ever heard. The reason was simple. It had a quarry-tiled floor so any recording there echoed as though it had been made in a large bathroom. The answer to the problem was a carpet and an indent was sent to the Quartermaster's store for one to cover the studio floor. The first reaction from the QM was: "Who uses the studio?" When he was told the announcers and engineers of FBS Tripoli, he remarked: "They only have Warrant Officer status and as such, are not entitled to carpets." Therefore he would be sending round some linoleum. After much argument, it was agreed a carpet would be supplied, but it took two years and two more indents before a 10-ton lorry appeared with three carpets! Harry Deadman became an expert carpet fitter overnight.

The humidity in North Africa was very trying for the staff in Tripoli and Benghazi and when the 'Ghibli', the scorching wind of North Africa blew, it coated everything with red sand. Every time anyone took a record out of the library rack, it was covered in a layer of gritty sand so the first rule a newcomer learned was to put the open end of the inner envelope at the bottom of the record sleeve. Although the outer cover would still be caked in dust, there was a fair chance that the disc inside would be playable.

In the early Fifties, German civilians were arriving in North Africa to fill skilled posts where Arab labour was not available. Soon, there were more than 1,200 in Benghazi. It was therefore agreed that a German section of the FBS Station should be established. Money was provided from the German welfare funds and the FBS technicians, with the assistance of the Germans themselves, rapidly established a

Anton Markfort, one of the former German POWs broadcasting to the German workers in North Africa from FBS Benghazi.   *(© Crown Copyright: FBS 900)*

small studio. Broadcasts in German began in June 1951 on a separate frequency and transmitter from 6.00 p.m. to 10.00 p.m. each day. The service proved very popular with the Germans as it was one of their very few relaxations.

In 1953, the FBS staff were putting the final touches to their Christmas programmes when the Technical Officer spotted what appeared to be a vast river crossing the neighbouring plain and heading straight for the station. He realised there had been a cloud burst on the mountains and the 'Wadi' had burst its banks. Within minutes, the engineers, with the aid of a large bag of cotton waste, managed to stop most of the water from entering the front of the building. The station had been scheduled to go on air at 12.30 p.m. and was already running half an hour late. A rapid examination of the transmitters and technical equipment was made and, after much mopping up, they were declared capable of working. The next problem was the mains supply. An emergency generator was just 20 yards away from the studio building and standing on a plinth five feet high and therefore, clear of the flood water. The cable which connected the generator to the studios was flooded and a German technician called Heinz swam to the generator towing another cable, which he managed to connect, putting FBS Benghazi back on the air. As the whole area was flooded, the next problem was to get the staff to and from the station. The FBS Benghazi duty driver took the Outside Broadcast vehicle and drove to the record library window, where the duty announcer managed to scramble into the back. This process of delivery – by what was known affectionately as Benghazi's Gin Palace – continued for three days, thus ensuring a normal Christmas programme for the Garrison.

In 1958, the Ministry of Defence decided that the Garrisons in Cyrenaica should be closed down and in June that year FBS Benghazi gave its last transmission after 12 years of uninterrupted broadcasting to the troops in the area.

However, due to a change of policy, it was decided to keep the Garrison in Benghazi and a small FBS station headed by Stan Challoner was once again established in 1960 to continue broadcasting to the British Forces in Libya.

Following the failure of HQ FBS Middle East to provide a satisfactory short-wave service to the smaller stations in the Middle East, it left Malta in 1951 and moved to Egypt.

It was late in 1953 that Lord Mountbatten, then Commander-in-Chief, Mediterranean Fleet, doubtless recalling his earlier success as Fleet Wireless Officer, Mediterranean, in relaying the late King George V's Christmas Message to the Empire, decided that the fleet should have its own VHF radio station. Their reception of the General Overseas Service of the BBC was poor and, therefore, frequency changes were necessary.

Neville Powley with Donald Peers by
the FBS Canal Zone sign – 1953.
(© Crown Copyright: FBS 899)

The Fleet Electrical Officer, Captain Robinson, had the task of setting up what became known as the Mediterranean Fleet Broadcasting Service (MFBS). The transmitter was situated on the roof of the Castille and the studio in Lascaris Ditch. The fleet's receivers were modified to receive music and the shore establishments had a service by landline. MFBS borrowed a spare FBS record library from Tripoli (40,000 discs) and Captain Lapper, Mountbatten's Assistant Secretary, with his wife's help, set up an indexed record library. The BBC sent them transcriptions of plays and such well-known programmes as 'Hancock's Half Hour'.

They had no producers and operated the equipment themselves. Lord Louis took a great personal interest in MFBS. When he left Malta, he broadcast a farewell message to the fleet from the studio in Lascaris Ditch.

Eventually, FBS came back to Malta in 1959 but, in the meantime, the volunteers of MFBS had filled the broadcasting gap. They admitted it was hard work but very enjoyable.

When the Malta headquarters closed in 1951, Wendy Barnes arrived in Cyprus as programme organiser. To young National Servicemen such as Ted King and

Irving Dee, she was not only the fount of all broadcasting knowledge but also a sort of elder sister. Their respect did not protect her from practical jokes however. The ground around the studio at Lakatamia was free-grazing for goats and when Wendy Barnes played 'Jingle Bells' for her Christmas children's show, the bells of the herd outside mingled with the music, more so when Ted King and Irving Dee pushed one into the studio. The terrified creature leapt on the continuity desk and came to a full stop on the record, which did likewise as Wendy Barnes shouted: "Get it out, get it out."

Plans were maturing to move the Station from Lakatamia into a ramshackle old house in the district of Strovolos, just outside the walled centre of Nicosia, when in 1952 the Lakatamia studio burnt down.

Fortunately, the fire did not reach the record library and, thanks to the help provided by the local villagers, a certain amount of equipment was saved. It was greatly to the credit of the FBS staff at the time that an emergency service was put into operation within 24 hours. The Station now consisted of two, mud-bricked, single storey buildings, which housed two turntables, a microphone and a salvaged transmitter. Additional equipment was rapidly moved from Headquarters FBS in the Canal Zone to Lakatamia. As the only serviceman living on the station, SAC Ted King found himself giving evidence before a court of enquiry into the fire, which appeared to have been caused by a cigarette end dropped during a studio party. The court exonerated him from any blame.

The building at Strovolos in Nicosia that housed No 4, FBS Cyprus – 1952

(© Crown Copyright: FBS 963)

Alan Kumm in the studios of FBS
Kato Lakatamia – 1951.
(© Crown Copyright: FBS 1364)

At the time, most of the staff agreed that the fire was a blessing because it accelerated the move into Nicosia.

The new Station was about two kilometres from the old Metaxas Square, located just off Dem Severis Avenue. It was a couple of hundred metres from Government House, the Governor's Residence (now the Presidential Palace). It was incredible that during the strife that gripped Cyprus from 1955-1959, FBS Cyprus, so close to the political core, came out generally unscathed. One theory was that No. 4 FBS was left alone because it was rumoured one of the Greek Cypriot studio technicians was a member of EOKA. Another, and perhaps more fanciful theory was that, because FBS broadcast the most up-to-date music on the island, and many of the EOKA supporters were keen listeners, they might have been alienated if FBS had been forced off the air. In fact, barbed wire and sandbags, typical symbols of a State of Emergency, were rarely, if ever, seen at FBS Cyprus.

In September 1953, Cyprus suffered a major earthquake in the Paphos area in which 40 people died. Bob Egby was on duty that morning and recalls the moment it happened. "I was on the early morning continuity shift playing 78 rpm records and giving five-minute time checks and our engineer Bob

MacDonald, was having trouble in getting our receivers tuned to the BBC. As a result, we missed the 6.00 a.m. BBC News Relay. Suddenly the earth moved, as if a giant hand was underneath the building. The lights started swinging, the water in the fire bucket slopped back and forth and a general feeling of panic broke out. 'Earthquake', yelled Bob MacDonald. In a flash he disappeared. I ran outside and experienced a complete feeling of helplessness as the ground heaved and fell. For 35 seconds it continued but it seemed like an age. Returning to the studio, I found the record was still playing and I casually announced 'If you are wondering what all that was about, we are too − Oh, yes, its 10 minutes after six o'clock'. Was it too flippant? I felt so at the time. No one ever briefed us on what to say in the event of a seismological event. It was only afterwards we learnt of the devastation and the injuries."

Earthquakes leave some people with odd fears. One FBS member used to make his wife and children go out in the garden doing 'Earthquake Drill'. He would have them cling to a water pipe, on the basis that if the ground opened up they would have something to hold on. Little wonder some thought FBS people were a shade odd!

The Cyprus Forces Radio Times of 1954 carried a balanced programme schedule, mixing popular and classical music with first-class radio drama from the BBC. There was a generous mix of international and local sport and magazine and feature programmes. Alan Kumm produced and presented the Mid-week Magazine and Irving Dee was responsible for the classical music output, with such programmes as 'A Plain Man's Guide to Music' and 'Opera Box'. Peter Buckle presented a programme called 'Last Chance'. The format, according to the Radio Times, was derived from the records, which were due to be deleted from the FBS Cyprus Library at the end of the year. Pat Selby, formerly of BFN Hamburg, presented 'Words and Music' and Kay Donnelly was still opening the ever-popular 'Letters from Home'.

When BFN Austria closed in 1955, John Parsons, Willis Toogood, Vic Widdowson and Pat Pachebat were transferred to Cyprus.

The programme schedules for that year showed a few subtle changes. Hedley Chambers, another recruit from BFN Hamburg, now became question master for the 'Inter Unit Quiz' with Peter Buckle acting as scorer. Ted King had replaced Alan Kumm as the producer of the 'Mid-week Magazine', Bob Egby, formerly with FBS Fayid, was in charge of the weekly film programme and Terry James presented Saturday nights 'Late Date'.

In the early Fifties, there was only a hint of the EOKA troubles that preceded independence. There were collection boxes for Enosis (Union with Greece) in the churches and one of the young Greek clerks, always complaining of poverty, took many holidays in Greece. Only later was it realised that he was training as an EOKA fighter. But in the old part of Nicosia, Greeks and Turks still fraternised and traded. 'Dad' Davis with his wife Penny, who lived in Larnaca, had numerous friends in both communities, unaware that it would soon be impossible to entertain them at the same time.

Bob Egby recalled the night when Cyprus changed forever. "On 31st March, 1955 we closed down the Station shortly after 11.00 p.m. by playing the Evening Hymn and Last Post. The Duty Engineer Alan Robson and I walked into Nicosia. Alan went to the famous Cosmopolitan Club and I went home to my wife. Our home was on the Larnaca Road, about half a mile from Metaxas Square. It was strangely quiet and we both mentioned this as we walked through the night.

"Shortly after midnight, the quiet was shattered by a number of explosions. Bombs had been thrown through the windows of the Secretariat, and at Wolseley Barracks in Nicosia. The Secretariat was an easy target, but the bombs aimed at the Signals room at Wolseley Barracks fell short. At the studios of Cyprus Broadcasting, two night watchmen had been overpowered, bound and gagged.

Dennis Phillips, Ian Fenner and Ken Doherty with the Outside Broadcast Vehicle FBS Cyprus – 1959.   *(© Crown Copyright: FBS 978)*

The intruders then dynamited the studios, including a fully soundproofed concert studio, the generator room and the transmitters. The place was ablaze. When you are in the radio business, it's demoralising to see a radio station being destroyed. The following morning came news reports that targets in Limassol, Larnaca and Famagusta had suffered similar attacks. Not all EOKA's attacks had been successful. One of their newly trained saboteurs had electrocuted himself by throwing a rope, damp with dew, over some high tension wires. It was April 1st, 1955 – All Fools Day.

"That day, the Governor, Sir Robert Armitage, issued a statement condemning the attacks and this statement was broadcast over FBS Cyprus. A few hours later, while the Governor was attending a large party at the Ledra Palace, a bomb exploded there and blew out windows and injured a number of people. In the days that followed, FBS Cyprus changed as indeed did the island itself. It was an uneasy existence that was to last five years."

With the commencement of the Emergency in Cyprus, it was decided to install a more powerful transmitter to cover the troops now stationed all over the Island. The War Office had stated that there was an old RCA 4750 transmitter, at a Royal Signals Establishment in the UK that could be offered to FBS MELF. The offer was accepted and the transmitter finally arrived in Nicosia. It was intended to become the most powerful transmitter in the area. However, it was discovered that pieces of the equipment were very clearly marked JCJC. This was the transmitter which had been installed in Cairo for the Middle East Forces Experimental Station in 1943. It had been shipped from Cairo back to the UK and used for normal Royal Signals purposes. It remained in use with No.4 FBS in Cyprus for 10 years.

As a result of the Emergency, many of the staff were issued with Smith & Wesson .38 revolvers, which they had to carry at all times. There were compulsory practice sessions on Saturday mornings at an army training ground, so that they did not injure themselves or their colleagues! Some of the staff later volunteered to become Special Constables and were often called out on emergency patrols when the Troubles were at their height. Pat Pachebat remembers that the order to carry a weapon gave him mixed feelings. "On one hand, I felt a sense of security that I could defend myself or others if attacked; on the other, I felt that, with a revolver strapped conspicuously to my waist, I was now an obvious target. At the time, I usually walked to work and felt very vulnerable whenever I heard a vehicle or the crunch of bicycle tyres coming up the hill behind me. I would not have hesitated to shoot in self-defence or in the aid of others had it been necessary but, thankfully, it never came to that."

Pat Pachebat recalls that despite the frequent curfews, which applied to everyone except duty personnel, there was still a lot of social activity on evenings when the staff could go out. "We had to carry our weapons, but once you arrived at a friend's home, they would be carefully put away on top of a wardrobe in the bedroom and left there until going home time. All too often, the weapon was forgotten and then one was faced with the embarrassment of returning the following morning to ask, 'Please may I have my gun'."

Pat's closest brush with EOKA terrorists or sympathisers came late one afternoon when his dog 'Tassy' suddenly went berserk in the back garden. "I rushed to the door to see two young men just finishing emptying cans of petrol over my car, which was parked in the drive. A few more seconds and I have little doubt it would have been ablaze, but luckily the fierce reaction of my dog and then my appearance with gun in hand was enough to make them turn and run. I must add that my older Greek and Turkish Cypriot neighbours were all extremely upset by the incident.

"Married staff worried about their families when they were on duty because the weakest and most defenceless were the main targets for the gunmen. Alan Kumm's mother-in-law had come to live with them. One day, walking down Ledra Street, she stopped to look in a window as two young soldiers walked past. Round the corner was a gunman who fired into the backs of the soldiers. She could only hold one of the young soldiers in her arms as he died. As he moaned "Mum, Mum," she comforted him by saying softly, "Never mind, son, this is Mum."

The bombing and shooting campaign was directed not only at the British but also at those Greek Cypriots who worked for them or were pro-British. One night, following the escape from prison of the notorious Nicos Samson, Alan Kumm's wife shouted that a man had been looking through the window. Apparently, a noisy manhunt was taking place in the nearby fields. Alan Kumm picked up a hockey stick and rushed out in a blind fury, only to pull up short realising that he could be facing one of the most ruthless men on the island. He turned tail and left the search to the Army.

Samson once saved Bob Egby's life. Bob had left Forces Broadcasting to become a freelance photo-journalist. "One of the problems with the terrorist gunmen was that, as they were captured one by one, new gunmen would come into town to take their place – and the new ones would not know who you were. Samson always called me Egby and one day he told me how he was talking with a new gunman in a coffee shop as I walked by. This new gunman saw I was an Englishman and said, 'Let's get him'. Samson replied: 'No, leave him alone, he's a reporter.' In those days a reporter was a reporter."

With the increasing number of troops on the island, due not only to the Emergency but also for the build up to Suez, the number of request programmes on FBS Cyprus increased. This did not please everyone. An article in the Cyprus

Kay Donnelly and Willis Toogood presenting the Children's Programme for FBS Cyprus in 1954.
The youngest listener on the left is Peter Donaldson.   *(© Crown Copyright: FBS 973)*

Mail complained: "We are getting a little too much of a good thing and some of
the request tunes are ridden to death. Couldn't some kind of rationing system be
introduced? When a tune has been played for the hundredth or even thousandth
time, could it not be blacklisted? Could listeners not be told that the record is in
danger of being worn out and is being put aside for the next three or four weeks
for recuperation and will the troops, their relatives and friends please choose
something else?"

On July 1st,1956, FBS Cyprus devised an audience research project which
would be carried out over a period of weeks. On the front cover of the Forces
Radio Times the readers were invited to fill in a questionnaire covering a
particular element of the week's broadcasting. The suggested comments ranged
from: "Wouldn't have missed this for anything," to "felt listening was a complete
waste of time."

In August 1956, FBS Cyprus became involved in the first 'Two-Way Family
Favourites' to be directed to the Middle East. The popular BBC Sunday morning
request programme between London and Cologne now included half an hour of
messages and records between London and Cyprus. The UK presenter was Jean
Metcalfe, with Kay Donnelly, chosen from six audition tapes, in the Nicosia

studios. For this first programme, five servicemen had their records chosen by a ballot held by 'A' Branch, Headquarters Cyprus District. For Kay Donnelly it was a very exciting moment; "It went off beautifully without a hitch." While Jean Metcalfe said at the time: "We'd looked forward to it for a long time because it seemed a pity every Sunday to send messages to people nearer home and not to Cyprus, which is so much in our thoughts."

Two other changes took place in 1956. The station now opened up at 5.30 a.m. and it also produced a French request programme introduced by Mary Tipler for the French servicemen and women who were stationed in Cyprus before moving on to Suez.

John Russell, who arrived as a National Serviceman in Cyprus, maintains that he owed his broadcasting career to the fact that he could fire a gun. At his audition, Russell who came from a theatre background, declaimed to the back row of the gods and Peter Buckle shook his head. Then a thought occurred. "Can you fire a gun?" he asked. John Russell said he could and was hired both to announce and to guard the female staff. He lived in a garret-like room above the telephone exchange which gave him the chance to flirt with the Armenian telephonist on the way up the stairs and the 'pleasure' of opening the station in his pyjamas when he overslept.

During the emergency, the scattered families, both service and civilian, relied more and more on the Cyprus station for news of EOKA incidents, curfews and government decrees and there were moments of sardonic humour. During the 1957 Wireless for the Blind appeal, RAF Nicosia and the Metropolitan Police, who were in Cyprus for the Emergency, were in direct competition for the coveted last record of the year.

When the RAF offered a pledge of an unbelievable £1,200, the girl on the phone checked with Peter Buckle in the studio. Buckle leapt at the offer, but she said prudently: "Listen to the request first." It was 'Praise the Lord and Pass the Ammunition' dedicated to Cyprus's militant prelate, Archbishop Makarios.

Discreetly, Peter Buckle said: "Sorry, no." The RAF sportingly paid up any way and chose an alternative. Some time later, when Peter Buckle told the story to General Sir John Harding, by then combining the role of Governor and Commander-in-Chief, the reply from that toughest of generals was swift: "You should have bloody well played it," he said.

During 1957, Leslie Knight left the Forces Broadcasting Service and returned to the UK. Since the early Fifties, he had been pressing constantly for improvements in staff and equipment in the Middle East and the Mediterranean but as short-term plans became medium term and medium term dragged on into a distant future, he became disillusioned. The two areas of Forces Broadcasting, BFN in Germany and the Near East Service based in Cyprus, were run as two almost separate organisations. So, in 1953, HQ MELF put forward his suggestions for an FBS head office in London.

The Army Council rejected them and Leslie Knight decided to leave the organisation that had achieved so much under his guidance during the past 14 years and Roy Morgan took over as Chief Broadcasting Officer of FBS Cyprus.

It could be argued that the Mau Mau emergency saved Forces Broadcasting in East Africa from closure. FBS Nairobi was able to prove its value to everyone from the GOC down.

Ian Redvers Brown, the Station Commander of the Forces Broadcasting Service at McKinnon Road in Kenya, is credited with one of the most laid back monthly reports in the history of the organisation. "Nothing to report today except that the station was destroyed by a herd of wild elephants."

It wasn't the elephants that brought about the station's return to Nairobi, but a run-down of the British troops.

When Peter Buckle arrived in Nairobi to take over as the Station Commander, he was still recovering from the gunshot wound he had received in Ismalia. He went to investigate the sound of shooting in the streets below his flat and received a bullet in the leg for his pains.

He had faced the terrorists of the Irgun and the Stern Gang, but admitted that the Mau Mau situation was very frightening. His staff were supposed to carry guns at all times and he possessed an old Smith and Wesson Five Chamber Revolver.

Following the "Beetle" Operation in Palestine, the role of the broadcaster changed in an emergency situation from one of pure entertainment to a medium through which the commanders could talk to the British families as well as the military. This was necessary on numerous occasions during the Mau Mau emergency.

In her book 'A Microphone and a Frequency', Doreen Taylor recalls the FBS involvement in an exercise codenamed 'First Flute'. During this exercise Ian Woolf, then Station Commander of FBS Nairobi, was caught up in a Mau Mau ambush. He switched on his microphone and kept the tape running. When he returned to the studio, he realised that his tape of the encounter, in which several terrorists were killed, had included women's voices. The recording of the incident was thought to be of such importance that it had to be vetted by Major General John Heyman, the Chief of Staff, who at first refused to agree to the broadcast. The General demanded that the women's voices be removed from the tape because the army did not like the idea of the public knowing there were women terrorists.

Radio interview at Nairobi

Wendy Barnes interviewing Joan Crawford for FBS Nairobi – 1956.

(© Crown Copyright: FBS 1144)

There was very little protection for the station and the emergency brought an atmosphere of unease. Wendy Barnes remembers that every Mau Mau cell had a leader, but no one knew who the local leader was.

One of Ian Woolf's innovations was to detach the Nairobi station from the Near East Command and have it report direct to Eaton Square in London. This gave it a certain amount of independence. He also decided that FBS Nairobi must keep its listeners up-to-date with what was happening in the wider world. During the Hungarian Uprising in 1956, the station managed to pick up the Budapest station on short wave and was soon transmitting the pathetic cries for help direct from Budapest.

One of the problems facing the engineering staff in Kenya was how to cover such areas as Nyeri and Nanyuke, the base of 70 Brigade who were fighting the Mau Mau in the Mount Kenya area. They decided to put up a huge aerial called a Lazy H. The site chosen was not ideal as the soil looked a bit like potting compost. Before they could lay out the aerial between its four masts they had to decide what to do with a large nest of wild African bees, which was hanging from a thorn tree right in the centre of the field. The engineers had been in Kenya long enough to know that wild bee stings, if there are enough of them, can kill.

The staff of FBS Nairobi, back row; Vic Widdowson, Larry Roberts, Paul Keable, Mike Farnes, Gordon Mills, Mike Robertson, Alan Parfrey, Stan Crabtree, seated Jean Williams, Joan Beard, Pat Pachebat, Sarah Ward, Margaret Evans – 1960.   (© *Private Photograph*)

The Chief Engineer parked his shooting brake near the tree with the back open and Roy Norris, one of the engineering team, took a long pole and knocked the nest down. He leapt into the back of the vehicle followed by a stream of angry bees, while his colleague attempted to emulate Stirling Moss. All would have been well except he had forgotten to close the window. As a result, Roy Norris ended up in hospital badly stung. According to popular opinion, the Lazy H system brought little improvement to reception in the Mount Kenya region.

Pat Pachebat arrived at FBS Nairobi in 1959. He was excited at the thought of managing his first station but shocked at its condition: "It consisted of four wooden huts,. One was for me, the programme organiser and the secretary; another housed the library and the presenters; the third contained the studio and the control room and the fourth was the transmitter hall. Outside there was a small structure that housed two-bucket latrines, one for each sex. There was no roof and there were many holes and cracks in the dividing partition." He set about lobbying the military for a rebuild, only to be told that no one had ever complained before! But they responded and when Pat left two years later for Aden, the Royal Engineers had built a new station with two splendid flush toilets.

FBS Nairobi had always been at the forefront of broadcasting initiatives and they decided to introduce Radio Tombola to their listeners in Kenya. With Major Brian Toy of the Royal Signals calling the numbers, they managed to raise several hundred pounds for the Command Welfare Funds. However, they will be remembered for their amazing ingenuity with the annual Wireless for the Blind Appeal. Pat Pachebat recalls: "We stayed on air all night from Christmas Eve through to New Year's Day. We had superb prizes donated by organisations like East African Airways and the Mount Kenya Safari Club and, at times, my office could have been mistaken for a menagerie with live geese, chicken etc in cages waiting to be snapped up by eager listeners. One seemingly harmless prize was a pair of pyjamas, which went for a few pounds. However, the new owner decided to auction the top and bottom separately, with the winners agreeing to meet dressed like that in one of the local hotels. At this stage, we wisely opted out."

Looking back at his time with FBS Nairobi, Pat Pachebat felt it was a wonderful character forming experience for a young manager setting out at the start of his managerial career.

On 7th October 1945, listeners to BFN Hamburg heard, for the first time, a new programme called 'Family Favourites'. At its peak in the Fifties, the programme had an estimated audience in the UK of around 20 million. The first request from London in 1945 was for 'Lilli Marlene' and the final request was broadcast on 13th January 1980. On 30th July 1995, as part of the BBC Light Programme's Golden Jubilee, a special edition of the programme was broadcast with former BFBS presenter Sandi Jones in London and Glen Mansell in Germany. However, this time the programme linked the families in the UK and Germany with their loved ones in Bosnia.

Cliff Michelmore and Jean Metcalfe in the Hamburg studios of BFN.

(© Crown Copyright: FBS 96)

Sergeant Chris Howland, who replaced Cliff Michelmore when he returned to the UK in 1951.

(© Crown Copyright: FBS 97)

Bill Crozier, a former staff pianist with BFN Hamburg, the longest serving presenter of 'Family Favourites'.

(© Private Photograph)

The members of Forces Broadcasting had witnessed many changes in the Fifties. They had said goodbye to BFN Austria, BFN Hamburg, FBS Trieste, FBS Fayid and FBS Lakatamia. They had been welcomed to BFN Cologne and FBS Nicosia. They had mourned the death of King George VI and joined in the celebrations for the Coronation of Queen Elizabeth II. They had played the music of Bill Haley and Elvis Presley and had covered the stories of Stanley Matthews and his Cup Final Medal; Gordon Richards and his first Derby victory; Roger Bannister and his sub-four minute mile; and Edmund Hilary and Sherpa Tensing conquering Everest. But the story that was to affect the future of FBS took place on October 4th, 1957 when the Russians launched Sputnik, which began the satellite era.

CHAPTER THREE

The Sixties

The Times They Were A' Changing

Bill Crozier of BFN Cologne was the best-known Forces Broadcasting personality in the early Sixties. Bill had replaced Dennis Scuse in 1957 as the Germany end of 'Two Way Family Favourites' and his mischievous style of broadcasting blended very well with that of Jean Metcalfe. He was also president of the '1800 Club', the daily request programme that had started in Hamburg in 1946 and was much favoured by National Service listeners. Their favourite demob record, played at least once a week was "Happy Days Are Here Again".

It was understood that if a record company could get their latest release on 'Two Way Family Favourites', then it was guaranteed a place in the Top Twenty. If it managed two plays in the space of four weeks, their record would be in the Top Ten. It therefore, was no surprise that record companies and song pluggers alike courted Bill. Each week bundles of the latest releases would arrive on his desk with subtle pleas for him to listen and possibly use one as his 'record of the week' on the '1800 Club'. The record companies hoped the chosen record would be uppermost in the minds of those requesting dedications on 'Family Favourites'.

Bill was meticulous in following the rules laid down by the BBC and no amount of offers would persuade him to play a record if he did not feel it was right for his programme. Usually on a Friday he would audition his growing pile of records in the Record Library and sometimes invite comments from his colleagues as to whether they felt the disc had 'hit' potential. On one occasion he was playing a one-sided song pluggers copy when he asked Ian Fenner, who would later replace him on 'Family Favourites', for his reaction. "I think the record is OK but with the name like that they haven't got a hope of getting played." Ian had just turned down "Love Me Do" by the Beatles!

As well as the records from the United Kingdom, Bill also received large packages of LPs from the record companies in America, so the listeners to BFN Cologne often heard the latest offering by Frank Sinatra, Nat King Cole or Ella Fitzgerald before the UK audience.

Bill Crozier joined BFN Hamburg in 1948 as the Staff Pianist, when he moved to Cologne, he took over Family Favourites from Dennis Scuse.   *(© Private Photograph)*

Another way of getting publicity for a record in the early Sixties was to send the artiste to Germany on a promotional tour. As a result, BFN was able to record in depth interviews with such performers as Frankie Vaughan, Cliff Richard and the Drifters, Petula Clark, Marion Ryan, Robert Earl, Ronnie Hilton and many others.

While BFN Germany's entertainment potential rose, the other Forces Broadcasting Stations in the Middle East and North Africa missed out because there was no syndication of programmes between stations.

Something had to be done to restore the balance.

In 1957 Leslie Knight, the architect of Forces Broadcasting in the Middle East, in his final brief to Lieutenant General Martin, requested that experienced staff, especially technicians be recruited and the salaries on offer be reappraised. At the same time he argued for more War Office money to be invested in equipment for Forces Broadcasting and a proper headquarters in the United Kingdom.

At the same time Ronald Icke, a former Station Controller of BFN Austria now based in London with the Forces Entertainment Service, wrote a 53 page paper on the way ahead for the Forces Broadcasting Service, which he submitted to the War Office under the auspices of the Institute of Professional Civil Servants.

In it he pointed out that only two stations, Austria and Germany, had been re-equipped in the past seven years and only then because the money was taken from the Occupation Funds available to the Military in those countries. "Other stations have to rely on the Treasury and will no doubt continue to operate aged, obsolescent equipment with apparently no change for the better. A persistent refusal to find funds for the reorganisation and re-equipment for FBS seems hardly excusable in the light of reports of the Select Committee of Estimates, which reveal so many flagrant examples of wasteful spending."

Among his other questions were: "How was the decision not to set up Forces Broadcasting Stations in the Far East reached, was it on security or political grounds or a complete lack of money?"

Icke noted that a small War Office Transcription Service had been operating in London since 1953, with two engineers, who recorded a few programmes each year. With an increase in establishment in 1954 they were able to virtually double their output, with programmes, which now came under the heading of Light Entertainment. As there was no budget, personalities taking part in the programmes did it out of the kindness of their hearts.

'P.S.15' the War Office branch that sponsored the Forces Broadcasting Service, wrote the following memorandum. "A new establishment is required to allow the most effective use to be made of the Forces Broadcasting Service by increasing the production in the United Kingdom of recorded programmes of special interest to the servicemen overseas and of programmes which will present 'the Army to the Army' and provide a closer link with home."

One of the problems facing the establishment of an FBS London Unit was that salaries offered in the United Kingdom for both programme and technical staff were far too low. At the same time the facilities that were being used were makeshift and obsolete. The single studio was not soundproofed, there was no proper Control Room and for Outside Broadcasts, there was one midget tape-recorder on loan from Army Public Relations and no recording van.

In 1956 a move was made to obtain £10,000's worth of new equipment but no money was put aside for new studios. The Forces Broadcasting Service was given such low priority by the Treasury that no progress was expected until 1960.

The programmes being recorded in London were of such poor quality that they were refused by BFN in Germany but other stations had to accept what they were given.

Ron Icke concluded that progress would not be made unless the Forces Broadcasting Service was taken away from the War Office and made the responsibility of the Ministry of Defence.

The Secretary to the First Sea Lord noted, on 20th March 1957: "Whilst Icke has raised many interesting points, under the present financial climate, I myself feel grave doubts as to whether an FBS will be sustained at all! There was, at one time, a proposal, that FBS should go to the BBC who would receive a Grant-in-Aid. I believe there are immense advantages, under the future outlook, in the BBC taking FBS over. For £x the BBC could produce a far better result than an independent organisation, struggling under service administration and paperwork. An independent organisation could, I think, only produce indifferent results, no matter what its staff considered the desirable criterion."

In 1958 the Executive Committee of the Army Council agreed that Forces Broadcasting's main defect was that it lacked a single head and a headquarters in the United Kingdom.

Two years later, Jack Knott, a former Director General of the Nigerian Broadcasting Service, was seconded from the BBC and charged with producing a report on the Forces Broadcasting Service. He was to be known as the Advisor to the War Office on Forces Broadcasting.

His report's basic recommendations were that the Service's name should be changed to the British Forces Broadcasting Service; that broadcasting control should be given to a director based in a London Head Office and that there should be improved salaries and conditions for all staff with a proper career structure. He also recommended that television should be introduced by the end of 1963 and that consideration be given to the role of FBS in war and what steps would need to be taken to enable it to carry out its task.

The idea of changing the organisation's name was greeted with absolute amazement in Germany. Since 1945, AFN and BFN had become synonymous with Forces Broadcasting in Germany. Manufacturers of 'top of the range' radio sets, Saba, Telefunken and Siemens carried a BFN marking on their dials. The question on everyone's lips in Cologne was; why change? Why not use BFN to incorporate the stations in Cyprus, Tripoli, Benghazi etc.? After all, the Americans had seen their radio service as a worldwide network. Despite the protests from Germany, in 1963 BFN Cologne became BFBS Germany.

In the past, in order to keep going, Forces Broadcasting had recruited staff largely on the principle 'learn while you earn'. Due to low rates of pay and a lack of security, many good staff left. There was no recognisable programme policy and no liaison between London and the overseas stations. In short, Forces Broadcasting lacked cohesion. Therefore, a Head Office, with full authority and backing on professional matters, could take the organisation forward into the Sixties.

In 1954 when Alan Kumm became a civilian with Forces Broadcasting in Cyprus, his annual salary was £208 per year and was supported by a Foreign Service Allowance of £800 tax-free. The 1960 Knott Report recommended that Grade V Programme Assistants start on £935 per year, which meant that recruitment of more professional staff for London was possible.

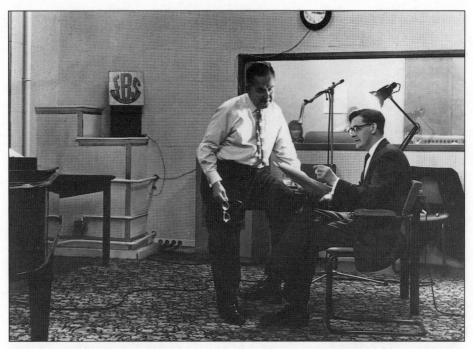

John Parsons and Lionel Gamblin in the London Studios of the Forces Broadcasting Service
– 1961.   *(© Crown Copyright: FBS 1160)*

A small team had been assembled in London made up of Jack Pickering, formerly of BFN Hamburg and the Middle East, another Middle East veteran, Terry James, and John Parsons, who had served in Austria and Cyprus. Two engineers, Howard Yentis and Bob Dawes, joined them.

By 1961 they were producing a 'Top Twenty Show" based on the latest information from the 'New Musical Express', which was recorded on a Tuesday afternoon and despatched that evening for the overseas stations. However, BFN Cologne preferred to use their programme, called 'The BFN Hit Parade' presented by Alastair McDougall. Jack Pickering produced and presented a Forces Motoring Magazine and Lionel Gamblin looked after the interests of Theatreland with a programme called 'London Showtime'. John Parsons edited a magazine 'In All Directions' and the Head Office team produced a series of fillers called 'London Miniatures' which lasted no more than eight minutes.

Following the approval of the Knott Report, the new Head Office took shape. In 1965 Pat Livingstone and Gerald Sinstadt joined the team in Kings Buildings to set up a serious music and a sports section. The Director of the new organisation was Bryan Cave-Brown-Cave, one of the earliest of the Forces

Broadcasters. Ian Woolf left BFBS Germany to take up the new appointment of Controller of Programmes.

The Head Office was to be known as BFBS London.

The War Office indecision highlighted in the report by Ronald Icke in 1957 became apparent again in the late Fifties and early Sixties. In 1958 Air Vice Marshal Heath wrote from the Arabian Peninsular to the Adjutant General asking for an update of the projected Forces Broadcasting Station in Aden. This had been agreed in July of 1956 but nothing had happened in Aden. There was only a radio station operating out of RAF Khormaksar and run by a group of enthusiastic amateurs. As Air Vice Marshal Heath remarked in his letter: "I do not know where the responsibility lies for the dilatory manner in which this business has been handled, but I would be most grateful, at this late stage, if you could provide the much needed boost to get something done as a matter of urgency."

Aden, in the early Sixties, was, in effect, a peacetime station with more Forces' wives and children than servicemen. There were hundreds of married quarters, ranging from new estates of houses to modern blocks of flats all freshly fitted with air conditioning and refrigerators. There were schools, shopping centres, churches and cinemas. For most of the Forces, the principal recreation, apart from shopping in the Duty Free Steamer Point area, was at the delightful beach clubs, where bars, restaurants and swimming pools had been built on the golden sands next to the sea. But all this was about the change. Egyptian-sponsored Arab Nationalism and Militant Trade Union politics were taking over.

At the end of 1963, as British officials and Arab rulers gathered at Khormaksar Airfield to fly to London for talks on the future constitution of a fully independent South Arabian Federation, a grenade was thrown at the High Commissioner fatally wounding one of his advisors, who threw himself between the grenade and the High Commissioner. Terrorism had begun and in the coming months, would grow.

One year earlier, Pat Pachebat, the Station Controller in Nairobi, received a signal from the War Office informing him that he had been appointed Station Controller (designate) for the new Forces Broadcasting Station in Aden. For the next three months, he commuted back and forth from Nairobi to Aden as he checked on the progress of the latest station for the Forces Broadcasting Service.

The Aden Chronicle of July 26 1962 ran the headline: "The world's most modern Forces Radio Station comes to Aden." The station, according to their reporter, had cost 2,300,000 shillings.

On first sight, the station looked quite attractive but the local contractor did a poor job and when the time came for Pat Pachebat to officially accept the building, he refused to do so because of poor soundproofing between the studios and the control room. For the next two years renovation work went on almost continuously. One of the strange features of the design was that the air-conditioning plant was directly above the continuity studios and caused a low rumble every time an announcer opened the microphone. Like most buildings in the area, it had a flat roof with no proper drainage system. It hardly ever rained in Aden, except in 1963 when one torrential downpour put the station off the air for twenty-four hours as water poured through the ceiling and cascaded over the control desk and studio equipment.

By the time Pat Pachebat left in 1964 the terrorist problem was beginning to escalate. BFBS Aden would soon become the only station in the organisation's history that had a machine-gun post on its roof and armed guards by its fortified front entrance. All the windows were covered with wire mesh to protect against bomb blast.

On May 3rd 1965 the station came under attack. Three Bazooka shells were fired into the station; one penetrated the outer wall of the concert studio, one shattered the front entrance door, and the third fell short of the building. John Nicoll, who was on duty at the time, was instructed by J.P.R.S. (Joint Public

The Studios of BFBS Aden at Steamer Point were guarded by members of the Parachute Regiment in 1965 – note the machine gun post on the roof of the studios.

(© Crown Copyright: FBS 1279)

The staff of BFBS Aden – 1965. Back row: Roy Norris, Len Collett, Adrian Sainsbury, John Nicholl, Kathy Emmett and the author. Front row: Mike Townley, John Campbell, Peter Buckle, Willis Toogood, Kay Donnelly and Barry Faber.   *(© Crown Copyright: FBS 1268)*

Relations Staff) to turn away enquiries in a non-committal fashion. The first our listeners knew about the attack was on a BBC News broadcast two and a half hours after the event. As a result of the attack, security measures, which BFBS had been requesting for some time, were finally put into place.

The station's inability to tell its audience what had happened was highlighted five months later when Peter Buckle, the then Station Controller, wrote to Headquarters Middle East Command complaining about the nonsensical way the Military were reacting towards BFBS. Buckle pointed out that his station was not allowed to broadcast material on the closing of the schools in Aden and yet information was chalked up at the main entrances to the camps that could be read by any local terrorist. He said: "I served with the Forces Broadcasting Service in Palestine, Egypt, Kenya and Cyprus and on each occasion BFBS achieved its main function of keeping troops and civilians advised and informed and played a major part in killing rumours and preventing doubt and discontent. In Aden we have done nothing. The JPRS News Bulletin is suspect and as a result, our local news is no longer trusted. If this curtain of silence is supposed to help the security forces, I fail to see how it has achieved its purpose. The local

Arab grapevine is more efficient than our broadcasts, and British families now rely on local tradesmen for up-to-the-minute accurate information."

The Army claimed in its reply that BFBS was short-staffed and not in a position to decide what was suitable for broadcasting on the local news. It said BFBS's local news was censored not only for good political reasons but also for military ones. It also claimed that BFBS was exaggerating the situation and on the very few occasions when the BBC beat it with the story, the more intelligent of their listeners had understood. However, as a result of this correspondence, incident reports on BFBS did speed up.

For the staff of BFBS Aden it was a time for fast reactions. As Paul Keable, the Station's Senior Engineer, recalled, "If you heard a bang, you flattened yourself." The staff checked their laundry with great care and insisted that the dhobi wallah unpack in front of them. They also told their children not to pick up toys in case they had been booby-trapped. Soon most of the town was out-of-bounds and people were living in a state of undeclared war.

The terrorists stepped up the pressure. They started by blowing up the South Arabian Broadcasting Station, which was opposite BFBS at Steamer Point. Peter Buckle was told that threats had been made against BFBS on the local Arab propaganda station, which was based in the Yemen. Apparently they were going to blow up BFBS at 1800 hours the following evening. As he was duty announcer and presenter of the evening request programme "Ask For Another", he recalled: "I kept one eye on the script and the other on the clock." Thankfully the terrorist attack did not happen that night.

When Rodney Burke, Peter Buckle and Kathy Emmett were packing up the radio station, the terrorists mortared the area and when the dust had settled, Kathy looked up and said: "I suppose you all expect me to go and make tea now?"

The original date for independence was to be 1st January 1968 and following a visit by Bryan Cave-Brown-Cave it was agreed that BFBS Aden would continue to broadcast until the last of the troops left. However, they would be housed in the AFBA (Aden Forces Broadcasting Association) building in Khormaksar. This move resulted in one member of staff resigning 'rather than work alongside amateurs'.

Peter Buckle's last letters to the Head Office in London gave an insight into the final days of BFBS Aden. "We recorded Sir Humphrey Trevellayn on 29th June and broadcast his 'panic out' speech at 19.10 hours, this means we will have no typists or assistants from the 18th July. Prepare not to receive monthly reports but prepare to accept scruffy longhand letters. This speed-up of the families has caused all sorts of confusion. People are being ordered home at twelve hours notice. The banks have been closed for a month so now we have to pay everyone in cash (if you can get it). Yesterday, apart from the usual grenades, mortars and small arms, the terrorists blew up an oil tank and a Viscount aircraft. There is no doubt who is winning. At this expensive rate, I reckon we'll all be out before the end of the year. Still, with all the shops shut, or out of bounds, we can save money. I only hope we are all able to spend it later – gin's still 4d a glass. I should worry."

In his final letter, he wrote: "I didn't realise that last week's attack was broadcast by the BBC. The energas fell around the station, all of them on the outside of the wire. The damage was negligible but the real nasty was when a second bank was discovered trained on the station. At 06.20 hours a major rushed into the station, moved the guard down the road and then told our duty engineer, Roger Beetham, to close down and clear out while the major's team dismantled the energas. Roger's reply was short and bore all the hallmarks of his Liverpudlian upbringing. 'Listen mate, you do your ********* job properly and ******* leave me to do mine.'"

In the final week, in true British fashion despite all the troubles that were happening around them, BFBS broadcast World Service Relays of the second Test Match between England and Pakistan at Trent Bridge.

BFBS closed down on Friday August 18th 1967 with Peter Buckle introducing the Evening Hymn and Last Post and the National Anthem for the last time in Aden.

The Observer Correspondent John de St. Jorre recalled the last moments of the British in Aden. "The NAAFI, Forces Radio and Cinemas, British Newspapers, Clubs and Security Reports have gone and with them, nearly all trace of British Rule. Even the peacocks from the Government House lawns have been packed off to the zoo. At midnight on 30th November the back alleys of Crater were as bright as if it were midday. Someone placed a blazing torch on the top of the hill that dominated Crater.

Militia men in khaki uniforms and peak forage caps waved their machine guns as they stood in front of giant pictures of Nasser and of the local commandos hurling grenades at the British Forces. The Service Quarters at Tarshyne, Khormaksar and M'alla Straight were empty and fly-blown – the British had gone. After all the bangs the end was a whimper: one of the few colonies which became independent without a formal and ceremonial handover."

For his efforts in running BFBS Aden for the final three years, Peter Buckle was awarded the MBE.

BFBS London started operating in the spring of 1965. Kings Buildings was situated on the corner of Dean Stanley Street and Smith Square. Close by was the Labour Party's Transport House and the Conservative Central Office. The

Kings Buildings, the London Headquarters of the British Forces Broadcasting Service as seen from Smith Square.
(© Crown Copyright: FBS 511)

building had an elegant façade but the facilities inside left much to be desired. The first floor studio, although it appeared to have adequate soundproofing, when Jack Dash of the Docker's Union, was rallying a group of strikers in the Square below, it was impossible to keep out the extraneous noises. The other studio complex was on the third floor with management and administration occupying the fourth.

The building was reputed to be haunted and on one occasion, a famous medium came in to be interviewed and refused to take the right-hand lift as she felt it had been taken over by an evil presence. The night watchman, who had been a former Marine Commando, would not go into the basement at night on his own.

As with all Ministry of Defence buildings, you had to show your pass to gain admission to the studios. The chief interrogator was a feisty Irish lady called Marie who demanded to be shown the pass of the then Prime Minister, Edward Heath, when he came in to record an interview. When he asked her "Don't you recognise me?": she said; "Yes, but I still want to see your pass." She was also not amused when ten passes were requested for a television team to enter the building and record a three minute interview with Sarah Kennedy.

At lunchtime staff and contributors would make their way to the local pub 'The Marquis of Granby', only to find it, on numerous occasions, full of trade unionists, who were listening to the amazing wit of Clive Jenkins, the Union Leader of the ASCMT (Association of Scientific, Clerical and Managerial Staffs).

BFBS London was made up of four programme departments, Features and Magazine, Light Music, Serious Music, Sport, an Engineering Department and a Personnel Unit.

Gerald Sinstadt, who had begun his career with Forces Broadcasting in Austria, was seconded from the BBC's Sports Department to set up a BFBS London Sports Unit. I joined them in July 1965, following my return from Aden, and became part of the production team of 'London Sportsdesk'.

The idea behind the programme was to add to the information currently being relayed to BFBS Cologne by the BBC Light Programme and to the other BFBS stations via the BBC World Service. From the very beginning Gerald Sinstadt

Cliff Morgan, the Presenter of London Sportsdesk with Henry Cooper and Harry Carpenter and the production team of Alan Grace, Geoff Frewer and Bryan Hamilton – 1969.

(© Crown Copyright: FBS 530)

Neil Allen of The Times interviewing Mary Rand and Lillian Board for London Sportsdesk – 1969.
(© Crown Copyright: FBS 520)

decided that only the top stories would be covered in 'London Sportsdesk' and in the first year Arnold Palmer, Jack Nicklaus, Gary Player, Margaret Court, Billie Jean King, Rod Laver, Cassius Clay, Rocky Marciano, Jack Dempsey, Jim Clark, Stirling Moss and Graham Hill appeared on the programme.

Gerald also encouraged many of Fleet Street's finest sports journalists to work for 'London Sportdesk' on a freelance basis. Ian Wooldridge and John Arlott looked after cricket; Brian Moore, Bryon Butler, Barry Davies and Geoffrey Green kept the listeners up-to-date with the latest from the world of football; Cliff Morgan, Bill McClaren and John Reason brought rugby to the fore; while Harry Carpenter and Reg Gutteridge concentrated on boxing.

It was on London Sportsdesk that Sir Alf Ramsey made his prediction that England would win the World Cup in 1966 and the BFBS reporters Sinstadt, Grace and Ken Doherty covered the amazing scenes at Wembley after England had beaten West Germany 4-2. BFBS Cologne had planned an Open Day for their German listeners on the day of the final. Realising the importance of the game, they arranged for television monitors to be available for those who wished to keep up-to-date with the match. More than 1,000 Germans visited BFBS and in the evening, Pat Pachebat was invited to the television studios of WDR in Cologne to talk about, or so he assumed, the Open Day. Instead the interviewer

Alexis Korner, formerly of BFN Hamburg, engineer Geoff Frewer and presenter David Gell discussing the programme 'Nice and Easy'.   *(© Crown Copyright: FBS 552)*

was much more interested in whether Pat agreed with him that a Russian Linesman had robbed West Germany.

In those days the Sports Unit was able to deal with the stars direct. Agents had not yet entered the equation. Many of Britain's finest sporting stars would agree to be interviewed for the princely sum of eight guineas. Some, like Brian Clough, then at the height of his fame, refused to accept payment. He argued that he and his team, Nottingham Forest, would always be available to talk to the Forces for nothing.

Gerald Sinstadt designed a series of programme called 'On Reflection' in which sports personalities would look back over their careers. In the Sixties, Graham Hill, Colin Cowdrey, Harold Abrahams, Sir Alf Ramsey, Peter Alliss, Chris Brasher, Sir Len Hutton and Stirling Moss all made their way to the BFBS studios in Westminster and often revealed unexpected facets of their character.

Whilst the Sports Unit was a hive of activity, the Light Music section headed by Jack Pickering was not far behind. The 'Top Twenty Show' with Colin Hamilton was one of the most popular music programmes to originate from London, 'On the Jazz Beat' with Humphrey Lyttelton, David Gell's 'Nice and

Humphrey Lyttleton with his producer Eggy Ley preparing for another programme in the 'On the Jazz Beat' series. *(© Crown Copyright: FBS 550)*

Easy', Wally Whyton's 'Hello Folk' and the Dave Cash Show were all well regarded by the service audience overseas. The Light Music section also produced a series of programmes called 'Banded Music Green or Yellow'. These were sixty-minute programmes of 'middle of the road' music without announcements and were designed to help stations who were suffering staff shortages. In their way they provided a good background sound and often saved stations from having to closedown during the morning or afternoon.

Another veteran from the Middle East, Pat Livingstone, headed the Serious Music section. She persuaded Eric Robinson to produce a series called 'Music For You', and Ian Wallace to present 'The Wallace Collection', while Gerald Sinstadt became involved in his second love, opera, with his very popular series 'Opera Notebook'.

The Features and Magazine Department headed by Mary Hill decided that the overseas service audience needed to know what was happening back in their part of the world and so a series of five minute newsletters was commissioned covering Scotland, Northern Ireland, Wales, the North of England, Midlands, the West Country, East Anglia and the South of England. These programmes were

Ian Wallace with Stan Challoner checking the records for 'The Wallace Collection'.

(© Crown Copyright: FBS 547)

extremely popular with the service audience. As only Germany could relay the BBC Light Programme's 'Woman's Hour', Mary Hill commissioned Hilda Bamber and Sheila Tracey to produce and present a magazine programme called 'Back Home' and this was to be followed later by 'Look Around Home'.

Ian Woolf, the Controller of Programmes, and other members of the broadcasting staff auditioned the various departments' output to keep the standard high.

BFBS London became the focal point for recruitment with training both in London and overseas. The Personnel Unit, staffed by Civil Servants, ensured that the broadcasters and their families were looked after.

On 4th January 1941 British and Australian troops entered Libya and a day later captured the town of Bardia. Seventeen days later they captured Tobruk.

Twenty-nine years later, the British Forces and BFBS left Tobruk and Libya for the last time.

BFBS Tripoli was the first Forces Broadcasting Station in Libya to go closing in 1966. It had played a vital role in entertaining the servicemen. Jack Knott received a letter from Wing Commander Coulson at RAF Idris: "I am writing to tell you how much we, at Idris, appreciate the radio programmes arranged by the Forces Broadcasting Service Tripoli. This is an isolated station lacking many of the amenities normally available at Royal Air Force stations in England. The FBS programmes do, therefore, make a major contribution to the maintenance of good morale in that they serve as a link with home. Your recent curtailment of broadcasting hours has been noticeably felt by Idris personnel and I do hope that you may find it possible to restore the cuts at an early date."

Three years earlier, it was not just cuts in broadcasting hours that were worrying the members of FBS in Libya. In November 1963 Sir Frank Markham, the Chairman of the Parliamentary Estimates Committee on Military Expenditure Overseas, expressed the view that FBS Benghazi was an expensive anachronism a frill in an already expensive Garrison. The Command Secretary of Headquarters Malta and Libya, who was lobbying hard for the opposing view said: "I felt it better not to mention to him that the Forces Broadcasting Service was contemplating opening up in El Adem!"

BFBS Tobruk opened in August 1964 and initially broadcast from 0600 – 0930, 1600 – 2300. The station had its studios in Tobruk and served not only the families in Tobruk but also those eighteen miles away at El Adem.

The studios were housed in what had once been an Italian Military Hospital. The continuity studio was said to have been the operating theatre and was reputed to be haunted. The only person who took it seriously was the Programme Organiser, Alan Hargreaves, who claimed to have seen a ghost and did not want to be left on his own there. One night, when Alan was alone on the station, the power failed (a common occurrence in Tobruk) as he was playing "The Archers". He grabbed a torch and departed the building fast letting the door slam behind him. He sought refuge in the Sergeants' Mess opposite the studios and downed a large gin and tonic. Only when the power was restored did he discover that the latch had dropped on the front door and he had left the keys in the studio! In the meantime, the station restored itself and "The Archers" continued where it had left off. Now it was a race to get the spare set of keys from the guardroom before "The Archers" came to an end. Unfortunately he lost the race and the dreaded tic, tic, tic of the run out groove was broadcast for several minutes.

In March 1967 Peter Attrill was posted to BFBS Benghazi and was just in time to replace Roger Dunn, who had gone off with the army on an exercise to find the Liberator Bomber, 'Lady Be Good', that had come down some 250 miles to the south during the Second World War. When they found it the aircraft was

The staff of BFBS Tobruk – 1969. Left to right: Paddy Hegarty, John Walker, Stephen Withers, John Hedges, Peter Holwill, Gordon Clarke, Tony Fawcett, Peter Blanchette, Reg Styles-Altieri. Seated: Kay Donnelly and Karl Sherriff. *(© Crown Copyright: FBS 1563)*

almost intact having been preserved by the dry desert air. Roger Dunn decided to bring back some of the live ammunition from the wreck. On returning to the station, he placed a round in the workshop vice in an attempt to remove the bullet from the casing. The workshop was adjacent to the continuity studio where the duty announcer David Lamb was broadcasting. When the round exploded the bullet exited the workshop through the studio and out via the external wall. It was said David Lamb was never the same again!

Jim Luxton had been an actor before joining BFBS Tobruk and used his many skills to dramatise, for radio, the story of 'Lady Be Good'. He then turned his attention to the rather sad story of a group of Germans who tried to cross the Siwa Oasis in Volkswagens and became bogged down in the sand. The story came to light when the bodies were found with a diary, which had been kept by a lady who was the last one to die. She had written things like: "Please someone come quickly, we only have three small tins of fruit juice left." Jim, who was friends with a German surveyor who worked in Tobruk, persuaded him to read extracts from the diary on the radio. This programme was being recorded after the morning closedown.

At the time there was an excellent PSI (Public Services Institute) shop in El Adem, which imported goods from Aden. That morning an RAF serviceman picked up the latest portable radio, and as he tried to tune it in the shop he heard what he thought was a call for help from someone stranded in the desert. He immediately called the Air Traffic Control Tower and told them there were people in trouble in the desert and they only had three small cans of fruit juice left. The Tower called out the Desert Rescue Team and three vehicles set off south into the desert. An aircraft was told to prepare for take-off. Only then did the Tower go back to the airman in the PSI shop to ask him to listen again for more information about the location of the distress call. Then someone thought to check the frequency and discovered they had to been listening to BFBS!

The BFBS Engineers had forgotten to switch off the transmitter on the morning of the recording!

On 5th June 1967 Peter Holwill, then in charge of BFBS Benghazi, received a request from Area Headquarters to broadcast an urgent message to families to pack a suitcase in preparation for evacuation. The station was duly opened at 11.20 am and a decision was taken to drop the BBC World Service programmes; "From the Editorials"; "Commentary"; and "Radio Newsreel" to avoid embarrassing the Libyan authorities. At midday, BFBS announced that all Army schoolchildren and kindergarten children were being kept safe in D'Aosta Barracks and they broadcast a constant reminder to dependants in the town of Benghazi to keep within their houses and have their suitcase ready.

Rioting broke out in Benghazi. Jewish shops were set alight as were the American Consulate and the Other Ranks NAAFI Club. The British Embassy was badly damaged and the British Council buildings. As many of the staff were outside of the Barracks when the announcements were made, Peter Holwill and Ted King were on continuous duty. They managed around three hours sleep in the first three days of the emergency. The following day, BFBS Benghazi began broadcasting the evacuation details for British and American citizens in Benghazi. They continued to play non-stop music interspersed with BBC News broadcasts and special announcements throughout the day and night.

On Monday 12th June, Radio Cairo started broadcasting worsening accusations against Britain and America. It called for acts of terrorism against their bases in Libya.

The following day the curfew, which had been in force since the start of the emergency, was relaxed and on 14th June BFBS Benghazi was able to inform its listeners that the Army schools were to be reopened and that families with cars would be able to go to the Army beaches during the afternoon.

Colonel Martin, the Commander Cyrenaica Area, in a letter to the Director of BFBS, commented upon the situation: "As you know I have always thought very highly of our BFBS in Benghazi. Their efforts from 5th to 11th June were quite remarkable."

Only two weeks later Bryan Cave-Brown-Cave, the Director of BFBS in London received a letter informing him that at the request of the Libyan Government, all service personnel were to be withdrawn from Libyan territory. The plan was to close down the Army schools in July and evacuate the families by the end of October 1967. BFBS Benghazi would cease broadcasting on 15th November 1967.

Mr. Cave-Brown-Cave's visit to Tobruk in 1967 produced a damning report on the behaviour and morale of some of the station's staff. He wrote: "The respect and esteem in which the station and its staff were held when I last visited El Adem/Tobruk eighteen months previously, now no longer exists. On all sides, from the Station Commander, El Adem downwards there was angry criticism of the behaviour, manners and dress of some members of the BFBS staff. To use the Camp Commandant's phrase, 'they are roaring about like young stallions'. They are involved in drunkenness and brawling. As a result team spirit no longer existed and the staff could only be described as in a state of anarchy."

The Director's final recommendation was: "the current Station Controller is not fit to fill the position he holds and he must retire in the autumn."

When Ian Woolf visited Tobruk in 1969 he commented on the improvement in the standards of broadcasting: "The Station is doing much more than just entertaining. It is a real beacon to the audience, giving out the information which they need e.g. the times the buses are leaving El Adem for Tobruk, the fact that the NAAFI has received fresh vegetables and that the newspapers are in." He then went on to describe life in Tobruk: "There is an atmosphere of neglect which is quite appalling. Tobruk reminds me of Aden before the Tedders launched their campaign for better amenities. There is only one communal centre in Tobruk itself; it is run by the Salvation Army and although they do a good job, the centre is in an appalling state. At the moment Tobruk does no good to our people or to Britain's image."

On 6th February 1970 Peter Holwill, the Station Controller of BFBS Tobruk, received a letter from Group Captain Terry at RAF El Adem: "The close and personal touch provided by BFBS has been a great morale booster, especially for families, during the curfew hours and the trying times which followed the change of Libyan Government. You have been an invaluable means of providing information and keeping everyone in touch with events. In such an isolated garrison area, with so few amenities, sound broadcasting has an increased importance. I know that this very fine service has only been made possible by a great deal of hard work, expertise, long hours and devotion to duty."

Major General Beckett, Director of Personal Services (Army), also wrote to Peter Holwill: "On the closure of BFBS Tobruk I should like to convey to you and your staff my grateful thanks for the very real contribution which your efforts have made to the morale and well-being of servicemen and their families in Libya."

On December 22nd 1960 Ian Woolf received a letter from the Command Secretariat in Rheindhalen: "It is understood that charges are not raised for advertisements broadcast through the British Forces Network in Germany e.g. those by NAAFI on Monday mornings and "Small Ads". I assume you have War Office authority for such free advertising and I would be grateful if you would send me a copy. On the other hand, if you have no such authority it may be necessary to ask the War Office to confirm it is their policy to waive charges. Can you say what would be a reasonable charge for a Small Ad based on the running cost of BFN during the time taken to read the advertisement and taking into consideration overheads and administrative costs in handling the advertisement?"

Ian Woolf's reply was brief and to the point: "No specific authority is held for the advertising you have in mind which is considered to form a part of the

Studio D in BFN Cologne was used for all the major request programmes including 'Family Favourites'.   (© Private Photograph)

service which BFN should provide under the terms of its charter (to inform, educate and entertain HM Forces overseas). I consider that this advertising comes under the information section of our responsibilities. Quite obviously NAAFI will wish to inform its customers i.e. BFN listeners of available merchandise, and it is in the interest of the Service to assist NAAFI in this way, because to assist NAAFI is, in the final analysis, to assist the Services."

One month later in February 1961 the Daily Telegraph's Bonn Correspondent wrote an article about a visit by the Head of the BBC Listener Research Department to BFN Cologne: "He is here to consider the problems of audience research in Rhine Army. To the average listener in West Germany BFN not only provides light entertainment for the troops but relays BBC news bulletins. These are not only listened to with appreciation by the Germans wishing to learn English but by Americans and others valuing objectivity.

The popular side is not unappreciated. The wire room of the central German Press office in Bonn regularly resounds with British pop music. Yet considering the volume of its output BFN is run on an astonishingly small shoestring. Its broadcasting team comprises eight members only, and its total staff including engineers is only 66. This nucleus turns out 119 hours of broadcasting weekly. Although 39 percent of the broadcasts are taken from the BBC Light programme, the rest is made up of locally produced programmes and the importance of BFN's disc jockeys should not be underestimated. More time is given to details of requests and messages than in regular BBC programmes thus preserving a sense of community and keeping people informed about friends and acquaintances."

In the meantime Ian Woolf's plans to increase his news collecting points began to materialise. First a small, unmanned studio was set up in Herford and allowed more news and information from 1st British Corps to be fed into the network. This was followed by another unmanned studio being opened in Spandau in Berlin.

The first Berlin reporter was Vic Andersen, who had been a regular freelance broadcaster in Cologne before moving to the City.

Then came the breakthrough that Ian Woolf had been fighting for. The Treasury had finally agreed to a permanent member of the BFN staff to be based in Berlin.

The decision came too late for Alastair McDougall to report on the building of the Berlin Wall but he was BFN's man on the spot when the Cuban Missile Crisis began on October 22nd 1962. Although Berlin could not, at this point, opt out of the network, he was able to give a feel for the pressures, which now affected the servicemen and their families in Berlin. As the Crisis grew, the Forces children in Berlin were being prepared for evacuation as they were throughout the BAOR. Families at BFN Cologne were also told to pack a suitcase, just in

Vic Andersen, the first BFN
reporter to use the new BFBS
Berlin studio – 1961.
(© Crown Copyright: FBS 1285)

case. Luckily the world stepped back from the brink when Mr. Khrushchev promised that the Russian missiles based in Cuba would be dismantled and shipped back to Russia.

In July 1963 President John Kennedy came to Berlin and visited the Brandenburg Gate and Checkpoint Charlie and made his famous "Ich bin ein Berliner" speech. Four months later, the man who had captured the hearts of the people of West Germany and Berlin was dead. As soon as BFN Cologne received the news, the station changed its schedules to sombre music. This was the first time this had happened for a foreign Head of State.

When Queen Elizabeth paid a state visit to the Federal Republic of Germany in May 1965, BFBS Cologne pulled out all the stops with Ian Fenner, Brian Bass, Alan Parfrey, Pat Pachebat and Alastair McDougall producing a series of Outside Broadcasts covering the 11 day visit. These included covering ceremonies at a variety of cities, from Munich to Hamburg, and making everything sound as if it was according to plan. Enthusiastic spectators continuously mobbed the royal party. In Koblenz, where the Queen gave her first address to the public, she reminded them that the first steamboat used on the Rhine in 1816 was made in Britain. When she had finished the crowd broke through the police cordon and the Guard of Honour was hastily deployed for crowd control. In Bonn, she laid a bouquet of roses at Beethoven's statue and in Cologne she was presented with a third–century AD Roman glass vessel and invited to sign the City's Golden Book.

During the early part of the Sixties, BFBS Germany's schedules had changed very little from the original format set up in Hamburg.

The Station still opened at 6.30 am with 'Musical Clock' and this was followed by a programme for the housewives called 'For You At Home'. At 5.00pm Bill Mitchell opened up his 'Kinder Klub' which was followed by the popular '1800 Club'. 'The Archers', 'The Dales' and 'Woman's Hour' were among the top programmes relayed from the BBC.

When John Russell arrived in Cologne in 1967 to take up his post as Senior Programme Organiser, he found, despite the changing world of broadcasting, BFBS Cologne was still steeped in the past. He knew he would face opposition from the older members of staff, but he felt it was time to axe some of the 'sacred cows'. First to go was 'The 1800 Club' in October 1967. As far as Russell was concerned, even the flagship programme of BFBS 'Family Favourites' was past its sell-by date.

Even the announcers' shift pattern was altered and a Radio One style of presentation took over. John Russell's brief to his producers was simple: "Make the programmes interesting, entertaining and relevant and increase the serviceman's awareness of what is going on in Germany".

With so many changes taking place, Bill Crozier and Alastair McDougall, veterans of the Musikhalle in Hamburg decided it was time to move on.

When Derek Hale arrived in Malta from BFN Cologne in September 1962, he was appalled with the deficiencies of FBS Malta. In a letter to the Command Secretary, he described the equipment as: "something which would disgrace the shelves of a radio junk shop. It is only through the extraordinary efforts of the engineer, Peter Blanchette, and the Station Controller, Peter Holwill, that the station stays on the air at all. It is my opinion that the equipment, when new, was not up to broadcasting specifications and never could have produced the required quality. The Station Controller is expected to do his own typewriting, his own filing, record ordering, indexing of records and at the same time, train volunteer announcers and controllers."

The attitude of the professional broadcaster towards the volunteer has always been ambivalent. On the one hand, most BFBS members will acknowledge the invaluable help of most volunteers. On the other, all professionals have a horror of those who are in the studio for the ego trip alone and who resent the sort of production and criticism that a professional takes for granted. Many of the volunteers who joined BFBS Malta, by sheer enthusiasm, reached a high standard of broadcasting in a very short time and some went on to a career with BFBS or joined other radio organisations.

For most found the radio station became the centre of their social life. Sometimes, it became a little too social. One night, sitting at home with his wife, Derek Hale turned on to listen to a play from the BBC Transcription Services. About ten minutes in, he realised the play was punctuated with heavy breathing and excited cries in a manner which the content seemed not to warrant. Realising the station phone was in the library and out of the presenter's reach, he jumped into his car and drove to FBS. The door was locked and he spent 20 minutes hammering before a dishevelled young man appeared. "Do you realise that your activities over the last half hour have been broadcast to the entire island?" he stormed. Inside the untidy studio they found that the microphone had a faulty switch. Apparently in the off position, it was still live!

If proof were ever needed of the importance of the newly created Head Office of BFBS then it came on 17th October 1963 at a meeting of the HOSC at the War Office.

The BFBS Director informed the meeting that he had recently listened to a tape recording of the programme output of FBS Malta, and he considered it to be of a deplorably low standard, which reflected badly on both BFBS and the Services in Malta. Inadequate staff and obsolete technical facilities, he claimed, caused the low standard. He went on: "I cannot agree to allow this situation to continue and that, unless the Services make provision in the estimates for the next financial year for a full-scale Class Three Station (i.e. the minimum size) to replace the present impoverished service, then BFBS will have to withdraw completely by the end of the present year."

Following this direct approach, the Committee agreed that on balance, they were slightly in favour of the establishment of a Class Three BFBS Station for Malta.

In the following February the Headquarters Malta and Libya wrote to the Under Secretary of State at the War Office supporting Cave-Brown-Cave's threat to remove BFBS from Malta, unless a new station was properly funded and set-up. "If BFBS disappears the only other broadcasting services available to Service families in Malta will be the General Overseas Service of the BBC and local television and radio. The GOS is not designed as a continuous listening programme and has no local appeal. Likewise, local TV and radio are broadcasting increasingly in Maltese. Following a survey we have ascertained that 70 percent of Service families listen to BFBS. The present station is rapidly disintegrating and will soon cease to function. The quality of programmes run by volunteers leaves much to be desired and in times of emergency, when a BFBS station is essential for the recall of troops to barracks and the dissemination of accurate news to the families, volunteer staff will not be available to man the station, since they will be carrying out their operational tasks."

However, with a Defence Review looming, the Treasury would only authorise the installation of a new VHF transmitter. The situation would have to continue until 1966, when equipment sent back from Nairobi and Tripoli could be repaired and then installed in Malta.

In 1964 when Malta gained her independence, it was assumed that, as the British had retained their bases on the island, it would be a long time before the British Forces would finally withdraw. The British presence, particularly at the dockyard, was important in a small island where mass immigration had not solved

Ted King, Kay Donnelly and Michael Aspel at the official opening of the new BFBS Studios in Malta.   (© *Private Photograph*)

the unemployment problem. So in 1967 when the British government proposed a swift reduction in the Forces on the island, the crisis took everyone by surprise.

Alan Hargreaves, who was now running the station in Malta, wrote to London and pointed out some of his problems: "We are not broadcasting commentary or Radio Newsreel for fear of upsetting the Maltese Government. The fuel supplies are running low and this is making it difficult for volunteers to get to the station. At the moment I am trying to work out a system that enables us to transport the volunteers home after their duty. I have been informed, but not officially, that the Maltese Government may regard BFBS as one of the privileges of the British Forces in Malta!"

Meanwhile, back in London, Bryan Cave-Brown-Cave, in a letter to the War Office, drew their attention to the importance placed on BFBS by the Commonwealth Office, especially during any internal security situation: "The vital importance of BFBS under these circumstances has been shown in Aden, Cyprus, Benghazi during the Arab/Israeli War, Nairobi and Egypt. BFBS is the only means that the Local Commander has of communicating rapidly with the servicemen and their families on the island and of keeping them informed. In Aden and Benghazi for example, BFBS was called upon to provide a 24 hour a day service. It is impossible to rely on volunteers to provide this service in times of crisis because of their own commitments. The only guarantee is a staff of professionals, whose duty it is to man the station as required."

The Ministry of Defence finally agreed that the studio in Malta should be re-equipped and refurbished and extra UK-based staff employed. But progress was slow and when the new Station Controller, John Campbell, arrived in January 1969, he found that the refit was still not complete. The main problem was that the building was listed and the exterior sacrosanct. To preserve it, he decided to prop up the roof, support the walls and gut the interior in one exercise. Within two weeks BFBS Malta was operating with a forest of props holding up the roof. When Ted King introduced "Two Way Family Favourites" from the studio, he found himself sitting on a crate against a heap of rubble.

With the new staff in place and a new VHF stereo system in operation, Michael Aspel, the London anchorman of Family Favourites, formally opened the new station on 2nd June 1970.

Having been twice threatened with closure, FBS Nairobi settled down in the early sixties. There had been some attempt at rebuilding and re-equipping the studios but attention turned to building a small out-station for 24 Infantry Brigade Group at Gilgil 80 miles north of Nairobi where reception faded after dark. The presentation team were all volunteers from the local regiments and

Keith Skues in the studios of the BFBS Nairobi – 1964.   *(© Crown Copyright: FBS 1152)*

their programmes were sent up on the daily postal run. The new transmitter reached Nakuru where the married families lived and although they were broadcasting five hours a day, many of the programmes that made headlines in the East African newspapers were not available.

One of these programmes was called "The Skeuball Special", a fortnightly comedy series written by Keith Skues, Peter Clare and the rest of their colleagues. Everyone on the station was involved. The programme ran for two years but gradually it ran out of ideas as many of the contributors were posted to other stations.

Kenya was, for many, a high spot in their time with Forces Broadcasting. They discovered anything was possible and, in a small community, they became public figures, but occasionally things could go wrong. On one particular day Keith Skues ran out of petrol on the Mombasa road and returned to find someone had stolen his wheels, while Lyndon Smith and Chris Denning crashed into each other as they drove in and out of the station.

This series of mishaps took their cars off the road at the same time. As Doreen Taylor wrote in her book; "A Microphone and A Frequency": 'As a joke, Lyndon

Smith bought a white horse and, complete with city suit, deerstalker and meerschaum pipe, trotted down one of Nairobi's main streets, followed by the rest of the announcers crammed into Peter Clare's two-seater sports car. When the horse stopped to nibble grass at a roadway island, the city traffic seized up, and in Peter Holwill's office the phone rang. "Please call your announcer in," pleaded the voice of a Nairobi traffic policeman. "They're causing an obstruction in the centre of Nairobi."

On 29 November 1964, BFBS Nairobi closed. The G-O-C British Troops East Africa, Major General Ian Freeland, recorded a farewell message for the station and his troops, and to complete the farewell programme Peter Holwill invited each member of staff to recount his or her most memorable moment. At the end Holwill made the closing announcement and the 'Evening Hymn' and 'The Last Post' followed.

In the morning Major John Ellis, Director of Army Public Relations in Nairobi, collect the General's message so that the civilian station, Voice of Kenya – anxious to build up its new Army audience – could rebroadcast it. He delivered the tape to the Head of the English language service of Voice of Kenya and was discussing the broadcast when an assistant rushed in. "Are our time pips accurate?" The department head looked up. "Within a minute or two I should think. Why?" Back came the reply: East Africa Airways have just phoned and asked if it's safe to rely on Voice Of Kenya pips, now that BFBS has shut down.'"

The headlines of the Sixties talked about England winning the World Cup, the last National Serviceman to be called up, the Beatles, Carnaby Street, Radio Caroline, the first Pirate Radio Station, BBC's 1, 2, 3 and 4 replacing the BBC's Light Programme and Home Service, Gagarin the first man in space and Nelson Mandela is sent to prison. All of these stories had been covered by BFBS but their stations were becoming fewer as Aden, Benghazi, Nairobi, Tripoli and Tobruk closed down.

The staff of BFBS Benghazi 1968. Left to right: Lance Daniels, Ted King, Peter Holwill, Colin Rugg, David Lamb, Brian Scott, Peter Attrill, Peter Blanchette and John Walker.

(© Crown Copyright: FBS 1572)

Gerald Sinstadt, whose broadcasting career had begun with BFN in Austria, returned to BFBS London in 1965 to set up the new BFBS London Sports Unit. He is seen here with Bertie Mee, Arsenal's double-winning manager, prior to the recording of a programme – 'Men At The Top'.

(© Crown Copyright: FBS 521)

CHAPTER FOUR

The Seventies

An Invasion and Two Farewells

In the spring of 1970, two men claiming to be record producers from a new record company visited BFBS Malta. One claimed to be the brother of Rita Moreno, a Puerto Rican actress who had made a number of films, the best known being 'West Side Story'. They said the purpose of their visit was to see whether BFBS Malta would include their most recent record release in their play-list. Tony Fawcett, who was the record librarian, pointed out that the records received by the stations came through the BFBS Head Office system. If they wanted their record to be considered, they should take it to London. Although, in those days, each station was able to prepare its own play-list, and locally produced records of merit might be included, this rarely happened.

The visitors asked, if they made a monetary contribution to the station funds, would that influence the decision as to whether their record could go on the play-list? Tony Fawcett pointed out that, apart from anything else, payment for inclusion of records was called 'Payola' which was illegal and it was definitely not part of the BFBS policy.

Several members of BFBS were involved in the last night of the Malta Amateur Dramatic Society's production of 'Salad Days'. It put a damper on the evening when news came through that a well-known national Sunday newspaper had included a double page spread detailing all that had happened during the visit of the two men who turned out to be undercover reporters.

Despite the newspaper's efforts, BFBS Malta and BFBS World-wide were completely vindicated, and Peter Holwill soon brought BFBS Malta up to full strength, taking charge for the third time in his broadcasting career.

In June 1971, Dom Mintoff and his Labour Party defeated the Right-wing government of Dr. Borg Olivier. Peter remembers receiving a telephone call from a member of his wife's Maltese family saying: "All the British troops will be gone by 1st January 1972." The British community on the island was astounded.

Mintoff relented a little and put the departure date back to 31st March 1972 and, by the middle of January, the service families and those of BFBS were on their way back home. Peter Holwill's problem was to keep the station operational until the end. When HMS Bulwark came into Grand Harbour to evacuate the troops, BFBS managed to present the first ever edition of 'Family Favourites' from the warship by using the Navy's communication system.

Back in London, Ian Woolf was trying hard to find out what was going on and the signals flowed to and fro. On 27th March, Mintoff struck a new agreement with Britain and NATO. The services could stay. Head Office rebuilt a team for Malta and, on 23rd June 1972, BFBS Malta was back in action.

In May 1971, a new and rather important programme was featured in the BFBS Bulletin called 'Ulster Calling'. The idea was to link the men currently serving in Northern Ireland with their families back in Germany. The programme was an instant success and featured a new name to the listeners to BFBS Germany – Gloria Hunniford. The reaction to this programme by the families in Germany was staggering and, a few years later, BFBS TV would use the same format with Pam Rhodes as the presenter.

Six years after BFBS had covered the Football World Cup in the UK, they were to achieve another landmark when a team of six set out to cover the 1972 Olympic Games in Munich. As they were leaving London, Ian Woolf remarked: "It will be a challenge," and it certainly was. They went on air at 6.30am every day with a roundup of the late evening and overnight results. This was followed by a programme at noon and a round-up of the day's events at 6.30pm. Despite having only two reporters, they were to record some of the best interviews of the games. Don Durbridge, from BFBS Gibraltar, recorded interviews with Richard Meade, the Individual Gold Medallist in the Equestrian Three Day Event and Mark Spitz, the American swimmer. The BFBS team took a gamble after Spitz had won his fifth gold medal and Don Durbridge, with the aid of an American coach, managed to record a 15-minute interview at the poolside with the games golden boy. That night, Spitz would win two more gold medals, but it was also the night of the Israeli massacre and by the morning, he had left Munich.

The Olympic Games were suspended and BFBS had a major story on its hands. They had an incredible stroke of luck when an old friend, Paddy Feeney of BBC World Service, offered them an interview that he had recorded with the Hong Kong Chef de Mission, which ended with: "I must go now, there are men with guns." Bryan Hamilton talked his way past security police to get into the Athletes Village, the scene of the massacre, and John Hedges, Don and Alan Grace rounded up as much information as they could and went on air with the full story of Munich's blackest day, beating the BBC's 'World at One' by 60 minutes.

Bryan Hamilton recorded an amazing interview with the 1500 metre Olympic Gold Medallist, Kip Keino of Kenya, which resulted in BFBS getting a rap over the knuckles for recording an interview with the winner before he had reached the obligatory press conference. As Bryan explained later, a very large Kenyan dressed in military uniform wanted to know who he was and when he discovered he was from BFBS, the Kenyan, who had been a fan of BFBS Nairobi, ordered Keino to do the interview.

Just before the BFBS team packed up to return to their various stations, Ian Trethowan, Director General of the BBC, called in to thank them for the many items they had supplied to the Corporation and remarked on the unusual methods employed.

On 7th March 1973, Ian Woolf, the Director of BFBS in London, wrote to all the BFBS stations: "The long awaited plan to implement a new pay scale for BFBS staff, as from 1st January, has not materialised. The government has put a

Ian Woolf, the Director of BFBS receiving an award from the American Forces Radio and Television Service. Presenting the award, on behalf of AFN is Pat Pachebat, the Station Controller of BFBS Germany – 1973.   *(© Crown Copyright: FBS 554)*

standstill on wages and salaries. Also, the recommendations of the working party in regard to increasing the size of the establishments have not been implemented."

At the time, the pay for a BFBS Grade V announcer was just under £1,000 a year, whilst BBC Local Radio stations were paying their equivalent staff considerably more.

BFBS Germany's Station Controller, John Parsons, was caught on the horns of a dilemma. His programme establishment was 12, but by April 1973, this had already been reduced to 10 following resignations and four others were planning to leave, either to join BBC Local Radio or the newly formed Commercial Radio. Having examined his options of either reducing the quality of his programmes or the quantity, he felt his only solution was to closedown the station from Monday–Friday from 9.00am to noon.

This was not acceptable to Headquarters BAOR. They suggested filling the proposed gap with direct BBC Radio Two broadcasts. At the same time, the military would canvas worldwide for servicemen with broadcasting experience to be posted to BFBS Cologne. They also suggested that the BBC should be approached to lend personnel to BFBS.

Most of the stations in the Forces Broadcasting Service had, at some time or other, reduced their broadcasting hours through lack of staff, but Germany, the flagship of BFBS, had never done so since it started in July 1945.

Back in London, Ian Woolf kept up the pressure on the MoD: "Unless something is done soon, the service will run down completely. Already the staff are thoroughly disillusioned and morale would further deteriorate if they were to realise, as they would, that the BBC was being used to prevent any radical action being taken to deal with the root of the trouble."

Another problem faced by John Parsons concerned the Berlin studio. He would be unable to man the studio in the present situation and the military, who were always looking at ways of saving money, suggested BFBS give up the permanent line to Berlin.

On 15th August, Headquarters BAOR issued a warning to all Commanding Officers about BFBS's shortage of staff. After explaining how the problem had come about, the note ended: "It has therefore been decided, with great regret, that it is necessary to accept a break in BFBS programmes from 9.20am to 11.00am daily from Monday to Friday, starting on Monday 3rd September 1973. It is impossible to forecast how long this cut will have to continue but the position will be under continuous review."

A little light appeared on the horizon for Forces Broadcasting, however, when the MoD agreed to a trainee scheme. The trainees would not have the qualifications required (i.e. two A-levels and two years experience) as a fully-

John Parsons, Station Controller of BFBS Cologne presenting a Station Plaque to mark 25 years of Forces Broadcasting in Germany to the Burgomeister of Cologne – 1970.

(© Private Photograph)

fledged Grade V, but they were a welcome addition to the staff, not only in Germany but in other BFBS stations as well.

BFBS Cologne closed down on Monday September 3rd but was back into full-time broadcasting on Monday 24th September with the Richard Astbury Show.

In October 1973, the first group of trainees assembled at Kings Buildings and a month later were on their way to their overseas stations. Nicol Raymond and Richard Clegg were sent to Cyprus, Nick Bailey to Gibraltar, Sarah Bawden (Kennedy) to Singapore, Richard Gwynn to Malta and Patrick Lunt to Germany. Although the trainees may have lacked experience, they more than made up for it with enthusiasm and an understanding of the concepts of modern radio. With the exception of Cyprus, the trainees were soon on air and all would make an impact in the next few months on Forces Broadcasting.

The day after Ian Woolf wrote to all stations about the standstill in salaries, the IRA planted a car bomb outside Kings Buildings in Dean Stanley Street,

Westminster, Headquarters of the Forces Broadcasting Service. It was one of four bombs; the others were planted outside New Scotland Yard, the Old Bailey and an Army Recruiting Office at Great Scotland Yard.

The Times News Desk received a call at 1.56pm from a man with an Irish accent, who said that three car bombs had been left on the streets of London and were due to detonate at 3.00pm. According to the caller, a Vauxhall Viva had been left outside the BBC offices in Dean Stanley Street!

The staffs of BFBS and the Service Booking Centre were ordered to leave the building immediately and everyone was ushered out through the side door into Smith Square. The broadcasters headed to their favourite studio 'The Marquis of Granby'. Only the Admin Officer, Arthur Lobb, stayed in the building and had to be persuaded by the Police to leave.

Bomb disposal officers smashed the rear window of the Viva and immediately detected the smell of explosives. Virtually all the space under the rear seat was filled with bags containing around 80 lbs of what was known as 'Co-op' mix and 30 lbs of blasting explosive. By 2.35pm the bomb disposal experts had cut the wires and made the bomb safe.

Two of the other bombs went off and more than 200 people were injured. The IRA had found it easy to plant the car bombs that day because there was a National Rail strike and parking restrictions had been lifted.

───────────

On October 12th 1973, Air Marshal Sir John Aiken, Commander British Forces Near East, unveiled a plaque in the foyer of BFBS Dhekelia, commemorating 25 years of Forces Broadcasting in Cyprus. Little did he or the assembled guests realise that the next time he would broadcast on BFBS would be at the start of the Turkish Invasion of Cyprus.

Following Independence, Cyprus returned to normal life with the members of Forces Broadcasting enjoying typical Cypriot hospitality with brandy and mezze the order of the day. But in December 1963, trouble broke out between the Greek and Turkish Cypriots. For Roy Morgan, the Station Controller, the main difficulty was getting his staff to the studios in Nicosia as some were marooned in their homes in the Turkish areas. Morgan and Kay Donnelly, who lived in Kyrenia, were unable to go home for three days. Roy Morgan recalls that the only way he could find out if the Kyrenia Pass was quiet was to ring a beekeeper friend, who lived at the top of the pass.

The following year, with the trouble escalating, the United Nations stepped in and a peacekeeping force was introduced to Cyprus.

That same year, BFBS Cyprus, after 10 years of waiting for a new studio complex, finally moved to Dhekelia in the Eastern Sovereign Base Area, into one

The first BFBS Trainees. Left to right: Sarah Kennedy, Rick Lunt, Nick Bailey, Richard Gwynn, Richard Clegg and Nicol Raymond – 1973   *(© Crown Copyright: FBS 542)*

of the most modern radio stations in the Middle East. At last, the staff could work in air-conditioned studios. It was not until four years later, when Ian Woolf visited the island, that he discovered that the Commander of the British Forces, Air Marshal, Sir Edward Gordon-Jones, believed the station was in the wrong Sovereign Base Area.

Despite the CBFNE's reservations, BFBS Cyprus did its best to cover the whole of the island and eventually built a small satellite studio in an old Sergeants' Mess in Episkopi to increase the news from the WSBA.

Life on Aphrodite's Isle continued at its usual sedate pace, interrupted only by the staging of the first Cyprus Rally, part of the World Rally Championships, in 1970, an event, which was covered by BFBS. However, internal problems on the island were beginning to escalate, which would change the story of Cyprus forever.

The Head of News in Dhekelia was John Walker and on 15th July 1974 he burst into Roy Morgan's office, where he and Alan Grace were holding their weekly programme meeting, with some startling news.

"I have just heard on CBC (Cyprus Broadcasting Corporation) that Archbishop Makarios is dead and a coup has taken place in Nicosia."

Air Marshal Sir John Aiken unveiling a plaque to commemorate 25 years of Forces Broadcasting in Cyprus, with him is Roy Morgan, the Station Controller and Alan Grace – 1973.

(© Crown Copyright: FBS 999)

Immediately thoughts turned to how the station could help, especially if the Troubles escalated into the dormitory towns of Limassol, Larnaca and Famagusta. However, deliberations were cut short with a call from Command Headquarters in Episkopi with the first of many statements that BFBS Cyprus would be broadcasting during the next few days.

"News of the outbreak of trouble was received at approximately 09.00 hours today, with the report that the Cyprus National Guard had seized and closed the Cyprus International Airport and taken over the Cyprus Broadcasting Station. This was quickly followed by reports that the Presidential Palace had been shelled and President Makarios killed. Fighting broke out in the major towns of Nicosia, Limassol, Famagusta and Larnaca."

The coup had been inspired by the Government of the Colonels in Greece and pitted Greek Cypriot against Greek Cypriot. However, it caught most people on the island by surprise.

The next telephone call turned BFBS Cyprus into a 24-hour radio station for the first time in its history. "While the situation in the Republic remains confused, the only means of getting advice, information and instructions to all

British dependants from the SBAs and retained sites (areas where the British lived and worked) is by announcements on BFBS Radio. Make certain, therefore, that you listen frequently. Switch on every 30 minutes during the day."

Once again, BFBS was to prove itself invaluable to the Command in an emergency because it was the only way they, or the High Commissioner, could communicate with families and visitors on the island, many of whom were staying with Greek or Turkish friends.

At a time of crisis, the role of a 24-hour radio station is vital. Many of the service wives were alone with their children, while their husbands were guarding the SBAs (Sovereign Base Areas) and other military installations. The fact that familiar voices, such as Richard Nankivell, David Davis, Keith Rawlings, Jim Luxton and John Crabtree, were bringing them the news was comforting.

Tension on the island grew with the news that the former EOKA gunman, Nicos Samson, had been elected President of the Republic. At the same time, correspondents to the BBC programmes were talking about unrest in Turkey and a possibility of the Turkish forces moving against Cyprus to protect Turkish Cypriots.

The WSBA Team at the Episkopi Studio. Left to right: Colin Rugg, Sue Smith and Jim Luxton – 1973. *(© Crown Copyright: FBS 1007)*

In BFBS Episkopi, Jim Luxton, the WSBA (Western Sovereign Base Area) representative had been warned by some friendly Turks to 'watch out'.

However, on July 19th 1974, BFBS was advised that it could return to its normal broadcasting routine. At dawn the next day, the Turks landed at Kyrenia. After shelling the town from the sea they made their way ashore, whilst airborne troops were landing on the plain between Kyrenia and Nicosia.

In Episkopi, Jim Luxton was ordered to Command Headquarters and given an envelope marked 'secret'. It contained instructions for the emergency and a statement that the Commander of the British Forces, Sir John Aiken, would broadcast.

At the other end of the island, in Dhekelia, Alan Grace, Senior Programmes Organiser, woke up to find the duty announcer, Richard Nankivell, and the duty officer, Lieutenant Philip Hanlon, on his doorstep who told him: "The Turks have landed and we've got to get the station on the air as quickly as possible." In 30 minutes, BFBS Cyprus was operational.

While Richard Nankivell broadcast the breaking news, Alan Grace rang round the staff. Within 10 minutes of being on air, Colonel David Woodford, from the Command Headquarters, rang through with a message: "All British service and civilian families are to stay put, get their documents together and wait for further instructions."

Using BFBS in an emergency was nothing new and it was something that the military understood.

Air Marshal Sir John Aiken, Commander of the British Forces Near East, used the BFBS Episkopi studio, which was close to his headquarters, to make his broadcasts which began with the phrase: "First let me identify myself."

During the first day, the BFBS staff were broadcasting a series of announcements to the families caught up in the fighting. In Famagusta, which had been badly hit, news was coming in of the concern of those trapped in the war zone. Because most of the listeners to BFBS knew the programme competition telephone number, the station was able to field the calls and pass on the relevant information to the Headquarters in Episkopi.

As the invasion gathered momentum, convoys were assembled to bring the families from Larnaca, Limassol and Famagusta into the bases. They were advised by BFBS to pack a suitcase and ensure they had all their documentation with them.

The population of the bases grew at an alarming rate and those living in quarters, including many of the BFBS staff, took in the refugees.

In Nicosia, many civilians, and tourists whose holiday had been cut short, were waiting for the news that would bring them to safety. It came in the form of another broadcast by Sir John Aiken: "I am sending a convoy of vehicles to

Archbishop Makarios, who initially was reported as having been killed in the Coup in July 1974, visiting Greek Cypriot refugees in Akhna Forest in the ESBA. *(© Private Photograph)*

Nicosia. Its destination is a place recommended by the British High Commissioner and the American Ambassador as one which is safe from the fighting at this time. Its purpose is solely that of saving life and evacuating to the British Sovereign Base Areas innocent people who find themselves in dangerous circumstances in Nicosia.

"I now address the Turkish and Greek Commanders in Cyprus: the convoy will be clearly marked with the British Flag, the Union Jack, a form of recognition you have come to accept during the past seven tragic days. Thus its identity will be unmistakeable. Military vehicles similarly marked will escort it. I ask the full co-operation of the Greek and Turkish Commanders and their troops in the execution of this purely humanitarian mission."

BFBS also broadcast instructions concerning the various evacuations in French and German for the many foreign tourists on the island.

One of those caught up in the problems in Nicosia was Squadron Leader Robin Turner, who had recently been appointed as the BFBS Padre, and his wife, Liz.

Life in the bases now meant queues and improvised sleeping quarters. Many of the BFBS wives worked in the Reception Centres, helping to process the British refugees so that they could be sent back to the UK. The children of the staff were enrolled to empty dustbins, clean toilets, help in the mess kitchens and collect clothes for the refugees.

With Cyprus Broadcasting off the air, BFBS had become the main source of news. Their broadcasts were picked up in Lebanon and Israel and relayed to stations throughout the world. The station was doing its best to stifle the various rumours that were flying around the SBAs and it was BFBS Cyprus which made the first announcement that Archbishop Makarios was still alive.

Many of the local staff of BFBS Cyprus were caught up in the fighting and were unable to come to work for many days. Andy Nicolaou, who worked in the BFBS Stores, was captured by the Turks and spent several months in a POW camp in Turkey. Upon his return to the station, the first man to greet him was his old Turkish Cypriot friend, the watchman, Mehmet Ibrahim.

Les Austin, the Station's Librarian, whose role was vital now the station had returned to 24-hour broadcasting, was one of those stranded in Famagusta. As he

Richard Nankivell taking part in a bed race for charity, with him on the road from Ayios Nikolaous is Richard Clegg (*second right*), his producer – 1975.   (© *Crown Copyright: FBS 1564*)

was waiting for news of the Famagusta convoy, he decided to wash-up the last of his dishes. Suddenly the doorbell rang and, as he turned away from the kitchen window, a bullet struck the wall exactly where he had been standing. Les still has that bullet at his home in New Zealand.

As was common at many of the Forces Stations in the Middle East, the wives of servicemen were employed in a variety of roles. In Cyprus, Sheila Lambert, the wife of a corporal in 9 Signal Regiment, was working on the evening shift as a Programme Assistant when the telephone rang and she was informed that she had just two hours to move her belongings from her quarter to the airstrip at Kingsfield near Dhekelia. For the rest of that shift, the announcer and engineer on duty found themselves doubling up.

Richard Clegg, one of the young trainees, was at home in the UK on leave when he heard about the invasion. He dashed down to Brize Norton and sat in the departure lounge until a seat could be found for him on a Cyprus bound aircraft. On arriving at Akrotiri, he had to wait again until a convoy was formed to transport people and equipment from the WSBA to the ESBA.

At the beginning of August, a ceasefire was called, but the BBC's World Service broadcast from London that it was holding firm could hardly be heard in Dhekelia because of a fierce battle taking place just three miles away from the radio station.

BFBS received many accolades for its efforts during the emergency and Jim Luxton was awarded an MBE. However, two years later, as a result of the 1976 Defence Review, the station underwent savage cuts with 60 percent of the staff either laid off or posted to other stations and the studio in Episkopi was closed but would re-open a few months later.

For Roy Morgan, the cutbacks were too much to take and, after 22 years in Cyprus, he retired.

———————————

In Cologne, in 1959, Alastair McDougall, Gerald Sinstadt and Bill Crozier combined to produce a programme called 'Let's Spend An Evening At Home'. It was the first time a station had devoted three and a half hours to one programme. It included interviews and competitions and Bill Crozier, a gifted pianist, playing listeners' requests live. The concept was to allow the listener to settle down for the evening to enjoy a relaxed form of broadcasting, knowing he would not miss any news.

Two years earlier, BFN Cologne had tried another experiment in broadcasting. It took virtually all the staff to a particular unit and the major programmes of the day - 'Musical Clock, 'For You At Home' and '1800 Club'; plus a documentary about the unit and a variety show - were broadcast from the unit's location. Both

John Russell talking to the Captain of the Lufthansa 747 during a recording of his programme 'The After Ten People' – 1971.   *(© Crown Copyright: FBS 503)*

programmes were extremely popular, but they over-stretched the resources and so, after a fairly brief period, they were dropped and BFN Cologne went back to the old trusted format.

John Russell's arrival in the late sixties had brought several changes and, despite opposition, a new BFBS Cologne had begun to emerge. One of his concerns was that visitors to the station had been unable to hear its output in the entrance hall: "One of my first decisions was to have loudspeakers installed in the foyers and in all the corridors and public areas, including the toilets, so that the building sounded like a radio station."

In 1968, John had persuaded the Allied Powers and the Berlin Senate to stage a combined, tri-lingual Christmas concert in the Kaiser Wilhelm Church at the end of the Kufurstendamm. The concert also featured stars from the Berlin Opera and the Berlin Philharmonic together with the choirs of the French, American and British Forces. These concerts were broadcast on BFBS, AFN, Sender Freies Berlin and the French Service.

Three years later, John Russell convinced an old friend of his, the Reverend Roy Trevivian, a producer from the BBC Religious Department, that the Christmas concert would be ideal for BBC Radio 2. It happened to be the year of the Bader Meinhof Gang. Two weeks before the broadcast, they had desecrated the church and threatened to disrupt, if not attack, the service as the Allied Commanders and the Mayor of Berlin would be in attendance: "I remember sitting in the Outside Broadcast vehicle with Roy Trevivian," said John Russell. "We were surrounded by armoured cars, water cannon and the whole of the Berlin Riot Squad, prepared for any eventuality, whilst fabulous music proclaiming the message of Christmas came from the interior of the church. Roy Trevivian downed a whisky at the end of the broadcast and declared they would never believe his story back at the Beeb."

Another of the Russell projects was a music and chat programme on a Sunday evening called 'The After Ten People', in which he interviewed some of the major characters who were visiting Germany. His producers were Bob Pierson and Andrew Pastouna and, on one occasion, the programme was recorded on an aircraft flying to New York and from New York itself: "Among my many notable guests were Steve Biko, the South African black activist, and Eartha Kitt," said John Russell. "I told her that I could not afford to pay her normal fee. In the end, we agreed that I would make available a car and a driver to take her and her daughter to the Cologne Zoo. As we used the BFBS staff car and driver, I suppose I could have been charged with a splendid misuse of MoD transport."

A cartoon drawn for BFBS by Corporal Dennis Edmunds about the popular 'Radio Roulette' – 1977

(© BFBS Archive)

In the early Seventies, Cologne was already relaying top BBC Radio 2's programmes, such as 'The Jimmy Young Show' and 'The Terry Wogan Show', and Russell felt it was time his presenters became involved in personality radio. The 'John Hedges Morning Show' was replaced by the 'Richard Astbury Show', which in turn became simply 'Asters'. Presenters were asked to take over the breakfast show for a three month run. The first to do this was Norman Rickard, and he was followed by the first double-headed breakfast show, presented by Sarah Kennedy and Andrew Pastouna. This programme was lively, sometimes irreverent, but a 'must' with the listeners. By the time John Russell left in 1972 to go to Cyprus, the door he had opened to the modern broadcasting world, allowed those who came after him to prosper.

Later, a new lunchtime programme called 'Midday Magazine' was presented by Kay Donnelly, while in the early evening the popular 'Five Thirty Report' was followed in August 1976 with the 'Six Twenty Five' programme, which incorporated requests, ring-in features, competitions, 'Schnell-Sell', 'Radio Roulette' with all its prizes and forfeits, announcements, 'The Archers' and 'Sports Desk'. It was almost a return to the days of 'Let's Spend An Evening At Home'.

Germany had been a breeding ground for inventive young broadcasters and Peter McDonagh took some of the Cologne ideas with him when he was posted to Malta in 1975 as Programme Organiser. Bob Pierson, another of Cologne's creative talents, joined him a year later as the new station manager.

While Germany was making rapid strides in modernising its programme sound, only Malta appeared to follow suit. In May 1975, 'The Richard Gwynn Early Morning Show' was followed by 'PMcD at Nine' and in the evening 'The Five O'clock Run' with David Burrows and Christine Pollard. In Cyprus, the programmes still had the old Sixties sound.

Pierson, McDonagh and Gwynn began to look at what John Russell had achieved in Germany and decided to produce a musical style which would match their young audience in Malta. At Bob Pierson's insistence, out went the BBC World Service relays and their 15-minute news packages to be replaced by three-minute news summaries read by the local announcers from the BBC 'rip-and-read' service. Instead of time-consuming trips with a portable tape-recorder, which involved travelling round island, there would be live studio guests and interviewees. In essence, the team wanted their audience to feel that there was a 'live' voice at the radio station. There was still opposition, though, from some officers and warrant officers who did not approve of 'bloody jungle music'.

Germany could not go 'live', however, because it had problems with 'Woman's Hour'. Frequent audience surveys had shown that the listening figures for this programme, 'Listen With Mother' and 'Afternoon Theatre' were deteriorating and Pat Pachebat, the Station Controller, decided that he had no alternative but to drop the programmes. This caused an almighty row. Brigadier Jimmy Hellier at 1 (BR) Corps sent a signal to every unit ordering them to protest by signal, or letter, or telephone call. Soon Pat's desk was submerged with letters from all over Germany, but he stood firm and defended his decision at the next Advisory Broadcast meeting. Thankfully, BBC Radio 4 switched to 1500 metres long-wave shortly afterwards and listeners in the western part of Germany were able to hear the programme once again. With the opening of BFBS 2 in 1990, 'Woman's Hour' would again be a regular feature of BFBS broadcasting.

In 1978, four years after BFBS Cyprus had gone to 24-hour broadcasting in the emergency of the Turkish Invasion, Bob Pierson and his team at BFBS Malta decided they too would bring 24-hour broadcasting to their listeners. It required a great deal of planning but it worked with the aid of the Schafer equipment

The BFBS Malta 'Listen In' Christmas Cartoon featuring, left to right: John McLeod interviewing the fish, Lance Daniels, Colin Nichol, Kay Donnelly, Hylda Bamber, Peter Holwill and Roger Dunn reconnecting the power supply – 1973.   (© *BFBS Archive*)

salvaged from Singapore which had arrived the previous autumn, and on 3rd January 1978 BFBS Malta began 24-hour broadcasting. In December of that year, BFBS Germany followed suit.

The concept of sequence programming and 24-hour broadcasting had changed the philosophy and sound of BFBS Malta. It would be known as Format 77. Ian Woolf was so impressed that it became BFBS policy worldwide.

It was resisted on some of the stations and two of the service's most popular broadcasters, Bill Mitchell and Terry James, took the opportunity to retire.

It had taken several years to turn around the style and sound of Forces Broadcasting but it would make future acceptance by the military much easier.

On February 22nd 1975, Dan van der Vat wrote an article for The Times about BFBS Germany. It was headlined 'The radio station that is forced to pretend most of its listeners do not exist':

"Although BFBS programmes were aimed at the 200,000 or so British soldiers, airmen and their families, it was in fact only a tiny fraction of the number of listeners in Eastern Holland, Belgium, Southern Denmark, West Germany, West Berlin, East Germany and even parts of Western Poland – a catchment area of more than 40,000,000 people."

BFBS Germany could not respond to record requests from all these extra listeners because of Performing Rights agreements. BFBS had to ignore its outside audience if the Performing Rights Society in West Germany was to turn a blind eye. The article praised two members of the BFBS staff for demonstrating how well the station had carried out its brief of entertaining the Forces and their families in a typically British way.

One was Richard Astbury who had been presenting what was known as the housewives' show for the past three years, taking live telephone calls, almost always from soldiers' wives, and conducting conversations full of double-meanings and risqué allusions while avoiding rudeness. His judgement ensured that his programme captured the largest audience of all BFBS Germany broadcasts and crowds of around 4,000 people turned up to meet him when he opened Army fetes. One of the most popular records of the time was 'Don't stick stickers on my paper knickers', which gave Richard Astbury the cue for another cheeky chat.

The other was Bill Mitchell, who had a rather different claim to fame. Several times a week for the previous nine years, he had been telling stories about 'Big Wood'. "His large postbag is a token of his popularity among adults as much as children", said The Times article. "His stories reflect nostalgia for an England, which if it ever existed, ceased to do so a long time ago. The strange world of

Richard Astbury, centre with Sir Harry Secombe and Richard Nankivell.

(© Crown Copyright: FBS 1565)

Asters and Uncle Bill has little to do with the mainstream of life in modern Britain yet it remains essentially British."

In 1976, a new and in some ways revolutionary programme was produced at Kings Buildings in London. It was called 'BFBS UK' and was presented by Tommy Vance. It had its roots in the Station Controller's Conference of that year when suggestions were made that a music/magazine programme should be the next step forward for the London production unit. When Brian Bass, the Controller of Programmes, and Mike Robertson looked at the various suggestions, they realised that they had the chance to raise the profile of BFBS London once more.

Brian Bass acknowledged that if he were to implement all of the conference's suggestions, he would need a newsroom staff dedicated to this one programme alone. In the end, he decided to let Tommy's personality carry the show through with a varied selection of guests and a mix of the latest pop music.

The programme had one interesting quirk. Although it would appear to be live on the various stations, it was recorded several days in advance. Tommy's trick was

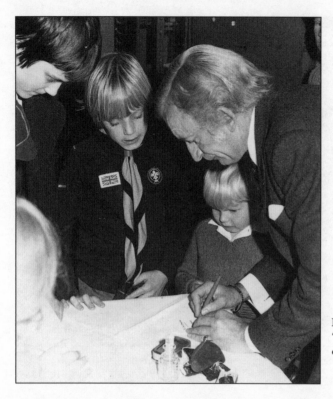

Bill Mitchell with some of his
'Big Wood' fans at the studios
of BFBS Cologne – 1976.
(© Crown Copyright:
FBS 1566)

to place a sign relating to the day of transmission i.e. Monday, Tuesday etc. on his desk. This would help him when he was recording the programme to connect with the day that it was to be broadcast on the overseas stations. Another little trick devised by Brian Bass was to mention occasionally that the programmes were recorded and urging listeners to get their requests in earlier than normal.

Occasionally, the team took the show to overseas commands and the response to Tommy and BFBS UK was amazing.

To Mike Robertson, the Senior Programmes Organiser of BFBS London, fell the task of investigating the whole range of publicity products for BFBS UK. Following the trend at the time, Mike had the BFBS Radio Logo printed on shirts, banners, mugs etc. As he put it later: "We were quite unashamedly aping the success of Capital Radio." Interestingly, the merchandise was snapped up, not just at major Outside Broadcasts by overseas stations, but also in the UK - where BFBS could not be heard – at events such as the Aldershot Army Show.

Mike Robertson's next move was to commission a series of eye-catching photographs of photogenic staff members wearing the BFBS merchandise, taken by Dennis King, then Julia Morley's 'Miss World' glamour photographer. On one occasion, a troupe of CSE dancers was rehearsing in the Queen Anne Footstool Theatre on the ground floor of Kings Buildings and one strikingly attractive blonde offered to model the BFBS sweatshirts. Dennis draped her provocatively on top of the A studio control desk and asked Mike whether he wanted her to be photographed with or without her bra. "Trying to sound nonchalant," said Mike, "I muttered something, but Dennis deciphered it as no bra please and after the adjustments were made, the photo shoot went ahead. Needless to say, large gold-framed studies of this particular photograph helped to adorn the rather drab corridor walls of Kings Buildings for several years to come."

For the next 10 years, BFBS UK would be the number one show originating from the London studios and became a forerunner for the Nineties programme 'Simon and The Squad'.

On Friday 16th April 1971, Basil D'Oliveira took part in the BFBS 'On Reflection' series. The main interviewer was Ian Wooldridge, who wrote in the Daily Mail the following Monday, 'Just the thing to give the troops but this D'Oliviera dynamite won't be heard in Britain': the article continued: "The

Anne Armstrong, the Soldier's Wives Campaigner with Tommy Vance in the 'BFBS UK' studio – 1976.   *(© Crown Copyright: FBS 534)*

sports unit of the British Forces Broadcasting Service – two men, one secretary and an ever-boiling kettle in a single cluttered office beneath Big Ben has just pulled off one of the major scoops of recent years. It is the first interview ever given by Basil D'Oliviera, in which he talks passionately about life under apartheid and the quite phenomenal political pressures to which he has been subjected behind the scenes. Quite what prompted him to change his mind and speak so forcibly in the BFBS's 'On Reflection' programme may never be known. Whatever the explanation, the result is D'Oliviera speaking with a brilliance, articulacy and conviction, which has never been heard in public before."

Another participant in the 'On Reflection' series was the Duke of Norfolk. Robin Marlar, the BBC cricket commentator and former England spin bowler, set up the programme and was joined in the studio by Brian Johnston. The result was an interesting look into the Duke's love of sport, especially cricket. Prince Philip also agreed to take part in the series and Bryan Hamilton, the producer, Ian Wooldridge and Frank Page, the interviewers, spent a fascinating time at Buckingham Palace. Shortly afterwards, however, Robert Neil was taken ill as he was due to interview Princess Anne, and Bryan had to get to the Palace as quickly as possible to take his place. Bryan recalled: "I must have looked a mess as my suit needed pressing, my tie should not have been allowed out on its own and my hair was in need of a good cut! As usual, Princess Anne put me at my ease and we recorded an excellent interview."

When Richard Astbury arrived in Malta, he found units closing down and all the Navy, Army and RAF quarters in the process of being handed back to the Maltese Government. He spent three weeks looking for suitable accommodation and eventually found a most attractive house at Qawra Point. There was only one problem. In that part of the island telephones were not available but Engineering Manager Peter Attrill soon fixed him up with a CB Radio, which was to prove vital. "I could not have wished for a better staff, both Maltese and UK based," he said. "Chief clerk Hector Frendo was in charge of the locals and knew every person in Malta who could do the station favours. John Crabtree was Programme Director and was to prove, with the experienced eye of Alan Clough, absolutely invaluable."

Before Bob Pierson left for Cologne, he introduced Astbury to the man who was to be his immediate boss, the highly distinguished Rear Admiral O.N.A "Ossie" Cecil, Commander British Forces, Malta. His clear brief from Westminster was to pull the British Forces out of Malta (after 180 years) without incident and he made this very clear to Richard Astbury.

"My first few months went very well. But as I became more aware of the local political scene, it was increasingly obvious that the Prime Minister, Dom Mintoff,

The 'On Reflection' team at Buckingham Palace. Left to right: Inez Clarke, programme secretary, Frank Page, interviewer, The Duke of Edinburgh, Ian Wooldridge, interviewer, Bryan Hamilton, producer and Ron Smith, engineer – 1976. *(© Crown Copyright: FBS 537)*

was keen to see the end of the British presence," said Richard Astbury. "The pro-British "Times of Malta" had published a story about a British businessman who was being sheltered by the Maltese Government when he was wanted for questioning in connection with the disappearance of his wife in Brighton. Then came another story of a British tourist who allegedly received emergency surgery in a Maltese hospital and had suffered after surgical instruments had been accidentally sewn up inside her. Prime Minister Mintoff was becoming more and more frustrated with the British press and this was made worse after a BBC interview with him was cancelled at the last moment."

In mid June, Richard Astbury was asked by Admiral Cecil to omit any news stories about Malta. The request had come via the High Commission from the Prime Minister's office. "For most of the day our news source came via teleprinter from the General News Service of the BBC (GNS)" said Astbury. "It was known as 'rip 'n' read' and presented locally by myself and other members of staff. In the evenings and over night we relayed BBC World Service. I felt very uncomfortable about a possible veto, particularly if a story were to be covered by the BBC and then omitted by us."

It was early July and he was sharing the early morning news reading: "On arriving at the station I immediately went to the teleprinter to tear off what I needed. As I looked down the various news stories I saw the names 'Mintoff' and 'Malta'. Dom Mintoff's daughter Yana had been arrested the previous afternoon in London for throwing horse manure from the Public Gallery in the House of Commons. I quickly checked whether it had been mentioned on our relay of BBC World Service and it had. 'BFBS credibility must be maintained', I thought and it was bound to be on the front page of the Times of Malta, so I'll use it in my bulletin!' We included it in the first few news broadcasts and heard nothing from anyone for the remainder of the day.

"Just as I was going to bed that night, at about 10.30pm, the CB Short Wave radio burst into life. I was to report to the British High Commission in Valetta immediately. I threw on some clothes and reported there within half an hour. What I had failed to understand was that my presence was to be discreet, hence the look of horror on the faces of those sitting round a long polished table when I walked through the door. Among the British hierarchy were the Chief of Staff, Norman Aspin, the High Commissioner and Admiral Cecil all agog at my loud BFBS tee shirt! The atmosphere was cool, quiet and controlled. I was told that the Foreign Office had ordered BFBS to cease broadcasting from midnight. No reason had been given, but the original request had come from the Maltese Government. I was escorted to St. Francis Ravelin by a British Army Colonel and, having deliberately delayed the process for as long as possible (10 minutes), I closed BFBS at 12 minutes past midnight. I was hardly able to believe what had happened. For the next three months, the station broadcast uninterrupted tone – believed to be a world record."

As he arrived at the station, the following day, Astbury was wondering what all the staff would say: "I thought that we must continue to communicate. Charly Lowndes, our resident 'academic' broadcaster, had expertise in printing and this gave me the idea of publishing a daily newsletter, transcribing the latest news from the BBC via our teleprinter. We also published the daily storyline of 'The Archers'. That was a basic start but we needed to give our radio audience more."

"What about the music and entertainment? I approached Peter Attrill and he agreed to build us a 'disco'. If Mintoff wouldn't let us broadcast the music, we'd take it to them. Three or four nights a week we were out around the island providing the services' clubs with an excellent disco. But that wasn't going to bring back our radio service. Negotiations continued in London, but our transmitters remained silent. The weeks turned into months and my frustration grew."

Another person who was becoming frustrated by the delay, was the RAF Commander, Group Captain Hall. By the end of August, he had persuaded BFBS

The final Radio Schedule for BFBS Malta
– 1979.   *(© BFBS Archive)*

to build a new studio in an underground installation at RAF Siggewi where he intended BFBS should broadcast, with or without permission from the Maltese Government. As Peter Attrill recalls: "As it happened, we were all saved from what could have been a difficult confrontation when the ban was lifted, but then we had to return all the equipment back to Floriana."

The lifting of the ban was great news for Richard Astbury: "Eventually, in the 2nd week of October we were given the go-ahead and resumed broadcasting on a hurriedly produced schedule prepared by Alan Clough. The winter months continued smoothly and thoughts were turning to March and our final withdrawal. It was a very sad occasion. Queues of locals turned up at the front door with flowers and gifts to say thank you and farewell. Having made the final closing announcement, we threw a cocktail party for friends of the station and it was almost over. The following afternoon I met representatives from the Malta government and handed over the keys. BFBS Malta closed for good."

In 1952, the Far East Land Forces Command (FARELF) set up a Forces Broadcasting unit and it was commanded by Captain Jack Ettridge. It broadcast for three hours a day to the thousands of Commonwealth troops who were serving up–country in Malaya. At the time they included Gurkhas, The King's African Rifles and the 1st Infantry Regiment from Fiji. The technical back–up for the unit was provided by the Royal Signals.

In 1964, after more than six months discussion within FARELF Command, the then Command secretary refused to support the case for a class-three BFBS station in Singapore. As a consequence, the case was never forwarded to London, despite the fact that the Director of Signals in the Far East had expressed his concern about a need to broadcast information to the British families in an emergency.

The Director was concerned that the recent creation of Malaysia had made itself felt on the programme content of the local broadcasting stations, leading to the isolation of British families from UK news, sports events, and entertainment at a time when wives and children were being left alone in Singapore by husbands serving in Borneo. He felt that the increased use of the national language would accelerate the trend for more local radio programmes.

Jack Knott, when advisor to the Forces Broadcasting Service, had made no recommendations about the future of BFBS Singapore as he was unable to visit the station. But in 1966 John Campbell was posted there with a brief to bring it into the Forces Broadcasting aegis. He was soon joined by James Nation, who created a new early morning show called 'The Yawn Patrol' to expand the English service. By the end of 1967, the service was broadcasting from 6.00am to 10.00pm.

The Singapore station was a purpose-built broadcasting unit that had been designed and run by Captain Jack Ettridge. Most of the new equipment came from BFBS Aden after it closed. BFBS Singapore was a bi-lingual station, but with the increase in the broadcasting hours for the English service on VHF, the Gurkha service had been relegated to Short wave. This seemed unfair, as the Brigade of Gurkhas was the main reason for a radio station in Singapore.

Peter Attrill had been posted to Singapore during the build-up phase, and was quickly involved in outside broadcasts of military events in Malaya. As he recalled: "It was no fun dragging all the kit by road, sometimes several hundred miles, just for one OB."

One of his main tasks each year was to fly to Penang and then travel south by Beaver, courtesy of the Army Air Corps to check at the various Gurkha Garrisons for signal strength. It was an exercise which was supposed to convince everyone in the Command that the Gurkha service was essential.

In 1970, the base at Singapore began to wind down. The bulk of the Gurkha Regiments would be going to Sek Kong in the New Territories of Hong Kong and the rest of the British Forces had left by November 1971.

Jack Ettridge, Station Manager, Forces Broadcasting Unit, Singapore with Vera Lynn (centre) and Jane Baker, the English Announcer – 1963. *(© Private Photograph)*

Peter Attrill and Bill Robertson checking the equipment in BFBS Singapore – 1970. *(© Private Photograph)*

The BBC were very unhappy at the loss of an outlet for the World Service and Lee Kwan Yew, the Prime Minister of Singapore, made public his desire to see the station reinstated. After discussions involving Ian Woolf, the Singapore Government and the High Commissioner, it was agreed that the station could be kept open and Peter Buckle, the Station Controller, offered to keep the station on air until it could be re-staffed.

The next few months were the oddest for any station in the Forces Broadcasting Service. BFBS Singapore had literally become a one-man station. In the morning, the BBC engineers at the South East Relay Station relayed a feed of their own service, while one of the former BFBS Indonesian engineers, who was now with the BBC, came in one day a week to maintain the equipment. For the rest of the time, Peter Buckle would open the station, set up the programmes, edit the tapes where necessary, answer the telephones, sweep the floors and feed the tropical fish. His constant companion was his transistor radio.

On Christmas morning 1971, he opened the station with: "Good morning everyone. Today is December 25th, it is Christmas Day, my name is Peter Buckle and I am BFBS Singapore".

In the meantime, Edward Heath had obtained an agreement through SEATO to form a force comprising British, Australian and New Zealand troops and BFBS was to be its official broadcasting station. The Australians and the New Zealanders contributed towards the costs of running the station and, by the middle of 1973, a new team was in place under Ken Doherty.

One of them was the newly appointed trainee, Sarah Kennedy, who could not believe her luck when she was told by Ian Woolf that she was going to Singapore: "I was not quite sure where it was, so I got out my old school atlas." 30 years on and Sarah can still remember the smells of the Orient, the monsoon drains that filled up around 4 pm every afternoon after the rains, and the amazing kaleidoscope of different cultures on the island.

It was not long before Sarah had her first encounter with the local wild life. As the early morning announcer, she had to make her way into the centre of the Army camp, enter the empty station, switch on the equipment and get ready for the first programme of the day. "On this particular morning," she said "I thought I had time enough for a quick trip to the loo before I set off 'Lilli Bolero', the World Service signature tune. I did not bother to switch on the light as I entered the loo and I was just getting comfortable when I realised I was not alone. I was sharing the loo seat with a snake! I believe I still hold the record for the quickest time between the loo and the studio."

Soon after Sarah arrived, she was invited, as a former Speech and Drama teacher, to teach Lee Kwan Yew's son English and this opened up a whole new world for her. Each Thursday, she would go to the Prime Minister's home and be

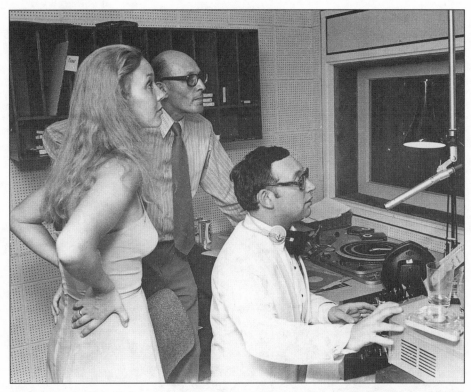

Sarah Kennedy, Ken Doherty and Roger Hudson preparing for the final moments of BFBS
Singapore – 1976.   (© *Private Photograph*)

frisked before being allowed in to a large room which contained two small chairs
for herself and the Prime Minister's son.

Prime Minister, Lee Kwan Yew supported the Forces station to the very end,
which came on 9th January 1976. It was a day of sadness for the BFBS team and,
in the last moments leading up to the final closedown at midnight, Sarah
Kennedy was joined by Roger Hudson and Ken Doherty for the final farewell.
First came 'Now Is The Hour' followed by 'The Evening Hymn and Last Post'
and the 'National Anthem'. The BBC carried the closedown live over its World
Service. Afterwards, there was a party when everyone indulged too much. Sarah
recalls: "I suddenly began to feel decidedly unwell and the nearest thing to hand
was the piano." A few days later, this instrument was packed and sent to BFBS
Hong Kong where its sterling service in an emergency was recounted repeatedly
until it was scrapped in 1985.

If the military authorities had intended the final withdrawal from Singapore to
be low key they were disappointed. Reuters followed the progress of BFBS

Singapore and wrote an article called 'Death of a Radio Station' which was syndicated worldwide.

Only Hong Kong and later Brunei would continue to keep the flag of the Forces Broadcasting Service flying in the Far East.

Mike Robertson and Catherine Head at the Aldershot Army Show with the BFBS 'Goodies'.
(© Crown Copyright: FBS 1168)

CHAPTER FIVE

The Eighties

An Injunction, a War, an Earthquake and an Interview that made the Headlines

In the autumn of 1980, NATO staged the largest exercise since the end of the Second World War in Germany. It was called Exercise Crusader. Invitations were issued to BFBS to cover it, not only with radio teams, but also with the new BFBS television service. A small team from the UK joined a team from Germany, led by Bryan Hamilton, and they worked alongside Pat Pachebat's television crew. At the end of four weeks, the teams were tired but happy with their performance.

During the exercise, Tom Scanlan discovered the full capability of the Uher tape recorder. He had been assigned to accompany a Royal Greenjackets' raiding party flown in by a Chinook helicopter. The landing zone was on one side of a vast muddy field bordering a wood. The helicopter landed and 40 soldiers leapt out followed by one intrepid reporter who set off in hot pursuit. With sounds of rifles, machine guns and mortars all around him, Tom was determined, not only to keep up with the Greenjackets, but also to keep one eye on the sound level indicator on the tape recorder. All was going well until he failed to spot a well-disguised ditch. He plummeted six feet with his trusty Uher taking his full weight. To Tom's surprise, the tape recorder kept going and recorded for posterity his phrase which began: "Oh my God…"

On 3rd October 1980, General Sir William Scotter, Commander in Chief of BAOR, wrote to Ian Woolf, the Director of BFBS: "I wish to congratulate you and your staff on the excellent coverage of Exercise Crusader 80 on both radio and television. I was very concerned that those soldiers not directly involved in the exercise and all the families in BAOR should have the opportunity of being able to follow the course of the exercise and thereby, feel involved. You ensured that this happened. The professional standards and cover achieved by your three teams were excellent and broke new ground in the field of troop information."

Four years later, the three teams would be working once more in Germany, this time on Exercise Lionheart.

Charly Lowndes covered Exercise Lionheart in 1984, in which two divisions were deployed in the field: "Finding 2nd Infantry Division Headquarters involved finding a grid reference, which turned out to be a village green somewhere in Lower Saxony. I stood there by my vehicle, map in one hand and a portable tape recorder in the other, wondering how I had gone wrong," he said. "Suddenly a camouflaged sentry emerged from a bush and challenged me. Satisfied, he led me into a farmyard where, invisible in the barns, the command vehicles were hidden with staff officers working quietly on folding trestle tables. The Officers Mess, in the cleanest barn, was laid for lunch complete with the Mess silver."

Eight years later Charly was covering Exercise Quadriga Gallop in which only the Headquarters and Signal Regiment of 4th Armoured Division took to the field: "Finding the location was still a matter of a grid reference, but this time the location – still a farmyard and various barns – was easy to spot," he said. "There were 16 bright orange portable toilets in a neat row in the yard. The German environmental movement had succeeded in confining the movements of the British Army to Portaloos, and the notion of operational secrecy took second place – after all, it was only an exercise!"

Peter McDonagh, editor of the Features and Magazine Department of BFBS London, commissioned Tony Craig, a left-wing Labour councillor on the Greater London Council, to record a half-hour special interview with Ken Livingstone, the council's Labour Leader. This he did on Tuesday 25th August 1981. As was the practice, Peter gave a copy on cassette of the rough interview to Tony Craig. On Sunday, 30th August 1981 a précis of the interview was published on the front page of the Observer. The media went mad. In the course of the interview Ken Livingstone had said: "If I was to make an appeal, what I would say to everybody who's got arms and is carrying arms in Northern Ireland, whether they are in the British Army or the IRA, is put those arms down and go back to your home. I think there would be no greater move for peace than if the British Forces just packed up and went home, and that would be one way of scaling down the violence. It would also help if those sectarian groups on both sides of the divide did the same thing."

The reaction from the newspapers was interesting: "Red Ken's Army row: Why won't he shut up?" Daily Mail, Monday 31st August. "Livingstone in Ulster Army Row", Daily Telegraph, Tuesday 1st September. "Oh God, he's at it again – party rebels launch bid to oust Red Ken", The Sun, Tuesday September 1st. "Charge Red Ken, his call to troops is sedition," Daily Mail, Wednesday, 2nd September. "Now Red Ken upsets the Army," Sydney Morning Herald, Wednesday 2nd

September and "Radio chiefs study Livingstone interview", Evening Standard, London, Tuesday 1st September.

The Daily Telegraph article stated: "Mr. Ian Woolf, Director of the Service, said consideration of whether the programme should go on air would be his first priority when he returns to his office. He will take into account whether the interview could have a demoralising effect on soldiers who serve in Northern Ireland and whether it would contravene the Incitement to Disaffection Act of 1934."

The interview was never broadcast. McDonagh was summoned to see Ian Woolf who said: "At least they have spelt my name right."

On 2nd September, the BBC carried the following news item: "The British Forces Broadcasting Service have decided not to broadcast a controversial interview with the Labour Leader of the Greater London Council, Mr. Ken Livingstone. In the course of the interview with a freelance reporter, Mr. Livingstone said that anyone carrying arms in Northern Ireland, British Army or IRA should put down his arms and go back home. Fears were expressed that the interview might be considered seditious. Tonight, however, the Director of BFBS, Mr. Ian Woolf, said that they had decided that the subject matter of the interview would not fit in to the series of programmes for which it was intended. It was intended to be on the subject of Local Government, but, said Mr. Woolf, it was more concerned with Mr. Livingstone's personal and political views on Northern Ireland."

Peter McDonagh was sent on gardening leave, and on his return was told he would be working only for the Music Department – no more Features and Magazines.

For many years the Ministry of Defence had wanted to get BFBS out of its system. In the Thatcher era, Departments of State were encouraged to hive off activities. They sought to reduce the number of civil servants and the BFBS staff were civil servants. To amalgamate BFBS with the Services Kinematograph Corporation made operational sense in that they were both there for the welfare of the troops.

For Ian Woolf, who started with the Forces Broadcasting Service in 1946 in Naples, it was to be the end of a long and distinguished career. Throughout his time, firstly as a Station Commander, then as a Controller of Programmes and Director of BFBS in London, he had fought against lack of staff and money in order to keep BFBS functioning. Now it was argued, once the amalgamation had taken place, a new man should be brought in to become Managing Director of the new corporation. It would be called the Services Sound and Vision

The Prime Minister, Margaret Thatcher with BFBS UK's Anne Armstrong at No 10 Downing Street.   *(© Crown Copyright: FBS 535)*

Corporation (SSVC). As far as the staff overseas were concerned, they would be responsible for their various budgets and, for the first time, could make local purchases of electronic equipment without referring it to the Treasury and the MoD's Procurement Branch. But would the new man at the top understand the business? They need not have worried; the first Managing Director, John Grist, was steeped in radio and television.

On 19th November 1981, John Grist wrote a report about the merging of the two organisations. He said: "When I joined the MoD, I was given a large weight of documentation that had accumulated over several years. What emerged from this reading was that BFBS had done a good job in the last 20 years or so but, for a variety of reasons, it sat uneasily as a small department in the MoD carrying out a function falling outside the mainstream of defence business. If a structure could not be found to support it and guarantee that the quality of broadcasting was sustained, it might be politic to move it from the Civil Service." The report concluded: "The MoD will continue to pay for the broadcasting to the Forces, with recognition that the ultimate responsibility for the policy and editorial style of the broadcasting must rest with the Ministry of Defence; a responsibility exercised by the Adjutant General."

In looking ahead, John Grist realised that the merger could save money and preserve and even enhance the radio and television service for the Forces. He recommended that more local stations on the lines of Rheindahlen, Bielefeld and Berlin should be added to the network in Germany, Kings Buildings should be vacated as soon as practicable and new accommodation found for a radio production facility in Central London. "This move", said Grist, "will be made easier following a recent statement from the Chief Engineer of BFBS who said that 'Given no major expenditure on equipment is made within the next two years, then most of the existing equipment will require replacement by 1984.'

While the MoD were still considering the implications of John Grist's report, their attention was suddenly drawn to problems in the South Atlantic.

In 1982, Argentine Forces invaded the Falkland Islands and South Georgia. The Prime Minister, Margaret Thatcher, despatched a Task Force to re-take the islands. Almost immediately, BFBS submitted a bid for a member of staff to travel with them and report back to the network. This was refused due to a shortage of places for the media on the various ships. BFBS was asked, however, to consider putting together a request programme for the men travelling south.

Mike Robertson carried out the initial negotiations and then handed over to the Local Radio Liaison Organiser, Alan Grace, to produce the programmes. "My first problem was to find a presenter. My first choice was Sarah Kennedy, a former member of BFBS, who had recently been voted ITV Personality of the Year with the show 'Game For A Laugh'. I was delighted when she accepted."

Fleet Street helped publicise the programme by carrying photographs of Sarah and news about the special request programmes. Soon, BFBS was receiving over 500 letters per day and this soon rose to 1,000. Each had to be checked for breaches of security. The Task Force request team discovered that elderly relatives were so proud of their grandsons they were passing on all sorts of confidential material such as: "my grandson is a gunner on board Fort…, the tanker for HMS Hermes."

The first programme was broadcast on 26th April 1982. Among the early requests was one for Prince Andrew, now the Patron of the SSVC: "Dear Sarah, please mention HRH Prince Andrew in one of your requests. I mean, his mother can hardly write in for a mention, can she?"

The BBC World Service had agreed that the programme, 'Task Force Requests', could be relayed using the BBC transmitters on Ascension Island, and three half-hour slots were made available. Such was the response that the BBC soon allocated the frequency on a daily basis and Sarah was joined by Nicol Raymond, who had been with BFBS Cyprus and was now working for BFBS television.

Sarah Kennedy in the Task Force Request Studio at Kings Buildings – 1982

(© Crown Copyright: FBS 513)

Once the casualties started to feed back to the UK, Alan Grace's task took on a more sombre role: "Each day, before we started work on the programme, I would check with the MoD and read the lists of intended recipients of requests. If any of them had been killed or wounded in the previous 24 hours, their names would be withdrawn from the programme."

With so many servicemen serving in the South Atlantic, BFBS decided to produce a series of special programmes dedicated to individual units or ships and these were sent down on radio cassettes. The first of these programmes was recorded in London with wives of the 2nd Parachute Regiment led by the CO's wife Mrs Sara Jones. Unfortunately, before the second programme could be despatched, news came through that her husband, Colonel H. Jones, had been killed at Goose Green.

Soon personalities from the world of entertainment were offering their services to host some of these programmes. Among them BFN old boy, David Hamilton; Diane Keen and Fiona Richmond; and the irrepressible sergeant major from 'It 'Ain't Half Hot Mum', Windsor Davies.

Once peace had been achieved, the MoD requested that the programmes continued for the men who were now on garrison duty on the islands or who were patrolling in the ships around the islands. When the last programme was broadcast on July 14th, the Task Forces Request Programmes had delivered 6,300 requests.

The 10-week war in the Falklands came to an end on June 14th 1982, and with it a need to restore impartial broadcasting for the island population.

For Patrick Watts, the Director of Broadcasting of the Falkland Islands Broadcasting Service (FIBS), it had been the most difficult time of his broadcasting career. The Argentines had taken over his radio station and allowed him to continue with two hours of broadcasting in the morning and five hours in the evening. The rest of the time was given over to a mix of news in English and Spanish with various instructions to the local population about curfews/black-outs and the confiscation of vehicles.

The Argentine Commanders feared the British Task Force would use the signal of the FIBS main AM transmitter to find its way to the Falklands, so they decided to reduce its power. Full power was restored for a dramatic rally to his troops from Major General Menendez just days before Port Stanley was liberated. It was also restored for the relay of the Mass to celebrate the Pope's visit to Buenos Aires.

David Hamilton, ex-BFN Cologne, and Nicol Raymond with the Task Force Request Programme's Mascot – 1982
(© Crown Copyright: FBS 515)

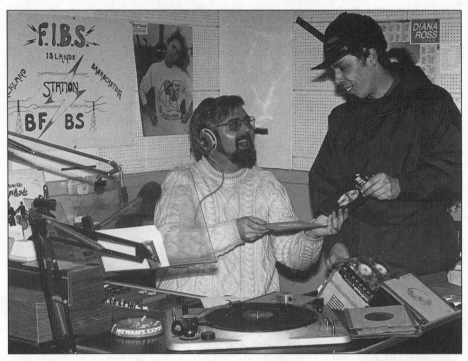

Terry Nicholas attached to BFBS from the BBC in the Studios of the Falkland Islands Broadcasting
Service – 1982   *(© Private Photograph)*

The Argentines had booby-trapped the local power station so FIBS – or LRA
60 Radio Nacional as they had renamed it – went off the air on 13th June and
power was not restored for three days.

The Argentine soldiers left the AM transmitter ticking over until the valves
packed up to keep the station guards warm at night and the FIBS short wave
transmitter was still working. When power came back, Patrick Watts began his
first post-war transmission on short wave by playing the National Anthem
followed by 'Land of Hope and Glory'.

Shortly afterwards, Patrick was approached by three British officers. They told
him that broadcasting would be vital for the moral of the thousands of British
troops who were now likely to remain on the Falklands and asked him to
consider sharing his studios with BFBS and working alongside them. In return,
Patrick was promised new equipment, regular supplies of the latest records, a
network of FM transmitters to replace the AM transmitter, a full-time engineer
and the use of the BFPO mail system and the NAAFI.

Patrick had a dilemma. He realised that the Military needed a quick answer,
but Governor Rex Hunt was still in Britain after his deportation by the

Prince Andrew with Jon Shilling, Peter Nairn and Jonathan Bennett outside the SSVC/BFBS
office in the Falklands – 1983   *(© Crown Copyright FBS 1546)*

Argentines, and the Falkland Islands Councillors had yet to reconvene following
the war. In the end, he said: "I took the decision myself for the amalgamation."
Immediately, his small team increased their daily broadcasting hours from seven
to 12. Each night, an Army major came in to talk about the danger of mines,
which were being discovered everywhere, the concerns over houses being
booby-trapped and the need for returning occupiers to ask the Royal Engineers
to check their properties.

Roy ffoulkes, BFBS London's Sports Editor, was the first broadcaster to
arrive in the Falkland Islands and soon discovered the frustrations of post-war
Stanley. Said Patrick: "I will never forget Roy's anger and utter frustration
when the power failed on a daily basis as he was mid-way through his daily
lunchtime programme."

BFBS was asked to support the new station and Mike Townley, then Engineer
in Charge in Cyprus, was dispatched to the Falklands. He arrived in Stanley on
July 31st, just six weeks after the end of hostilities, to find a desolate scene. Among
his many problems was the aerial farm, which was known to be heavily mined.
He installed a small FM transmitter and drew up plans for future improvements.

As Mike recalls: "In those early days, the flight from Ascension Island's Wide-awake Airfield was by Hercules aircraft with in-flight refuelling over the South Atlantic. The Hercules would go into a shallow dive to catch up with the refuelling V bomber which was flying at marginally over stall speed and the fuel was pumped as quickly as possible to fill the tanks before both aircraft hit the ocean!"

The next BFBS engineer to arrive was David Young, bringing with him the promised new equipment. Although most of it had been used previously in Gibraltar, Patrick Watts found it to be a thousand times better than he had in his FIBS studio.

The next broadcaster to arrive on the island was Charly Lowndes, who started the 'Early Morning Breakfast Show'. This became so popular that people living on the farms would set their alarms in order to hear Charly go on air at 6.00 a.m. Another benefit for the locals was the BBC's rip-and-read news, which came by telex and was read by Charly. This was followed by an early morning weather forecast. Patrick Watts discovered just how popular Charly had become when Mrs Thatcher arrived in 1983 and Patrick joined the official party for a visit by helicopter to the outlying farms. "At Goose Green, we all trooped along after the PM and Dennis Thatcher and we arrived in the hall where 118 people had been detained during the occupation. One farmer came rushing up to me to ask who the visitors were. I pointed out Mrs Thatcher and her husband and the Commander of the British Forces before being interrupted by the farmer: 'Yes, that's fine,' he said. 'But which one is Charly Lowndes?' "

FIBS and BFBS increased their broadcasting hours from 12 to 18 and then 24 hours a day. The sharing arrangement with FIBS continued until 1985, when BFBS moved first to Lookout Camp in Stanley before moving on to Mount Pleasant.

The popularity of the BFBS/FIBS Radio Service was highlighted when Lana Whitney from Fitzroy Farm wrote to Pete Johnson, BFBS Falkland's Programme Organiser: "I hope you won't mind my writing to you, but being a great lover of Country and Western music, and due to the fact that now the time has changed to winter time and the 'Country Folk' programme is being broadcast at 2 p.m., I am no longer able to listen to it. At 1 p.m. our electricity on the farm goes off bringing everything electric to a halt, including my radio. I believe the programme is repeated again in the early hours of the morning, but as our electricity does not come on until 7 a.m., I miss the repeat as well. Is there any chance of 'Country Folk' being put on at a different time? P.S. I will give you my electricity time just in case: 7 a.m. until 1 p.m.: 5 p.m. until 11 p.m."

It was not just 'Country Folk' that appealed to the Falkland Islanders. The whole range of BFBS London programmes were available to them including 'Alan Freeman's Classics' and the popular 'John Peel's Music'.

David Allen with his special 'Country Folk' guest, Dolly Parton – 1982

(© Crown Copyright: FBS 551)

With the Falklands War over, the main priority for Mike Robertson, the Station Manager at Kings Buildings, was to organise the move to Bridge House in Paddington in such a way that the overseas stations would not notice the join. They had to maintain normal daily output and much of it came on tape from BFBS London. The delivery of these tapes was crucial.

The withdrawal was carefully phased over a period of four months. Everything from in-house programme research and production to recording and multi-distribution of the weekly output to stations had to be running smoothly at Bridge House by 1st April 1984.

The success of the move from Westminster to Paddington was due, in no small measure, to the amazing flexibility of the BFBS Kings Buildings' staff and their freelance presenters. Jazz, Classical and other reasonably non-topical popular music programmes were recorded well in advance, multi-copied and stockpiled to await normal despatch. Topical programmes such as 'London Sports Desk' and 'Sitrep' had to be despatched as quickly as possible from Kings Buildings after recording. These, and one or two other speech programmes, were the last to move.

Producers and technical operations staff were "day-released" to Bridge House on a rota basis as the new equipment was installed. There, thanks to the forward planning of Colin Rugg, identical studios and control rooms hastened the learning process.

The biggest problem for Mike Robertson was the removal of the record library. "Les Austin and his record library staff were superb and the smooth transfer of the huge record library at Kings Buildings was a feat in itself," said Mike. "Hundreds of crates were ordered and filled with records not required during the run-up to the transfer target date. These were transported to the new "rolling shelves" library at Bridge House. Most programmes from BFBS London relied on recorded music and discs either had to be retained at Kings Buildings or sent to Bridge House during the run-up to meet programme needs at either of the locations."

Alan Freeman with producer, Dennis Astrop getting ready for a special edition of 'Alan Freeman's Classics' – the subject – Johann Strauss – 1983

(© Crown Copyright: FBS 587)

In the weeks following April 1984, only administrative mopping up and the removal of surplus equipment was carried out at Kings Buildings. What had been the first home for the BFBS London production unit in 1964 was now handed back to its original owners and, for many of the staff, the walk from Waterloo station across Westminster Bridge to Kings Buildings would become a memory.

Belize was one of the few radio stations broadcasting to the troops that was operated by volunteers, both servicemen and wives. In 1979, Mike Robertson, visited Belize to see what assistance BFBS could give to the station. "I was expecting to see a basic set-up but when I got there I had no idea just how basic it was," he said. The equipment was well past its sell-by date but the volunteers, with boundless enthusiasm, viewed their station in the same way as the staff of BFBS Cologne saw theirs.

On Mike's return, he made a series of recommendations about upgrading the equipment, increasing the number of BBC Transcription discs, ensuring that the total output of BFBS London was made available to Belize and that a member of staff should be sent out to undertake presentation training.

The next visitor from BFBS was Alan Grace, who arrived in his capacity of Local Radio Liaison Organiser with the object of setting up a series of link programmes with families back in the UK. The Queen's Regiment, whose families were back in Canterbury, was the first to benefit. He recorded a series of voice dedications which were put together by BBC Radio Kent and broadcast in a special programme on Christmas Day 1980. Shortly afterwards, dedications from the wives and children of the soldiers was recorded in Canterbury and the assembled programme sent out to Belize for the station to broadcast. At the time, only those based in Airport Camp could hear the direct transmission, so cassette copies were sent to the other camps at Holdfast, Salamanca and Rideau.

John Bussell, the Controller of Radio in London, took up Mike Robertson's suggestion and a BFBS staff member visited the station to train the volunteers in their presentation skills. Later, he sent BFBS staff on a four-month unaccompanied tour to maintain and improve station standards.

Up until November 1984, the transmitter used in Belize was an old military one on loan from the command. This had a very limited range and was unable to reach many of the hirings in Belize City. At the lowest point during Marc Tyley's time in Belize, the entire output was dependent upon a cassette recorder playing out tapes, which were brought in by the volunteers. After several reports from Roy ffoulkes and Marc Tyley, John Bussell was convinced that BFBS had to invest in new equipment for Belize if the organisation was serious about building up a proper radio service. Gordon Mills, the Senior Engineer from BFBS London

Gordon Mills and Marc Tyley at the BFBS Studios in Belize – 1984   (© *Private Photograph*)

arrived with a new transmitter, which he began to install. He also identified another problem concerning the feeder cable, which was old and contained too many connections and the aerial currently in use was far too low. He extended the aerial mast and modified the turntables that had just arrived from Germany.

The success of this operation persuaded John to create an accompanied post in Belize and in 1988, Dave Raven, who had just finished a tour in the Falkland Islands, became the first Station Manager of BFBS Belize.

One of the problems in Belize was to find suitable family accommodation as the quarters on the camp were allocated to service families only. As Dave Raven's accommodation in the Falklands had been akin to a large garden shed, he was determined to do better in Belize. By chance, Dave heard about a house on the Moho Cay, an island just 300 yards from the mainland with a ferryman to take him to work. His house on stilts was probably the most exotic BFBS quarters in the history of the network.

The successful coverage of the two major exercises, Lionheart and Crusader, had caused Whitehall to reassess its view of BFBS's ability to cover major military events.

In January 1984, Alan Grace, as a former Head of Sport, was asked to join an Army PR team covering the preparations of the young servicemen and women representing Great Britain in the 1984 Winter Olympics in Sarajevo. The result of the combined operation was a series of interviews on radio and television back in the UK.

Four months later, another invitation was issued to Dick Norton, then Station Controller of BFBS Germany, this time to cover the Queen's Review of the Royal Regiment of Artillery, which happens only once during the reign of a sovereign. Originally, BAOR had requested television coverage only, but with five days to go to the review, Dick was asked also to provide a radio commentator. Alan Grace was the only one in the organisation at the time and was flown from the UK to Dortmund the day before the dress rehearsal. The whole event provided massive media coverage in both Germany and the UK and gave BFBS the chance to help the BBC when the Bonn correspondent's tape recorder broke down during the Queen's Address.

Six weeks later, another BFBS team led by Charly Lowndes covered the 40th Anniversary of the D-Day landings, including a fascinating interview with Major Johnny Howard, who had led the attack on Pegasus Bridge.

In August 1984, Alan Grace was informed that he was to be the new General Manager of BFBS Hong Kong, and would also be responsible for the radio stations in Brunei and Nepal. His first task, according to John Grist, would be to persuade the Command to give more support to the English service of BFBS Hong Kong. Without it, posts would be lost.

Alan, like his predecessors James Nation and John Campbell, failed to convince Major General Derek Boorman, the then Commander British Forces Hong Kong. Whilst giving total support to the Gurkha Service, he felt that British servicemen and their families were well catered for with Radio, Television, Hong Kong (RTHK), Commercial Radio and the BBC World Service.

After some discussion, however, his successor, Major General Tony Boam, agreed to support the BFBS English service if an audience survey conducted by his headquarters proved its popularity.

Tom Scanlan, the Programme Organiser in Hong Kong, had fought to obtain at least one new recruit from Britain and more money to tempt freelances to work for the English service, but was posted to Germany before he was successful. Marc Tyley replaced him, but there was still a need for another permanent announcer. John Bussell, the Director of Radio, recruited Alan Jennings, a New Zealander, then broadcasting for Two Counties Radio in Bournemouth. The combination of Tyley and Jennings changed the sound of

BFBS Hong Kong. Their office resounded to music and ideas and some of these were to wash off on the Gurkha Service, especially their Programme Organiser, Kishore Gurung. Within weeks, the local press were reporting favourably on the station's new sound and within a year, BFBS Hong Kong had been voted the best English Service Radio Station in the Colony.

Marc Tyley and Alan Jennings were irrepressible. At a Cathay Pacific reception, they removed a huge model of a 747 Jumbo jet from the foyer, took it to pieces and put it in the back of the station vehicle. "Next day," said Marc, "I phoned the Cathay PR office and told them they could have their plane back providing we received a cheque for 10,000 Hong Kong dollars made payable to the Wireless for the Blind Fund. They thought this was a great publicity stunt and immediately agreed. What they were not expecting was that Alan and I would arrive carrying this eight-foot long model aircraft along the streets of Central to their office. Cathay Pacific and BFBS got fantastic coverage in all the main newspapers and the Wireless for the Blind Fund received a very handsome cheque."

The success of BFBS Hong Kong prompted an invitation to participate in the annual pedal car marathon for the Media Cup. It was an event normally won by RTHK but they had reckoned without the resourcefulness of the BFBS team who, after serious training in their favourite watering hole, 'The Bull and Bear', took the event by storm and won. RTHK immediately lodged a protest but this was withdrawn following a visit from Janet Gerslick, the BFBS lunch time presenter and a very persuasive lady. BFBS were to retain the cup the following year.

BFBS Hong Kong, with its studios in Sek Kong in the New Territories, was considered by some of the local media to be isolated. So greater visibility on Hong Kong Island was needed. Roger Dunn, who could build a studio out of fuse wire, cables and a couple of turntables, had already created a small temporary studio complex in the Prince of Wales building at HMS Tamar so John Dunn could broadcast his BBC Radio 2 programme live from the colony. All that remained was to persuade Roger to turn the mock-up into a fully operational studio. This he achieved in a matter of weeks and soon the BFBS Tamar studio was providing the Sek Kong station with a series of excellent personality interviews including: Peter Ustinov, Derek Nimmo, Freddie Trueman, Paula Wilcox and Max Boyce.

Kishore Gurung suggested that the visit of the Queen and the Duke of Edinburgh to Nepal in 1986 was such a major event that it should be covered by live commentary. This was quite a challenge but was accomplished with the help of the Nepalese Government. It was a notable first with Kishore interviewing many of the famous Gurkha VCs who, in some cases, had travelled many days to meet the Queen. Shortly after this, Kishore was despatched to the UK to cover

The Avenue of Guns, the highlight of the Queen's Review of the Royal Regiment of Artillery – 1984 *(© Crown Copyright: FBS 1547)*

The BFBS Pedal Kart Team (No 5), with Alison Taylor at the wheel for the start of the Pedal Kart Derby in Hong Kong – 1986 *(© Private Photograph)*

the Centenary parade of 2nd Bn of 2nd Gurkha Rifles at Church Crookham, Hampshire, with Prince Charles taking the salute. This was another memorable broadcast, aided by the engineers from BFBS London. By this time, Gurkhas units were serving in Belize and the Falklands and Lieutenant Pushpa Rai was sent to train Gurkha broadcasters in each location so they could have their own programmes on the local BFBS stations.

In 1988, news reached BFBS Hong Kong of an earthquake in East Nepal and the Gurkha Service made full use of the BFBS satellite station in Dharan Cantonment, the site of the British Army Camp in East Nepal. Extended reports were broadcast by K.B. Rai, the Gurkha Service's reporter in Kathmandu, and the audience response was overwhelming, not only in terms of the appeals for help made by BFBS, but in the recognition of the effort by the service to alleviate some of the worries.

A Gurkha officer in 10th Gurkha Rifles, one of many who called the Hong Kong station, expressed a deep concern about the safety of his son, who lived in

Each year BFBS Hong Kong entered a team for 'Trail Walker', a gruelling run over the hills of Hong Kong to raise money for various charities. In 1986 BFBS won the Minor Units Event. The team, left to right, Staff Sergeant Krishna, Adrian Almond, Alan Jennings and Sergeant Sonam.

(© Crown Copyright: FBS 1397)

Dharan Bazaar. K.B. Rai managed to contact the boy's headmistress and received an assurance that he was safe, putting his father's mind at rest.

Both the English and Gurkha Services broadcast appeals for clothes, kitchen utensils and money and the station became one of the main collecting points. Alan Grace recalls: "Many Gurkha officers and soldiers had families in the areas that were devastated by the earthquake. Everybody on the station, but especially the Nepali staff, pitched in from the first news of the earthquake to make sure that, with the assistance and support of the military command information machinery, we were able to provide fast and accurate details."

A few weeks later, Alan Grace flew to Dharan and was amazed to find the BFBS Station and the rest of the army camp untouched by the quake, whilst Dharan Bazaar was devastated with many buildings flattened.

The Gurkha broadcasters were hard working but resistant to change. They were far from happy when they were given a brand-new state-of-the-art studio, in Sek Kong, with the proviso that they should produce more live broadcasts. Up

In 1987 Princess Margaret, the Patron of SSVC visited Hong Kong and met members of the BFBS Hong Kong staff. The Princess is talking to Marc Tyley and waiting to be introduced to her are Heather Tyley, Eddie Wallace and his wife Julia, Barney Gladwell and Kishore Gurung.

(© Crown Copyright: FBS 1395)

WOI Shanta of BFBS Hong Kong rehearsing a Gurkha children's choir – 1986

(© Private Photograph)

until this point they had recorded much of their output. Within a week of their live sequence programming, however, the number of appreciative telephone calls they had received astonished them. When the news was announced that the Commander British Forces Hong Kong, Major General Gary Johnson, a fluent Nepali speaker, would be prepared to take calls live from the Gurkha soldiers on any subject, the audience figures for the programme 'Phulbari' were the best ever.

On 19th May, 1985, the Sony Radio Gold Award for Outstanding Contribution to Radio Over the Years was presented to Mr. John Grist, Managing Director of the Services Sound and Vision Corporation, for BFBS's "Superlative contribution to radio for decades." The presentation, at the Grosvenor House Hotel in London's Park Lane, was made by Lord Wilson of Rievaulx and was the only gold award given that year.

The variety and excellence of BFBS Radio and its programmes also became known to a wider civilian audience thanks to a highly reported media event held in October at Expo '88 in Brisbane, Australia. Earlier that year, Pat Pachebat accepted an offer from Anthony Mora, the Executive Director and Founder of the

Australian Academy of Broadcast Arts and Sciences, to include BFBS Radio stations in the 7th PATERS – the official media event of the Australian Bicentennial Year. Mike Robertson arranged for all BFBS Radio stations to send their best editions of locally produced programmes to London where they were copied and sent to Brisbane for final judgment by Anthony Mora and his media panel.

A few weeks later, they learnt that they had won nine major awards in a variety of categories. Mike Robertson, the Station Manager of BFBS London, went to Brisbane to accept the awards on behalf of BFBS Radio. "It was a wonderful chance to show off BFBS," said Mike, "although, when I first arrived at the massive Expo '88 site, I was alarmed to find that I was the only radio representative who had reported in. I wondered if the whole thing was a scam! However, other radio people from successful stations arrived later in the day so I knew all was well. A generous sprinkling of Director Generals from various broadcasting organisations and ministers from the Australian and New Zealand Governments sat around me before it was my turn to do my bit on stage and receive the prizes."

BFBS Germany's 'The Saturday Sports Programme' devised and produced by Paul Chapman, the Cologne Receptionist and presented by Dusty Miller, the Station's Admin Officer, took first prize in the International Open category. The station also took top honours for the Best Original Listener Contest programme.

Lord Wilson of Rievaulx presenting John Grist, the Managing Director of SSVC with the Sony Radio Gold Award for BFBS's contribution to Radio – 1985

(© Crown Copyright: FBS 1196)

Charly Lowndes and Jonathan Bennett, two of the PATER award winners combining for the
Queen's Birthday Parade in Berlin – 1987   *(© Crown Copyright: FBS 1290)*

An edition of 'Brains of BFG' produced by Alan Clough and presented by Charly
Lowndes – and the 'Berlin Breakfast Show' presented by Baz Reilly won in the
Small Market category. Jonathan Bennett of BFBS Germany and ABC Radio
Sydney shared the Best Small Market Local News and Current Affairs
programme prize, beating CBS Radio News, New York. Finally, the judges gave
the International Open Award for the best Investigative Reporting programme
to BFBS London's 'Seven Days' presented by the former leader of the Liberal
Party, Lord Steel.

On 6th March 1988, three members of the IRA were shot and killed by
members of British Special Forces in Gibraltar. On 28th April, Thames Television
broadcast a documentary programme called 'Death on the Rock' which led to
widespread criticism by the press. An inquest into the deaths was held which was
to have consequences for BFBS Gibraltar.

On Sunday 17th September 1988, Bryan Hamilton, the Station Manager, was
summoned to the Convent for a meeting with the Governor, Air Chief Marshal
Sir Peter Terry, where he was informed that an injunction was being placed on

BFBS Gibraltar and Gibraltar Broadcasting Corporation preventing them referring to the killings or saying anything which might influence witnesses at the inquest. Bryan's problem was that the news heard by the British Forces in Gibraltar was relayed from the BBC who had not received an injunction. He therefore had to arrange for all news bulletins to be faxed to him so that his team, none of whom had ever read the news before, could broadcast an edited version. At the same time, his staff was told to monitor all BBC World Service programme joins in case there were to be any references to the 'Death on the Rock'.

On the instruction of Alan Protheroe, the Managing Director of SSVC, Bryan employed a QC to put their case to Gibraltar's Attorney General but he found against BFBS. The injunction was lifted once the inquest got under way. Gibraltar Broadcasting Corporation had continued to broadcast a full BBC news bulletin throughout.

During the latter part of the Eighties plans were under way to move the well-established radio stations in Cologne and Dhekelia. It had been felt for some time that BFBS Germany was too far away from its audience and plans were drawn up for its move to Herford. At the same time, BFBS Cyprus in its custom-built radio station was seen as an expensive anachronism and it was overstaffed. Within two years, both stations would be razed to the ground.

In 1989, another milestone passed in the long history of BFBS with the closure of the smallest, but certainly the most picturesque, of radio stations: BFBS Dharan. Situated in the eastern part of Nepal, BFBS Dharan began when an army warrant officer, Alan Richardson, set up a rediffusion service within the camp and, in 1967, asked BFBS in Singapore for some help and guidance. It was James Nation who came to Richardson's aid by supplying him with three hours of programmes a week.

In recent years, BFBS Dharan had received the total output of BFBS London and, without a full-time member of staff, had produced a good standard of broadcasting due to its excellent volunteers.

On Friday, 10th November 1989, an East German Government Minister casually announced that travel restrictions for East Germans were being lifted. "Did this mean that the people were free to leave East Germany?" The official replied: "Yes," he supposed it did.

The Brandenburg Gate seen from the top of the Reichstag the night before the Berlin Wall came
down – 1989   *(© Copyright – Andy Carnall*

In the early evening, thousands of people took to the streets and headed for
Checkpoint Charlie. German radio and television began broadcasting newsflashes
that people were on the move and soon East Berliners could be seen climbing
the infamous Wall.

The full impact of this momentous occasion hit the BFBS Berlin team the
following day. Each reporter was given an area of the city to cover with the brief
"be back with something for the 1 o'clock news." Alan Phillips was to get the

story from Checkpoint Charlie but, with Berlin now one enormous traffic jam, he had to abandon his car and run to get there. Having recorded a short descriptive commentary on what was happening, he realised that he would never make it back to the studio on time so he headed back to Checkpoint Charlie and persuaded a Royal Military Police corporal to let him use his telephone. He called the station and prepared for his report but, just before he went on air, the feed of the station output disappeared from his telephone earpiece. Hoping the line was still there, he took his cue from the RMP's radio and delivered his report.

Baz Reilly had taken off with 7 Flight Army Air Corps to see the historic moments unfolding beneath them: "It was like midnight on New Year's Eve - only better."

Cathy Hulett covered the Staaken Crossing and June Wilde reported on the traffic crossing the Glienicker Bridge: "One man from East Berlin is riding a horse across the bridge, while others are making the journey on foot," she told listeners. Back in the studio, Patrick Eade was putting the reports together for the lunch-time programme. Soon, he was inundated with calls from around the world wanting to know what was happening. Shortly afterwards, a postcard arrived which read: "British friends! We don't want to miss thanking you for your interest and Mrs Thatcher for her will to help the refugees from the DDR. We know where our friends are, sooner or later we'll make it up to you."

Patrick Eade and Alan Phillips in front of the Brandenburg Gate on the day the Wall came down in Berlin – 1989   *(© Crown Copyright: FBS 1571)*

In the meantime, Alan Phillips went to the Falkenseer Chaussee to see a West Berliner attacking the Wall with a power drill and managed to take out a small section before the police stopped him. In the days that followed, the BFBS team were out and about recording interviews with the former Chancellor of West Germany, Willi Brandt, and the West Berlin Mayor, Walter Momper.

The Berlin Wall had disappeared as if by magic and in the days that followed, BFBS Berlin produced a number of special programmes such as 'The Rise and Fall of the Berlin Wall' and a few months later, 'Charlie Comes in from the Cold – the closure of Checkpoint Charlie'. The BFBS Berlin team of Alan Phillips, Patrick Eade, Baz Reilly, Robin Merrill and Jamie Gordon had left their mark on the people of Berlin. However, the life of the station was to be short-lived as, with the inevitable draw down, the Forces would be leaving Berlin and, with them, the members of BFBS.

The opening of the Akrotiri Satellite Studio in 1989 by the Chairman of the SSVC Sir Gordon Pirie. Left to right: Akrotiri Liaison Officer, Air Vice Marshal Bill Bailey, Deputy Managing Director of SSVC, Lizzie Hoskins, wife of the Akrotiri Station Commander, Colin MacDonald, the BFBS Akrotiri Representative, Aidan Donovan, the BFBS Western Sovereign Base Representative, Sir Gordon Pirie, Dorothy Bailey, Lady Joanna Pirie and Group Captain Brian Hoskins, Commander Officer of RAF Akrotiri.   *(© Crown Copyright: FBS 998)*

CHAPTER SIX

The Nineties

Out with the Old and in with the New

An alternative network had been the dream of every Station Controller and Programme Organiser since the first Broadcasting Advisory Committee Meeting was held in Germany in 1948, but it was not until 5th February 1990 that BFBS Chalfont went live in Germany via a 52,000-mile trip by Intelsat to Osnabruck, Bielefeld, Hohne, Lippstadt and Munster.

Colin Rugg's Engineering Division in Chalfont built the studio from scratch in just two months as Peter Attrill's engineers in Germany erected satellite dishes, tested decrypters and chased the best available signal.

The BFBS 2 schedule included documentaries, drama series and serials, light classical music and relays from the BBC of the 'Today' programme, 'World At One', and 'PM'. It was an instant hit with listeners in Germany. One family in Hohne commented: "We have needed a good current affairs programme and 'Today' is great and 'Around the Horne' brought back some lovely memories of Sunday lunches in England."

Initially, BFBS 2 was on the air five days a week but on 7th April 1990 it was extended to cover Saturdays and Sundays. As a direct result of its success, plans were made to extend to a 24-hour round-the-world stereo service to Gibraltar, Hong Kong, Brunei, Cyprus, the Falkland Islands and Belize.

The alternative service was here to stay.

The dates 26th February 1954 – 31st October 1990 opened and closed a massive chapter in the history of Forces Broadcasting in Germany.

The need for economies, and the philosophy of 'West of the Rhine' that followed the Berlin Airlift and the intensification of the Cold War, led to the closure of BFN's operation in the Musikhalle in Hamburg and the setting up of a much smaller headquarters in Cologne. History recalls that the Brigadier who formerly opened the new studios arrived by special train. Was it an indication of

The Entrance Hall of BFN Cologne in 1954 with Tom Cousins, ex-BFN Hamburg on the stairs
and Charlie Werner behind the Reception Desk – 1954   *(© Crown Copyright: FBS 335)*

the enhanced stature of BFBS within the military community that the closedown
speech was given by a four-star General?

The last evening in Parkstrasse was one of mixed emotions, a chance to
meet old colleagues and yet sadness for those German staff who were being
made redundant.

BFBS Cologne had been a family station, with the British and the Germans
working in harmony and sharing the many triumphs and a few disasters. In his
speech, General Sir Geoffrey Howlett, the chairman of the SSVC, recalled the
Hamburg Days and paid a well deserved tribute to the German staff, which
had provided the backbone of continuity and had given the station much of
its character.

Pat Pachebat, a former Station Director of BFBS Cologne, listened to the
Cologne output for the very last time: "To hear the reminiscences of those who
had worked there was very moving and I had the privilege of being the final
voice leading into the special piece of music that we used on virtually every
BFBS radio station at closedown, the evocative 'Evening Hymn' and 'The Last
Post'." It was the end of an era.

Three months earlier, BFBS London had begun planning a new show to occupy the traditional slot for the 'flagship' programme out of BFBS London on weekday afternoons. It was to be a radical departure from what had gone before. 'Simon and The Squad' presented by Simon Guettier, Rory Higgins, Janet Gerschlick and Alison Taylor was the first network show on BFBS using more than one presenter. It went out live in Germany and was broadcast as a recording a day or so later on all other BFBS stations. The Squad tried to incorporate elements of comedy, sport, news items, music and showbiz in a real pop tabloid style that hadn't been done before. They would also chat among themselves about the day's news or some silly story. This is the norm in radio now, but back in 1990 it was new and was very exciting.

The planning for the new show started on August 1st, but the next day an event took place that was to change the way the whole of BFBS was run. Saddam Hussein ordered his army to invade Kuwait. This shocking military action, the first major conflict in the post-Cold War order, was to bring BFBS back to its wartime roots and launch it into a brave new world of satellite broadcasting.

BFBS started short-wave transmissions to the Gulf on August 13th. They were able to transmit to Saddam Hussein's reluctant 'guests' and the growing number of British troops in the region thanks to 'space available' airtime on the BBC World Service frequencies. The broadcasts became a magnet for listeners from Finland to Japan.

Producing and presenting request programmes in a crisis requires careful planning to avoid security breaches. Charles Foster, then the Network Editor Music, issued the following instructions to his presenters: "For all military requests, Saudi Arabia is OK, but not specific locations such as the Tornados in Dharan. Oman, Bahrain, UAE, Qatar should be referred to as the Gulf. For the military and civilians trapped in Kuwait/Iraq, the generic 'somewhere in the Gulf' is to be used. Military personnel should be referred to by their rank and Christian name and in all cases, the full UK address, if available, should be read out."

BFBS London broadcast three, half-hour shows of requests and dedications. The morning edition was a relay of a special Gulf part of the Simon Bates Show from BBC Radio 1. He broadcast the BFBS address for dedications and hundreds of letters were received every day. The requests were sorted and arranged by a member of staff and a producer was sent to Egton House to help the BBC make sure they had the names, ranks and units correct.

When Rory Higgins was sorting out his request mail, he found a letter from a refinery near Baghdad. The writer was a 'Bacon, Lettuce and Tomato' or a member of the 35-strong British Liaison Team marooned in Kuwait since August 1990. The team had been split up: some were still in Kuwait, others at strategic

Simon Guettier, seated with three members of 'The Squad' and the Network Editor Music, Charles
Foster. Left to right: Liz Hutchinson, Alison Taylor, Rory Higgins and Charles Foster – 1990
(© Crown Copyright: FBS 1569)

locations around Iraq. The release of some French hostages had given him the
first opportunity to get mail out of Iraq uncensored. The letter was about
reception of BFBS. "Radio Moscow tends to drown you out at times but that
could just be the Russian radio we listen on!" The letter continued: "We've been
tuning in to BFBS twice a day now since you started transmitting to OP
GRANBY – pity it's only half an hour because it really is a morale booster –
believe me! Finally, could you please read our messages on either of your
afternoon programmes as hostage life doesn't begin until 9.00 a.m."

Broadcasting to the Gulf from the UK was fine in one respect but a live local
BFBS was needed. The men at the front were asking: "When are you going to
get here? The Yanks, American Forces Radio Service (AFRTS) have been here
for ages."

BFBS had been ready to go live in theatre since August. They had a transmitter,
studio, news relay service, tapes, records and even the staff as nearly everyone in
BFBS had volunteered to do their time in the Gulf.

Just one day after BFBS had started its short wave transmissions, Colin Rugg, Director of Engineering, and Brian Scott, Chief Development Engineer of BFBS, produced a detailed and costed plan to put FM in the Gulf. However, there were other points of view – one MoD expert asked if BFBS had thought of using oilfield data transmitters for broadcast purposes.

Bob Martin was on leave revising for an Open University examination when he realised that, with the build-up of British troops for the Gulf, BFBS could well be involved. He decided to volunteer and returned to work.

The use of satellites was mentioned during a meeting with Colin Rugg and Brian Scott, but it was more a hope than a reality. The ideal satellite would be Arabsat but, unfortunately, Iraq happened to be a major shareholder in this system. Also, there was no equipment in the United Kingdom, either transmitter or studio, ready for deployment.

On arrival in Riyadh, Bob Martin met the Commander, General Sir Peter de la Billiere, who said he wanted a BFBS station on air within two weeks. "I tried to explain to him the problems of using Arabsat, but he left me in no doubt about his views on having a BFBS station in theatre."

Bob heard through the grapevine at command that the BFBS presenter Alton Andrews was on his way. "As we had no resources available, I contacted AFRTS,

Bob Martin, the first BFBS Engineer to arrive in the Middle East. Within days, he was preparing the ground for the setting up of the BFBS Middle East Station – 1990

(© Private Photograph)

who already had 40 people in the area compared to one from BFBS, to see whether we could share resources when Alton arrived." Through his contacts, Bob arranged for Alton Andrews to broadcast for two hours each day for BFBS on AFRTS.

The Sunday Telegraph reporter, and now Executive Editor, Con Coughlin, reported on the effectiveness of Alton Andrews's show under the headline 'Disc Jockey takes G.I.s by storm.' He reported: "An obscure British disc jockey has become an unlikely cult figure among American G.I.s in search of a little light relief from the monotony of desert duty in the Gulf. A two–hour afternoon request programme on Oasis Radio, the American Armed Forces Network, has become required listening for thousands of American soldiers. They liken it to the radio programme made famous by Robin Williams in the film 'Good Morning Vietnam'. Alton broadcasts his afternoon show from a converted ship container in the middle of an American military base in Saudi Arabia, which serves as Oasis Radio's main studio. Although he dresses in American Army combat fatigues, his American colleagues call him 'Jeeves'. His sense of humour would not exactly have British people rolling in the aisles. When he plays 'I Can't Stand the Rain', for example, he will say something like: "No chance of that out here in Saudi Arabia." The Americans love his quirky sense of humour and as one marine from Brooklyn put it: "We just really dig his accent. We don't hear nothing like that where we come from."

Meanwhile, Bob Martin had found a suitable site for the BFBS studio just outside Al Jubayl at Camp 4. This was to be the R & R centre for the troops from the desert so a good audience was guaranteed. Also, the staff would benefit from the protection of the camp's guards. He named the new station BFBS Middle East as it covered the area.

"I had numerous meetings with the Saudis to obtain frequency clearance," he said. "I explained that the only way we could supply a service was to deliver the station output by satellite to the transmitters, which would be deployed in the troops' location. The Saudis wanted to know where it was going to be received and, trying to think of a solution that would be diplomatically acceptable, we told them it was to be a service to the Royal Navy, who were in international waters."

However, on November 7th, Bob Martin received a signal from Brian Scott explaining the problems as seen from Chalfont: "As at 09.30 today, nil repeat nil funds have been allocated for BFBS operations in Command by our financial sponsors RAF, AMP (F&S). Grateful if Command apply increased pressure on MoD to start the ball rolling a.s.a.p."

On November 17th, Chris Russell, the Senior Programme Director in Cyprus, joined Bob Martin to help set up the new radio station, but he had several problems to resolve. First, he had to obtain permission from the Saudi authorities to broadcast, then he had to check on the availability of lines from the Saudi Telecommunications Authority and the availability and suitability of the Arabsat Distribution Network. Within three days, Chris had discussed with the military's legal expert the status of the men from BFBS/SSVC: "We discovered that SSVC staff really need Geneva Convention identity cards for that remote but chilling prospect of being captured by the enemy." The wearing of uniforms was also discussed and it was agreed that this would make it easier for the Saudi authorities at checkpoints and while walking around the bases during alerts.

By now, the military were producing a newspaper called 'The Sandy Times' and the 25th November issue ran a headline 'Radio Gulf, the struggle continues'. A week later, it informed readers that BFBS Middle East had been given the go-ahead.

Robert Fox, writing in the Daily Telegraph on 26th November, reported on a visit to Saudi Arabia by a Parliamentary delegation led by Michael Mates, the chairman of the Commons Committee on Defence. The delegation had been visiting the British troops in the desert and Mr Mates said their main complaint was a shortage of entertainment for the few minutes they had spare. In particular, they wanted their own radio programmes from BFBS. Most units said they could get the Iraqi propaganda station known as Baghdad Betty – which they dismissed with a laugh – and the American Forces programmes.

By Friday November 30th, Russell and Martin had two lined and carpeted ISO containers in Camp 4 with power available and the prospect of telephone lines.

Meanwhile, back in London, the new 'Simon and the Squad' programme was launched with part of it broadcast to the Gulf on short wave. The first shows were light and fun with guests ranging from Fred Harris, a children's presenter on BFBS TV, and the man with the number one record of the day, Timmy Mallett.

But soon they found themselves covering big news events too. On the 22nd November, when Margaret Thatcher resigned as Prime Minister, Rory Higgins was despatched to Downing Street to report for the programme from outside Number 10. He took along a mobile phone, which was the size of a house-brick in those days, but achieved a 'first' by doing so.

On December 2nd, Chris Russell and Bob Martin were in the offices at HQ BFME when they were informed that the Americans had detected that Scud missiles were on their way. Lieutenant Colonel Glyn Jones, the Senior Staff Officer, suggested they closed the windows and said he would have just enough time to write a couple of letters. It was assumed the missiles were Saddam's answer to the American offer of talks and were targeted at Riyadh to provide maximum terror and effect. Only later did they discover that the missiles fell well short of the city.

A few days later, Chris learned of consternation at HQ BFME over a front-page article and a leader column in the Daily Mirror condemning him as crass for banning Christmas carols and broadcasts of festive church services to avoid offending the Saudis. Back in the London studios in Paddington, the BFBS Middle East Station Controller was soon being jokingly referred to as 'crass' Chris.

When Peter McDonagh, the Director of Radio, arrived in Al Jubayl on 16th December, he found the equipment still in the ISO container in a half-built state. The only sign of occupation was Peter Ginn desperately struggling to make sure the station would be ready for the official opening. McD had just decided that a little 'music while you work' would help the situation when the door of the container was opened by a British squaddie in full battle order. "BFBS?" he asked laconically, "Yes," said McD. "So you got here then?" With that he disappeared into the night. This, in squaddie talk, was the highest token of approval. Back in Germany, home for many of the men serving in the Gulf, BFBS produced a regular request programme 'It Ain't Half Hot Missus', derived from the material airmailed by the men in the desert. BFBS was deeply aware of the need for support for the families left behind in Germany while their men were at war. This made Glen Mansell's mid-morning show the main forum for wives and families in Germany to air views and grievances. His 'care line' gave them direct access to senior officers who were able to explain entitlements, discuss problems and reassure the callers.

On December 17th 1990, BFBS Middle East (Desert Radio) opened with a two-hour lunchtime show presented by Peter McDonagh, with special guest Sir Harry Secombe, who was touring the camps for Combined Services Entertainment on a 'grip-'n'-grin' exercise. Also present was Brigadier Patrick Cordingley, who wanted to talk morale. McD cautioned against this. "I've been talking to the lads," he said, "and what with the sand and the missing kit and the rationed water and the lack of facilities, they'll probably eat the station and us in it."

Outside the studio sat the Band of the Royal Scots, whose Director of Music, Major David Price, popped his head round the studio door to say: "I was thinking I might open up with 'Force One', the BFBS signature tune, followed by a medley of Christmas hits and carols." McD, remembering the comments in the English press about the inadvisability of playing Christian music in a strict Muslim country, started by saying no and then asked: "Which ones are you thinking of playing?" "Well we've got 'Deck the Halls', 'Winter Wonderland', 'Hark the Herald', 'White Christmas' and 'Jingle Bells'. "Just a moment", said McD, "I will give you a hand cue to begin but don't be surprised if the titles are different. Just go ahead and play your Christmas medley." And so the station opened its first live concert with a medley of 'Summer Songs' by the Band of the Royal Scots, which included 'Summer Pleasures', 'Sunshine Wonderland', 'It's A

Christmas Lunch outside the BFBS Middle East studio. Enjoying the spread, left to right, Bob Martin, Alton Andrews, Dave Boyle, Chris Russell, Mike Burnett, the SSVC Video Librarian and Stuart Wadsley – December 25th 1990 *(© Private Photograph)*

Good News Week', 'The Green Fields of Summer' and 'Ring Out Those Bells'. There were no complaints from higher authority!

The station was still waiting for its own telephone lines from Cable and Wireless, despite much nagging by Chris Russell, so he was forced to send the first part of the band concert to London by pointing a newly installed Mercury payphone receiver in the direction of the band which was about 50 yards away. Apparently it worked, as London appeared satisfied.

The station was broadcasting a mixture of BFBS 1 and 2 and many of the presenters were familiar to listeners to BFBS in Germany including Richard Allinson, Dave Rodigan, Bob Harris, Dave Boyle and Simon Guettier. Sometimes news had to be obtained by ringing the Bridge House newsroom using a Mercury telephone box just outside the studio. The BFBS Engineers had discovered problems with the satellite and asked Mercury if they could put an 'out of order' sign on the box so it could be used for interviews with local radio stations in the UK.

The build-up to war continued and the celebrities flowed through the BFBS London studio doors. The programme 'Simon and the Squad' began inviting well-known TV actors to come on the show playing the characters they had made famous. As Simon Guettier recalls: "We first had Gordon Kaye and Vicki Michelle from TV's 'Allo Allo' playing their characters Rene Artois and Yvette Carte-Blanche; they were excellent. Later, from the same show, we had actors Guy Siner and Richard Gibson as Lieutenant Gruber and Herr Flick. Probably best of all was actor Tony Robinson appearing as Baldrick, the antihero character who'd been a huge success in 'Blackadder'. His deadpan humour came across brilliantly. The Squad admired all those who could improvise while staying perfectly in character."

There were many highlights. England footballer and goal-scoring machine Gary Lineker came on the programme and was astounded when Simon told him that they would be taking questions for him live on the phone from British Forces in the Gulf. The lads were equally surprised to find out that they really were hooked up to a football legend.

The Sandy Times of 21st January quoted an article in The Times about BBC disc jockeys being told to play it safe. Apparently radio executives had drawn up a list of 67 pop records considered unsuitable for broadcasting during the conflict. These included: John Lennon's 'Give Peace A Chance' and 'Imagine'; Elton John's 'Saturday Night's All Right For Fighting'; Cher's 'Bang, Bang'; and Eric Clapton's 'I Shot The Sheriff'. Paul Gambaccini, the well-known BBC disc jockey and broadcaster for BFBS London, said: "It's ironic that they should ban 'Give Peace A Chance'."

However, BFBS Middle East was in such close contact with its audience that the station suggested they help compile 'Saddam's Top Ten'. The most requested records were: 'Eve of Destruction' by Barry McGuire; 'Nothing's Gonna Stop Us Now' by Starship; 'Eve of War' by Jeff Wayne; 'Bang Bang' by Cher; 'Stop the Cavalry' by Jonah Lewie and – in an oblique joke about the nine seconds 'grace' to don your gas mask in the event of a chemical attack – The Hollies with 'The Air That I Breathe'.

Chris Russell kept a fairly detailed diary during his time in the Gulf and on December 23rd he noted: "Highlight of the day – the RSM Pete Rose, spotting the Cable and Wireless man, ordered him to rig up a phone for us. At last, we have a temporary phone line, not the three we ordered but something disappearing into a junction box. Nobody knows how it is being accounted for, but it is there and we don't now need to go charging 400 yards to the camp office to make a phone call."

On Boxing Day, BFBS Middle East was visited by General Sir Peter de la Billiere, who once more stressed how valuable he holds the service to be, but pushed for a transmitter for Tabuk and for better coverage for the men in the Gulf.

The work was exciting but very tiring for the presenters. The station had to be kept on air 24 hours a day. On 17th January, the BFBS staff at Al Jubayl received news that in future all 'on air' warnings about attacks would be 'live' and not recorded. The first time it happened, the Station Manager, Jonathan Bennett, had to run across to the studio whilst everyone else took cover. A recording of that first air-raid warning was unearthed recently in which, according to Jonathan: "You can hear the air-raid sirens wailing in the background and the fear in my voice; both were absolutely real." The following day the log records: "A Scud missile being taken out by a Patriot Battery, only 10 miles south of Al Jubayl." Another entry: "The MD in Chalfont has approved that all ex-service members of the SSVC should carry weapons and was now awaiting authorisation." However, the military were not so sure that it would be a good idea!

On 19th January, the station logbook records: "An explosion nearby at approximately 03.30 and 23 minutes later, a suspected chemical attack." At 05.00 Jonathan Bennett was still in his NBC kit and created a world first by broadcasting from inside his specially adapted suit. As he recalled at the time: "I was scheduled to go on air at 05.00 and it became obvious that we would still be in the full kit. By then the respirators had a microphone speech module built into the side of them, designed for military communications admittedly, but I reckoned it would work so I told Alton Andrews to come to the studio with me (we were operating a buddy-buddy system whereby no-one was ever left alone during an attack). I pointed the microphone at the side of the respirator and off we went! The hardest part was not being able to see the microphone in front of me and wearing headphones on top of the NBC suit hood, but it worked!"

One of the first arrivals in Al Jubayl from BFBS Hong Kong was Dave Boyle, who quickly made a name for himself with his non-stop banter and musical taste. He soon found that, not only were the British enjoying his style of broadcasting, but the Americans were listening too in preference to their own station. As one marine put it: "I don't want any more hourly reminders of wearing sunglasses in the desert." He teamed up with Alton Andrews and was soon creating hilarious havoc in the desert. Calling themselves 'The Blues Brothers', after the film, they visited forward positions clad in sunglasses, black trilby hats and black suits, with Dave Boyle handing out visiting cards in English and Arabic, with the legend: 'Breakfast DJ: Combat Trained!'

Another of Dave Boyle's achievements was to acquire a pool table for the office. His reasoning was simple: "In the event of a Scud missile flying over, it will make a good bomb shelter."

As ever, the BFBS Engineers also demonstrated themselves to be handy in a crisis. Geoff Evans, a broadcast engineer based in Hong Kong, managed to source a satellite feed of the BFBS TV operation in Cyprus then built a low powered

TV transmitter using odd radio spares. The 'TV' service was a great boost for troops staging through Camp 4.

The Times for 30th January 1991 reported: "Today BFBS is the place everyone wants to be. Politicians and celebrities clamber over each other to appear on interview programmes, and the studios in Paddington are alive with activity day and night. The Gulf conflict has also reminded military commanders of the importance of having their own broadcasting organisation, closely integrated into the life of the services."

With the beginning of the Gulf War proper, things took a slightly different turn. In consultation with their producers, 'Simon and the Squad' had decided to continue their format largely unchanged. Experience told them that in dangerous and stressful times, the British Forces actually appreciate some normality and their humour in such situations is legendary. But Simon Guettier remembers: "We had to make some changes. We started a feature where we would phone up the spouses and partners of our listeners at the front and put them on air. After a chat, we'd naturally invite them to send a message to their loved ones in the Gulf. Understandably these messages frequently became very emotional, with our phone guest sometimes sobbing on air. When this happened we felt very moved ourselves and anyone listening couldn't help but notice a tremor in our voices as we tried to continue as normal."

It wasn't too long before British politicians became aware that through BFBS UK, and their live worldwide show in particular, they had a perfect vehicle to talk to the troops in the Gulf and families in Germany. In one hectic week, BFBS had the leaders of the three main political parties appearing on 'Simon and the Squad'. First was the newly appointed Prime Minister, John Major. "I think it was felt that with such high-powered guests, having three or four squad members in with him at once would be inappropriate, so I was told on the day that I'd be doing the interview alone," said Simon Guettier. "Nervous already, this made me more so. I remember deliberately trying to avoid going near the studio until the last minute, thinking that putting the interview to the back of my mind would help my nerves. So I decided to skulk around the office until the last minute. Normally, I would get into the studio at least half an hour before we went live. With some 10 minutes to go, I glanced out of the office window only to see the street outside lined with policemen! Worse still as far as my nerves were concerned, when I finally got into the studio it was packed out with camera crews from BBC, ITV and Sky TV - so much for hiding from reality!"

The Prime Minister appeared to be more nervous than his interviewer. He had decided to come to BFBS London as our live link to Downing Street was too much of a challenge for the rather creaky connections with transmitters in Saudi Arabia. He spoke directly to the British Forces he had committed to war and

The Prime Minister, John Major settling down for his live broadcast from the BFBS London studios to the servicemen and women in the Gulf – 1991

(© Jeff Baynham)

took questions from Richard Nankivell in BFBS Herford and Jonathan Bennett, who was joined by two serving soldiers from the BFBS studio in Al Jubayl, Corporal Paul Saunders of the RAOC and Company Sergeant Major Jennie Reynolds, Queen Alexandra's Royal Nursing Corps. Most of the questions dealt with matters of great importance but there were some lighter moments when a listener in Germany, who was one of Mr. Major's constituents, wanted to know whether he had been in the local pub, 'The Pike and Eel' for a glass of Cidrax. The PM obviously knew of the place and invited the serviceman to join him there for a drink once the war was over. In closing, Simon Guettier remarked on Mr. Major's support for Chelsea, whilst he, Simon, supported Spurs. The Prime Minister's reply: "I'm extremely sorry to hear that and perhaps it would be indelicate of me to remind you of the result at Tottenham just a few days ago when Chelsea won 3-0!"

Next, it was the turn of Neil Kinnock, the Leader of the Labour Party, to join Simon on his programme and lastly Paddy Ashdown, the Lib-Dem Leader, presented himself for interview. Simon Guettier's memories of that week were of three very sincere men who wanted to reassure the forces in the Gulf.

At the time of the conflict, there was a record in the charts by Beverley Craven, called 'Promise Me'. Although it was written long before the crisis in the Middle

Company Sergeant Major Jenny Reynolds of the QARNC and Corporal Paul Saunders in the BFBS Middle East Studio preparing to put questions to the Prime Minister – 1991

(© Private Photograph)

East, Simon played it frequently on the show as the lyrics seemed particularly relevant and poignant. "For some reason, and pretty much on the spur of the moment, I said on air that I would play the record every day until the first British troops arrived home when the war was over," he said. "It's a song – and a time of my life, that I will never forget." The closing lines of the song are:

Promise me you'll wait for me I need to know you feel the same way too and I'll be home, I'll be home soon.

As the weeks went by, some of the BFBS staff were concerned that, despite their very best efforts, not all of the British troops could hear the station's output. Soon letters began to arrive on the editor's desk of the Sandy Times. Said one: "I don't want it to sound nasty, but how is it the Americans have been blasting their radio signals all over the desert, courtesy of AFRTS, and we can only pick up BFBS in Jubayl and Riyadh? It would be nice of BFBS to beam some of their programmes to us further north in the desert." Another wrote: "As comforting as it may be for all of us out here to think that HQ BFME and other PONTIs (people of no tactical importance) are listening to Simon Guettier, it just isn't the same. Also while we're ticking, cheers to the RAF for destroying the only decent radio station in the desert, 'Baghdad Betty'." The editor felt it was necessary to

Jonathan Bennett collecting interviews from the Kuwait/Saudi border – 1991

(© Private Photograph)

reply: "We share your frustration. The fact is that from mid-January, we would, technically, have been able to provide a full BFBS service to cover the desert localities. It was essential, for purely operational reasons, to conceal the fact that 1st Armoured Div was working with the American VIIth Corps and not with the American Marines. If we had opened up a radio station for the forward forces, we would have given the game away. We can tell you now, but at the time we simply had to hold our tongues for the real reason. If lack of BFBS radio contributed to fewer casualties, then I am sure you will agree that the deprivation was worth it."

BFBS Middle East closed in June 1991 and the ISO container, which had been their home for several months, was left to rust in the sands of the desert. In the meantime, the MoD, expecting a long haul in the Gulf, approved the building of a state-of-the-art transportable, air-conditioned studio, which was completed just as the Gulf War ended. It served for some time as an extra studio at the BFBS Headquarters in Paddington.

In an interview with Charly Lowndes, General Sir Peter de la Billiere stressed the importance of a local BFBS station. "I think Forces Broadcasting is of fundamental importance in an operation of this nature where English language broadcasting is not readily available. It makes a great contribution to morale. Until we got BFBS, the servicemen had nothing to listen to except American Forces' programmes and the fearful harridan known as 'Baghdad Betty', who, between pop music records, broadcast doses of crude propaganda from the Iraqi capital."

"The other side of it is that it also gives the more senior commanders, who can't possibly get round a force of 45,000 people an opportunity to get a personal message across to every service person."

"If I had to choose which I would want (out of newspapers, video-tape news reviews or broadcasting), I'd put broadcasting at the top of the list. BFBS did a superb job out here. I made very heavy demands of them. We were stretched over thousands of miles... and they responded magnificently. I am very proud of them. I was very grateful to have them along!"

Following the experiences in the Gulf War, the Armed Forces seemed increasingly likely to have to act 'out of area' using expeditionary forces and BFBS, therefore, examined how it could support this new kind of commitment in Europe. Instead of serving a barracks-based, static deterrent force in Northern Germany, BFBS might be needed, at short notice, to supply news, entertainment and music to troops on exercises or operations in alien surroundings anywhere from Norway to Turkey who were living in cramped, temporary accommodation and working long hours with minimal recreation and welfare facilities.

BFBS had found it very difficult to move people and transmitters to the Middle East. The military system during the build-up to a war just did not recognise a bunch of enthusiastic civilians and their equipment. Despite the fact that the commanders wanted BFBS, it took high level lobbying to gain the necessary clearance.

With the ACE Rapid Reaction Corps emerging in the new Europe, Charly Lowndes wanted to show that BFBS could offer a mobile package of news, command information, music and the odd laugh so BFBS Rapid Reaction Radio was born.

Charly had his own views on what was required. "We needed a small, portable facility for broadcasting anywhere," he said. "We needed a studio and transmitter, capable of being maintained in the field by available support – which meant a standard military vehicle. It would be manned by a small team who had enough basic military training to survive in the field without being a burden to the military community around them: first aid; nuclear, biological and chemical warfare; camouflage and even the art of the field latrine."

BFBS borrowed a three-ton lorry, a box body and a generator from 16 Signal Regiment, and a Land Rover from 21 Signal Regiment. 4 ADSR provided BFBS

The Old and the Bold of Forces Broadcasting gather at the National Army Museum for the 'Battledress Broadcasters' exhibition – August 1993   *(© Soldier Magazine)*

with monitors and NBC kits. They were using a mobile transmitter that still had the shrapnel holes from an exploding ammunition dump at St. George's Lines, Kuwait City. The BFBS engineers, Peter Ginn, Alan Boxx and Graham Seymour, fitted out the box body as a studio, and in the lorry was a small transmitter and on a nearby hill-top, a bigger one. Then a chain of transmitters and receivers took the programme back to the network centre in Herford. The BFBS Rapid Reaction Radio team could be heard from Brussels to Berlin and became a force for the future.

In 1992, with the Gulf War over, discussion in the Headquarters of BFBS in Chalfont centred on how to celebrate our 50th Anniversary, which was due in the autumn of 1993, and Alan Grace was given the role of exhibition organiser. "Peter McDonagh, the Director of Broadcasting, suggested that we should set up an exhibition in Central London and the National Army Museum in Chelsea was extremely interested, provided there was a series of interesting exhibits. First, we went through the photographic archives of the Imperial War Museum, then we started contacting veterans of Forces Broadcasting who had given so much of their time to the service."

It was decided that a central exhibit should be based on Gladys of B 4 and the Royal Corps of Transport Museum agreed to lend BFBS a vehicle of similar age. Then Roger Dunn had the task of finding equipment used in the Mobile Studios in 1944. Other exhibits included a plaque of BFN Hamburg that had hung in the garage of a former engineer, Ron Chown, since 1948; a copy of the Forward Forces Radio Times dated November 6th 1944; an original poster from the Irgun Zveui Leumi, the terrorist organisation in Palestine, advising British soldiers and FBS broadcasters to go home, and a delightful poster from BFN Hamburg advertising Trevor Hill's Children's programmes.

The exhibition, called 'Battledress Broadcasters', opened on August 17th 1993 with the help of many former members of the service including: Leslie Perowne of B 4, Dennis Scuse of ABS Athens and BFN Cologne, Arthur Appleton and George Bayley, formerly of BFN Northern Italy now with the BBC in Northern England; Gordon Cox and Brian Johnson of FBS Palestine; Alastair McDougall, Robin Boyle, Trevor Hill, and Ron Chown of BFN Hamburg; Douglas Brown of BLA 3 and the much travelled Peter Buckle of Palestine, Nairobi, Cyprus, Aden and Singapore.

Roger Dunn, one of the organisers of the 'Battledress Broadcasters' exhibition, checking out some of the early FBS equipment at the National Army Museum – 1993   *(© Private Photograph)*

Princess Margaret, the Patron of the SSVC, attended the final day of the exhibition. Raymond Baxter, Anton Rodgers, David Jacobs, General Sir Peter de la Billiere and Lieutenant Sonam Sherpa, who represented Gurkha Broadcasting, talked to her about their memories of Forces Broadcasting.

The exhibition proved very popular with visitors to the National Army Museum. The most popular question was: "Is Family Favourites still going and what happened to Bill Crozier and Jean Metcalfe?"

Dusty Miller, one of the Gulf War veterans, found himself exchanging the desert of Saudi Arabia for the jungles of Belize. His task was to increase the local output and introduce a breakfast show while continuing to train the volunteer staff. At the same time, he streamlined the SSVC TV videotape system, which increased the efforts of BFBS Belize and 'The Link With Home'. When his efforts in Central America were over he received the Commander British Forces Commendation for "Bringing Forces local radio to life and making members of the garrison more aware of service news in Belize and at home."

Four years later, Dusty was to take over the running of BFBS in the Falkland Islands and saw the start of BFBS television after Martin Bowd, the BFBS Engineer, installed a new satellite dish and a computerised TV delay system. The programmes arrived live and were stored in the computer and broadcast four hours later at the correct time (Coronation Street arrived at 3.30pm and was broadcast at 7.30pm). Live sport and news really was live. The advent of satellite to send TV meant BFBS could send more audio streams and, as a result, BFBS Radio 2 became a real possibility. After much negotiation, it was agreed that the medium wave frequency, previously used to get the single channel around the islands, would now be needed to send out BFBS Radio 2.

Unfortunately, one area of the islands (Ajax Bay) could not pick up the FM frequency because they were shielded by the surrounding hills. This meant they would lose the local information broadcast on FIBS and BFBS Radio 1 when the MW frequency was taken over by BFBS Radio 2. As a result, a brand new transmitter with its own frequency was purchased by the Falklands Government and installed for the one family occupying the farm at Ajax Bay. As Dusty commented at the time: "It must have been the first and only time a Government anywhere in the world sanctioned the purchase and installation of a transmitter for just one family!"

Despite the success of the BFBS operation in the Gulf, the Ministry of Defence had decided that the status and modus operandi of The Services Sound and Vision

Dusty Miller, the Station Manager of BFBS Belize handing over the keys of the station to Baz
Reilly – 1992   *(© Crown Copyright: FBS 1555)*

Corporation, of which BFBS Radio and Television was just one part, should be
scrutinised in detail. A team of management study "experts" descended on
Chalfont and published their main recommendations.

The BFBS service was, effectively, only governed by a three-page document
called 'The Blueprint' which gave a vague guidance about programming,
payment and the like. SSVC had a monopoly, there was no formal contract and
money was always paid up front. The far-reaching financial changes
recommended by the MoD study also coincided with the collapse of the Warsaw
Pact and major cuts in the Armed Forces.

Under the new rules, the MoD and the Treasury threatened SSVC/BFBS with
the possibility of Forces Broadcasting going out to competition. The new
Managing Director, Air Vice-Marshal David Crwys-Williams (hot foot from the
MoD financial planning staff), his Deputy MD Colin Rugg, and the new Finance
Director, Julian Portman, mounted a robust defence and as a result of their efforts,
the MoD agreed to an initial single-tender five-year contract.

There were other major hurdles to overcome, however. In a nutshell,
SSVC/BFBS was only just keeping itself from financial disaster. The Corporation

had one main asset: its 120-acre estate near Gerrards Cross. They had no liquid reserves as SSVC/BFBS had done all work "at cost" under 'The Blueprint'.

The MoD's decision to cut its budgets, throw non-BFBS work out to tender and pay after the event forced the Corporation to borrow to plug a £3million cash-flow gap and to look at new ways of raising cash to survive.

David Crwys-Williams and his team's strategy was to cut overheads drastically and identify what BFBS and SSVC expertise could be marketed to new customers. Studios were rented out, training and PR videos made for other government departments, masts maintained for mobile phone companies and an audio-visual company was bought and expanded.

The real stroke of genius however was Colin Rugg's and Brian Scott's plan to provide satellite services from Chalfont Grove, not just for BFBS but also the new telecommunications companies burgeoning as a result of the de-regulation of that industry. The Corporation, backed by a very supportive board, persuaded the local council to grant planning permission for up to 23 large satellite dishes in a spare field – no small achievement in an affluent residential part of the Green Belt. Teleport London International (TLI), as the new venture was called, was a great success and within three years became the fourth largest firm of its type in the UK. When SSVC finally sold the Teleport, associated studios, its broadcasting engineering arm and the Chalfont site to Kingston Communications in 1998, the proceeds wiped out SSVC's considerable debt and filled the organisation's coffers with several million pounds.

SSVC – and thus BFBS – now had financial independence from the MoD. BFBS had a fresh lease of life and a new management style and discipline was established. Most importantly, considerable financial responsibility and authority was delegated to a smaller, very enthusiastic and highly skilled group of broadcasters.

Although BFBS had been relaying programmes to SFOR in Bosnia and Croatia since the early Nineties, the only local presence in the Balkans from BFBS were short visits from radio and TV to record items or entire programmes for broadcast, either by BFBS UK or BFBS Germany.

In 1992, the first Inmarsat programme broadcast from Bosnia was from Gornji Vakuf by Chris Pratt and Peter Ginn, who linked the Prince of Wales Own Regiment with their home base in Osnabruck in Germany with a programme 'Calling From the Balkans'. At the time, it was speech links only along with live interviews and music played in at Bridge House in London by Christina Bray.

The success of this programme set the scene for future links with the Balkans. Chris Pratt recalls one of the more interesting acoustic problems: "The recordings took place while bullets and mortar shells were flying over the factory where we were based as the two ethnic factions decided to attack each other. I decided not to use the sound effects microphone as this may have upset our audience listening back in Germany."

In 1996, BFBS Banja Luka was set up in a portacabin that had been used for the first post Dayton elections in the country. The signal went via the experimental codecs to the UK and was sent back for transmission in Bosnia via satellite.

During the latter part of the Nineties, Germany supplied the lion's share of the personnel for operations in the Balkans and the programme 'Calling the Balkans' became the most popular request show on the BFBS Network. Glen Mansell, presenter of the programme, made regular trips to the Germany based units on detachments there and using the newer, and more compact Inmarsat, became BFBS's first self-sufficient producer/presenter of live programmes from the region. The BFBS service to the Balkans continued in this format until 1998 when problems developed in the Kosovo region of Yugoslavia and the Organisation for Security and Co-operation in Europe – OSCE – were ordered out of Serbia, Montenegro and Kosovo. British forces, based in Macedonia, were deployed during this operation and BFBS were asked to provide a service to the area and relay radio and television programmes to the troops based in the Former Yugoslavian Republic of Macedonia – FYROM.

It was decided that a temporary containerised studio would be built, with office accommodation, and would be deployed using the new V-Sat technology to deliver programmes from the theatre via satellite back to the UK. This would then be fed into the BFBS network system and sent back out by satellite to receivers and broadcast from low-powered transmitters at each forces location.

It was ironic that on the day BFBS was to begin its first local broadcasting in an operational theatre since the Gulf war in 1991, most of the audience had moved 40 miles away. Chris Pratt recalls the first show from BFBS Skopje: "It was lunchtime on Saturday June 13th and Patrick Eade and I presented a double-headed show made possible by the amazing work carried out by our engineering team. The first show was an instant hit with requests coming in to our new little studio, thus starting a trend which was to continue until the present day."

During this time, the BFBS team ventured into Kosovo to collect stories and dedications but soon BRITFOR moved to other locations and it was decided that BFBS should move from Skopje to Pristina. With just a four-day break in transmission, BFBS's latest station was on air on 12th September 1999.

Unfortunately, the Temporary Field Accommodation (TFA) build did not go to plan and, for six months, the life support systems were very Spartan. The showers were a 15-minute drive away so the broadcasters had to wash with bottled water and use a Portaloo in temperatures that dropped to minus 27C.

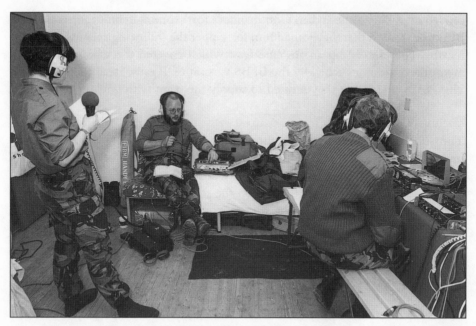

Caroline Young, Charly Lowndes and Cathy Pearson preparing for a live broadcast from the Balkans
– 1995   *(© Crown Copyright: FBS 1221)*

Chris Pratt's lasting impression of his time as the Kosovo Project Manager was having to hold a torch as John 'Jevo' Jevons, wearing pyjamas, dressing gown and slippers in minus 20C, helped him refuel the BFBS generator. Chris said: "Jevo undertook the task every day during his time in Kosovo until the generator was replaced with one that had a larger fuel tank and only required one top-up per day."

Another of the Kosovo Station Managers was Aidan Donovan whose memory of Kosovo, apart from hard work, centred on food. "We had been issued with the yellow military ID cards. This allowed us access to the other international locations," he said. "The advantage of this was that we were able to enjoy the culinary delights of the other nations: the Swedes and Finns, great for fish; the Italians, the best pasta, and the Germans, sauerkraut and 'bratties'. One day, however, Aidan, with Darren Carrington and Michael Anderheider, the engineer from BFBS Germany, were returning to barracks when they passed the headquarters of the Indian Special Police Unit. Rumour had it that this contingent had a snake-throwing unit that they used as an intriguing method of crowd control. They stopped their car and were ushered into the guardroom and eventually were shown into the commander's office. He inquired: "Who is it you want to meet?" To which Darren replied: "No we want to eat." When the team offered to publicise the Indian Commander's forthcoming tennis tournament on BFBS, he insisted that they joined him for supper the following evening. As Aidan recalls: "They served up an absolute feast which covered the whole table." The next unit to be approached by the BFBS version of 'Ready, Steady, Eat' were the Hungarian troops, but they refused to supply the team with goulash.

The success of BFBS to cover the stories that really mattered prompted an invitation from the MoD for Bryan Hamilton, then Head of News at BFBS London, to travel with a United Nations team to Rwanda. He was based in the football stadium in Kigali that had been the scene of an appalling massacre only a few days before. After reporting on the exploits of the UN contingents made up of Canadian, American and British troops, he travelled further afield in search of a story that would bring a message of hope. Not far from the capital, he met a Belgian missionary who was running a home for orphans. These children had rags for clothes but were cheerful. When Bryan asked them to sing a song that he could record, he was amazed by the enthusiasm they showed. When they had finished, he went behind one of the mud huts to check his tape only to discover that one of the youngsters had followed him. The little boy had never heard a

Chris Pratt and Patrick Eade by the BFBS Skopje sign. Note the large piece of unexploded ordnance alongside the sign! – 1999

(© Private Photograph)

radio or a tape recorder and was enthralled by the sounds coming from Bryan's magic box. Within minutes, the rest of the children surrounded Bryan and were soon following him everywhere he went. As he remarked later: "I felt like the Pied Piper of Hamlin."

For some years, BFBS had tried and failed to get a foothold in Northern Ireland until one day Peter McDonagh remembered the 'Returned Granby Asset' or the portable studio. He decided that it would be a good idea to send it to Northern Ireland as a feeder base for the network, where requests could be played for families in Germany and news items could be sent back to the London Headquarters. With the help of the military, it travelled from Paddington to Lisburn in Northern Ireland.

Jonathan Bennett was the first Station Manager of BFBS Northern Ireland. His brief went something like this: "There's no money for this operation, officially you're on an extended OB from BFBS UK, so do the best you can and try and get the General to pay for it." He went away from the brief wondering just why he'd volunteered.

Bryan Hamilton recording a group of orphans in Rwanda – 1994   *(© Private Photograph)*

"My concerns increased on my first meeting with the GOC, General Sir Roger Wheeler, who had only just arrived in post," he said. "The setting up of the station had been agreed by his predecessor, so imagine my reaction when his first question to me was 'and what are BFBS doing here then?' Yet again I went away wondering."

Experience in Berlin and Brunei had taught Jonathan that the best way to achieve his goal was to get the top man on his side. If you did that, the rest soon followed. Thus he targeted the GOC relentlessly, taking every opportunity to show what 'his' station could do. Training in the black art of TV reporting gave more opportunities and, by the end of the first year, the good general agreed to the funding. "Beyond this, I developed a deep respect for Sir Roger," he said. "His term saw the first IRA ceasefire and he was walking a knife-edge every time he dealt with the media. He also came to genuinely appreciate just what BFBS could do, and they developed a good personal relationship. A relationship that developed further following the black day that the Chinook crashed on the Mull of Kintyre. BFBS Northern Ireland played a big part in the aftermath with the GOC making a public declaration of sorrow from our studio. BFBS was the only media invited, by the general, to attend the dedication of the memorial cairn at the crash site.

'Ulster Calling' was a continuation of a programme originally produced by BBC Northern Ireland in 1971, one its presenters having been a young Gloria Hunniford. BFBS Northern Ireland revived it and very successfully too. Jonathan Bennett recalls: "At its height we ran two shows a week, much of the success being down to Station Assistant, Emma Davies. Having found the money to employ an assistant, Emma came into BFBS with a great sense of humour and, being an army wife, a good knowledge of what made soldiers tick. The amount of recorded dedications from Northern Ireland to Germany increased massively when Emma was given the task of gathering them in. Donning a short skirt, she would arrive at somewhere such as the Maze prison clutching her tape recorder, word would get around that 'The BFBS bird was here' and the guys would queue up, waiting to give their dedication."

Ulster Calling was a large part of the justification for setting up the very first permanent BFBS transmitter in the UK. Girdwood Park, a bleak barracks in the very centre of Belfast, was home to a succession of Germany based units and BFBS managed to convince some serious doubters that a 'FM induction loop' system (a leaky wire) would serve the barracks but not go outside. Doubters were eventually convinced, largely because the GOC told them they would be, and the system was installed.

General Sir Roger Wheeler, the GOC Northern Ireland with Jonathan Bennett, Peter McDonagh and Alan Protheroe, the Managing Director of the SSVC at the opening of BFBS Northern Ireland – 1993 *(© Crown Copyright: FBS 1556)*

Jonathan Bennett, the Station Manager of BFBS Northern Ireland with Station Assistant Emma Davies – 1993
(© Crown Copyright: FBS 1557)

When Marc Tyley arrived at Bridge House in 1993, he was aware that, apart from the Sony Lifetime Award from the Radio Academy to BFBS and the PATER awards, the trophy cupboard was fairly bare. He began to look for programmes that might stand a chance, not only with the Sony Radio Awards in this country, but also in the global arena at the New York Radio Festival.

In 1994, BFBS entered the New York Festival and within three years had achieved gold status with three entries: 'Mark and the Manger' – the Mark Page Christmas Special; 'The Swamp' – a BFBS promotion produced by Stephen Bumfrey; and the 'BFBS Branding Package' – produced by Andrew Wright and Paul Daniels.

In 1995, 'The State of the Nation', the programme by Stephen Bumfrey and Hannah Cox, won bronze at the Sony Awards. The next big challenge was to involve the overseas stations and 'The James Watt Breakfast Show' picked up a bronze medal in New York, beating off Chris Evans along the way.

———

In the spring of 1994, it was decided in Chalfont that BFBS should cover the 50th Anniversary celebrations of the D-Day Landings. A team from Germany and a team from UK met at Arromanches to plan the coverage. This time, unlike the 40th Anniversary commemoration, a major programme would be coming from the battlefield sites and commentary on the Queen's visit to Arromanches.

The first problem was accommodation. All the hotels and guest houses in the immediate area had been booked by British, Canadian and American veterans and so, with the approval of the mayor, Dr. Jean-Michel le Comte, the BFBS team camped in the local caravan site.

The team, which was led by Bryan Hamilton, included Tom Scanlan, Patrick Eade, Charly Lowndes, Alan Phillips, Margaret Hayes, Phil Collins and Alan Grace, arrived on June 3rd. Plans were finalised for coverage of the celebrations, not only at Arromanches, but also at Omaha Beach. On the Saturday, two days before the big event, Alan Phillips presented a show from the centre of Arromanches with many of the veterans who had fought on day one of the D-Day landings among his guests. On June 6th, the team were up early to make the most of the time available. The main problem concerned the tide. At this time of year, the beach was clear at 11.15 a.m. but the tide would return at around 5.50 p.m. Gladys, the Outside Broadcast vehicle, was to be the only vehicle on the beach and at 11.30 a.m. was driven down a ramp onto the beach. The next problem was to connect the power supply and, more importantly, the broadcast lines. With 15 minutes to go to the first broadcast, the team discovered they had lost their lines. Phil Collins checked and caught a Belgian TV team, who had not booked sufficient lines for themselves, removing the cables and replacing them

Hannah Cox and Stephen Bumfrey after winning a bronze at the Sony Awards for their programme
'The State of the Nation' – 1995   *(© Andy Harding)*

with their own. They also had plans for our power supply system. Following a broadside from the Gulf War veteran, they backed off and connection was made with Germany and the network with two minutes to go. Because of a lack of line-up time, however, the quality for the first part of the programme was far from good.

The major event of the day was the arrival of the Queen, the Duke of Edinburgh, Prince Charles, The Princess Royal, the Duke of York, Princess Margaret, the Duke of Kent and the Duke of Gloucester, who would be meeting the veterans, who were drawn up in a hollow square on the beach, with their backs to the sea. Suddenly news came through that the Royal party was delayed at the American celebrations. Would the Queen be able to inspect her veterans before the tide came back to the beach at Arromanches?

Alan Grace was commentating on the events. "As soon as the Royal party arrived, I found myself with one eye on what they were doing and the other on the tide, which was moving ever closer to the beach," he said. "The Royal party were determined to meet as many of the veterans as possible and, just when I had visions of the Royal Range Rover and our own Outside Broadcast vehicle becoming bogged down on the beach at Arromanches, the Queen moved off towards the esplanade and the final part of her visit." Patrick Eade, Alan's co-

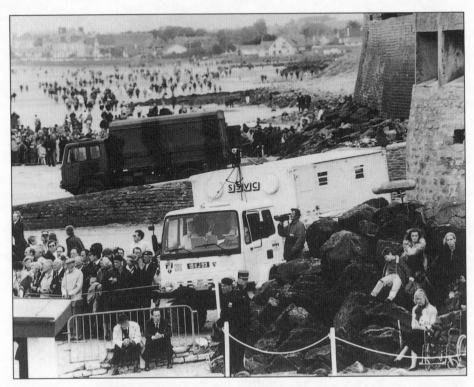

The BFBS Outside Broadcast Vehicle known as Gladys 2 on the beach at Arromanches waiting for the start of the Queen's inspection of the Normandy veterans – June 1994   (© *Soldier Magazine*)

commentator, remembers the Queen's address to the men on parade: "Veterans of the Normandy Campaign, you deserve your nation's thanks. May we, your fellow countrymen, be worthy of what you did for us." At this point, Brigadier David Nelson-Smith led the march past of the veterans to the stirring sound of 'Old Comrades'. By now the tide was coming in but both vehicles managed to get off the beach with minutes to spare. Instead of commentating on the final part of the celebrations, the BFBS team had to hand back to the studios to prevent the sea from making their withdrawal impossible.

The outstanding memory for all of the BFBS team was the superb hospitality offered by the French, not only to the veterans, but to the broadcasters as well.

———————

Having arrived in Berlin in 1992, Aidan Donovan's main task was to plan and execute a smooth draw down of the BFBS presence in the city. At the time, BFBS

Berlin was housed in Spandau and it had to be handed back in pristine condition. As a result Aidan and his small team became experts with vacuum cleaner, dustpan and brush.

The Berlin Officers' Club was to be the venue for the last BFBS Berlin party and each member of the staff was presented with a magnificent picture of the Brandenburg Gate at dusk.

The final broadcast from the Spandau studios was very emotional with the studio packed with former staff members and film and television crews from a number of television stations. Among the guests was Heidi Brauer from East Berlin, who had been the station's biggest fan, even when it was forbidden for people living in the east to listen to BFBS. The final record from BFBS Berlin was Spandau Ballet's 'Through the Barricades' which seemed to fit the occasion as the words were very pertinent to Berlin: "Father made my history, he fought for what he thought and would set us somehow free. Born on different sides of life, we fear the same, feel of all this strife."

The song was very symbolic of what Berlin had been through and where it was going.

In the autumn of 1996, Tony Davis, who had recently taken over as Station Manager BFBS Gibraltar called a staff meeting. Apparently word had filtered through that the station would be closing down on 31st March 1997. Gibraltar's military future was also in question as the resident battalion had been pulled out some years before and there was no RAF squadron based on the Rock.

Nicky Ness, a locally employed broadcaster, and other members of staff, began to think of ways to save the station.

The Command was incensed that a decision had been made without full consultation and they wanted to keep their radio station. "With the aid of Peter McDonagh, I began to figure out a way to keep the service running in a skeleton format, at least until the powers could be persuaded to reinstate the station," said Nicky Ness. "The turning point came at a Burn's Night in the Sergeants Mess when I found myself seated next to the business manager for the Gibraltar Amenities Fund. This was an initiative to generate non-public money within the garrison, which could be used by the military who were based there." That night the GAF agreed to use their non-public profits to fund Nicky Ness's post and allow for a part-time administrator. BFBS agreed to take her on as a 'stringer' who would feed stories back to the network. The Gibraltar Nuffield Trust (a local military charity) also agreed to fund a presenter for the breakfast show and George Pusey agreed to work for them for next to nothing to secure the future of the station.

A room was earmarked in HMS Rooke and somehow the Command found £40,000 to convert the new location using labour provided by Royal Engineers, who were visiting on their annual exercise. It took them just four weeks. BFBS persuaded the MoD to pay for equipment that would allow 'a room with a microphone' so the Commander British Forces (CBF), could talk to his Forces in an emergency.

For a time, Nicky Ness worked on her own in South Barrack House. From 1st April 1997, the station was no longer on the broadcasting contract, but she persevered and was amazed by the support she received. The MoD establishment did not think it would ever work, but Nicky and her volunteers managed to pull it off: "In reality," she said: "We never decreased any of our on-air hours and even the twice daily news magazine programme was sustained. The volunteers kept going, even though they did not know, from month to month, whether the station was going to survive."

The move from South Barrack House to HMS Rooke was hilarious and happened in October 1997. Although the 'room with the microphone' was ready,

The Staff of BFBS Gibraltar with Station Manager Nicky Ness in the passenger seat of the OB vehicle just after their move to HMS Rooke – 1999   *(© Crown Copyright: FBS 1558)*

there was no budget to pay for the move and so Nicky pulled in a lot of favours: "I don't know how many trips I did up and down the hill and moving the satellite dish was done on the back of an RAF pick-up truck with four RAF lads holding on to it for dear life."

BFBS Gibraltar never went off air and the transition was seamless.

Although the new regime still cost BFBS around £70,000 per year, it was a huge reduction on the £300,000 that had been spent in the previous year. In 1999, the BFBS staff finally managed to get their contract status reinstated and they threw a big party in the Caleta Hotel to celebrate.

Rory Higgins had begun his broadcasting career as a freelance for BFBS Hong Kong. When he left the colony in 1985 he did not expect to return, but in mid-January 1996 he was back on the plane to Hong Kong with a brief from the Director of Broadcasting, Peter McDonagh, to manage the station as the Forces went through the draw-down process and to remain on air for as long as possible up to the handover.

He still had 17 radio staff (mostly Nepali). In his first weeks, he closed the transmitter at Brick Hill, which had served the resident Army battalion in Stanley Fort.

Throughout 1995, the General Manager, Ian Martin, and his Senior Engineer, Dave Richardson, were involved with the planning. The idea was always to draw down from north to south, first in the New Territories and then Kowloon, leaving the Prince of Wales Barracks as the last redoubt. The last month of the draw down was covered by a huge plan which dictated where and exactly when every remaining member of the Forces community would leave. BFBS had to be out by midnight on the 30th June 1997.

The programme challenge for Rory in Hong Kong was to work with the presenters and the engineers to ensure that BFBS, possibly the most high profile expression of Forces life in the colony, continued as usual until the last day. BFBS needed to simultaneously 'draw down' whilst retaining the quality of output. At the same time, there was the difficult task of making some locals redundant and encouraging the freelance English staff to remain until the handover.

"As the major military plan for the handover became clear we were able to plot the withdrawal of BFBS from Hong Kong," said Rory. "We had been asked by the Command to continue broadcasting up to the last moment of British sovereignty, if possible. Our plan in 1995 was that the Nepali service would close when Sek Kong closed, as that was when most of the Gurkha troops would leave."

The English service would move its operation down to the Prince of Wales Barracks in the Central district of Hong Kong Island as they already had a small studio set-up there and it was to be the last piece of real estate to be closed. "It was thought that, in the last days of British rule, we should move our studios into a container and on to a ship in the harbour so that we could transmit until the last moment."

In April 1995, the Hong Kong service began recording short 10-minute programmes for Gurkhas in Bosnia. These programmes were played out live from Hong Kong to Bosnia via Bridge House in London. BFBS continued to carry a small amount of Nepali broadcasts using tapes supplied from the Gurkha Service in BFBS Brunei.

In March 1997, many British personnel and the families left. The last few months were to be witnessed by a 'hard core' of the garrison and ceremonial troops who would be flown to the colony in the last few weeks.

In the months and weeks before the handover, BFBS gained a higher profile as local expats realised BFBS would be going. A 'save The Archers' campaign started and Rory Higgins put the government radio station, RTHK, in touch with the BBC to sort it out. Visiting journalists from all over the world were also looking

Rory Higgins and Damian Watson with the All Black Super Star Jonah Lomu in the studios of BFBS Hong Kong – 1996
(© Crown Copyright: FBS 1559)

for new angles on the handover. BFBS provided an interesting footnote of colonial history. Many people said: "We don't care about the military leaving, but BFBS – that's another matter!" Rory was interviewed by BBC Radio 1 and Five Live, Japanese TV, Chinese TV, Reuters TV, Finnish TV, ITN, the Guardian, the Boston Globe, the Independent and the Daily Telegraph.

"We still managed to do important radio jobs though. I remember dealing with an emergency in late 1996," he said. "An officer's elderly mother and his mentally handicapped adult brother were visiting Hong Kong. The officer left his visitors at his quarter and went to work. An hour or so later, the mother rang him to say his brother had gone missing. After nearly 24 hours of searching and with the Royal Hong Kong Police now involved, he called BFBS. We made the announcement and within a few hours the brother was found near Kowloon City. He was spotted by a teacher who was driving along listening to BFBS and matched the man with his description."

The Christmas of 1996 was the last Wireless For The Blind Appeal. The star prize led to a furious bit of on-air bidding by two Chinese people for a British

The famous First Day Cover, which was auctioned for Wireless for the Blind in 1996 and signed by the Commander British Forces Hong Kong and the PLA General.

(© Crown Copyright: FBS 1560)

Army first day cover signed by the Commander British Forces and the incoming PLA General. The loser was so angry that he threatened to sue BFBS. Fortunately, Rory Higgins was able to calm him down and remind him that the appeal was for charity and supposed to be fun.

In April 1997, BFBS had a visit from the Australian Cultural Attaché, Sir Les Patterson – the comic alter ego of Barry Humphries, the man behind Dame Edna Everidge. The BBC were making a comic-documentary about Sir Les's final visit to the fleshpots of Hong Kong. He approached BFBS because he had had a good interview with Jamie Gordon a few years before. Rory remembers: "I presented a live show where he was very crude and funny with on-air callers. I set it up for him to visit the Black Watch and the Royal Navy on Stonecutters Island. The CO played the game and met him as a VIP and showed him around. It made marvellous television. At the end of the day, Sir Les took his teeth out and Barry thanked me for being such a good comic straight man!"

Around two weeks before the handover, the studios were ripped out and BFBS retreated to a containerised studio outside A Block. They invited the press to publicise the event and well over 50 journalists attended. On 29th June the last show from the container was presented and the team filled it with equipment from the studios upstairs. It was then moved to an RFA (Royal Fleet Auxiliary) for shipping back to the UK. BFBS had pre-recorded the sequences for that day. Damian Watson produced and presented a two-hour network show called 'Disconnect HK' which was heard in all BFBS locations worldwide. So all the programmes bar the final one would be played down the line from the UK.

On the final day, the remaining office equipment was thrown in a skip to prevent the PLA from benefiting from our generosity. The office was empty apart from a small amount of broadcast equipment stacked in the corner. BFBS just had a small mixer and a couple of microphones for the final broadcast, covering the British handover ceremony on the waterfront. The BBC outside broadcast people provided the parade effects. The output of the desk was piped up the final BFBS transmitter in Hong Kong, which was on the top of the headquarters. It was also piped back to the UK for simultaneous broadcast around the world on BFBS Radio.

"The day of the 30th June dawned and we looked out nervously at the hot, overcast weather shrouding the harbour," said Rory Higgins. "For the final time I took the Star Ferry across the harbour and walked into the barracks armed with several passes. We spent the morning cleaning out the office and moving our OB equipment to the balcony. The British spent a huge amount of time making sure that the military facilities were handed to the Hong Kong Government in spotless condition. The barracks had been renovated and painted in 1997. We were to hand the keys of our office into the guardroom before we left at

Corporal Colin Mathews of the Black Watch, Commodore Peter Melsen, Chief of Staff HQ British Forces Hong Kong in the Mobile Studio known as the 'Love Shack' at its official opening in May 1997. *(© Crown Copyright: FBS 1561)*

midnight. The military headquarters staff set up their final office in the same guardroom. We had witnessed a dress rehearsal on the weekend before the handover and I had taken notes at that stage. I was also very lucky that a major in the Black Watch had prepared some commentary/press page notes. I wrote an introductory 'scene-set', which was to be followed by a 10-minute package by Damian Watson, pulling together some of the final political developments before handover. A studio manager in the UK played it in. The rest of the commentary was to include an emphasis on the military involvement in the story of the British in Hong Kong. I was very keen to make reference to and remember the British and Chinese who had fought together during the Battle For Hong Kong during the Second World War. There had been quite a bit of press speculation about what the final tune of BFBS HK would be – much of it, I admit, fuelled by me! Some thought we would play Monty Python's 'I Like Chinese', others Peter Cook and Dudley Moore's 'Goodbye'. Those suggestions were amusing, but I knew that we should play 'The Last Post' and 'Sunset'."

Officially the barracks, the last to remain in British as opposed to Hong Kong Government, hands would be handed over to the PLA at around 2200 hrs. On

Rory Higgins interviewing the last Governor of Hong Kong, Chris Patten just before the final withdrawal – 1997.   *(© Crown Copyright: FBS 1562)*

television, Rory Higgins saw their ceremonial troops come across the border in the early afternoon. This caused some consternation, as they were not due for a few hours after that. In reality, a small number of PLA had been been in the barracks for a week or so. Their soldiers had annoyed members of the Black Watch by putting up a large clock which counted down to the handover second by second. Not surprisingly, it was put out of action by the Jocks in short order!

The actions of every member of the garrison were controlled during the last few days by a huge draw down document. It ran to many hundreds of pages and BFBS movements were charted down to the last minute. The only UKBCs – Damian and Rory Higgins – were booked on the last flight.

"At dusk, around 1800hrs, we began our broadcast," Rory said. "The eyes and the ears of the world were on Hong Kong. Thirty years after most of the rest of the empire, the flag was going down. The British ceremony was to be a tribute to Hong Kong. There was music, dancing and song. The Governor, Chris Patten, made a moving speech followed by the Hong Kong Symphony Orchestra playing Elgar. Then the British Forces marched on as the rain began to bucket down. The Royal Navy were represented by the men and women from the Hong Kong

Squadron, HMS Chatham and the Royal Marines Band. The Black Watch represented the Army, and the Queens Colour Squadron, the RAF. There were also Pipes and Drums and an Army band. The parade included the lowering of the flag at sunset. As the military marched off the parade square and as we approached 2000hrs, I said farewell to the audience in Hong Kong. I spoke on behalf of the British Forces that had served in the territory and especially on behalf of the BFBS people. I wished the people of Hong Kong well and told them that we would never forget them. I finished by speaking in 'Chinglish' and saying "Bye Bye". 'Evening Hymn' and 'The Last Post' marked the end of BFBS Hong Kong."

Rory Higgins still remembers his last journey in Hong Kong: "As the special ferry crossed the harbour towards Kai Tak Airport, junks and other boats serenaded us. People throwing parties aboard sang 'Rule Britannia' and wished us good luck. The special ferry dropped us off at the side of the runway where tents had been erected to allow us to change out of our wet clothes. In the tent I filed a live report to LBC radio. We were then bussed to the special BA charter flight and we took off around 0100hrs. The BA pilot welcomed us on board with the words that Britain was proud of us! Shame it was a dry flight."

Countess Mountbatten of Burma, General Sir Geoffrey Howlett and David Crwys-Williams at the 50th Anniversary Celebrations of BFN/BFBS Germany in the Musikhalle in Hamburg – 1995.

(© Ivor Wynne-Jones)

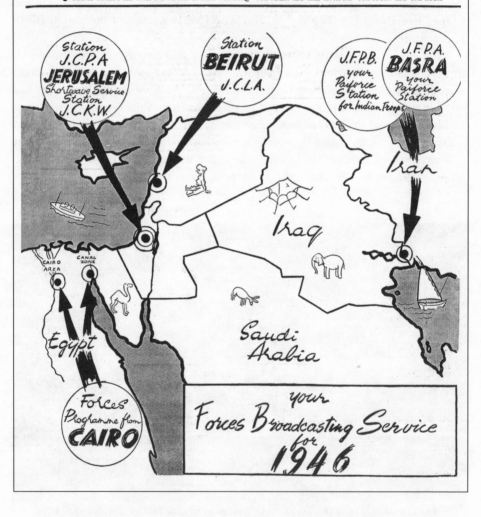

CHAPTER SEVEN

The Millennium

Return to Basra

In the late 1990s the military realised that BFBS radio and television, along with NAAFI and telephones, had an important welfare function in operational areas such as the Balkans. They all became elements of the 'Operational Welfare Package'. The armed forces also realised that there would be more operations of this sort in potentially dangerous areas where BFBS was also expected to deploy. The first example of this was in Kosovo in 1999.

BFBS Radio had been gearing up since Autumn 2002 for a possible call to the Middle East as part of this welfare package. Chris Pratt, Peter Ginn and Martin Bowd decided to recover whatever equipment was available from Kosovo, Bosnia and Oman. Although they had no idea what would be needed or how much, it proved to be a wise move. In the middle of January 2003, five personnel, mainly engineers, were selected to attend an NBC course at RAF Cranwell. Unfortunately, Peter Ginn, veteran of the first Gulf War, had recently undergone a minor heart operation and failed the fitness test.

Following a meeting with David Crwys-Williams, the managing director, Chris Pratt and Dave Ramsay flew out to the Gulf to see how many transmitters would be required for the radio service and how many individual satellite systems would be needed for the TV service. Within two weeks, Martin Bowd had joined them and it was decided that the newest BFBS station would begin life within Op Telic at Camp Arifjan. The first site to get BFBS radio was Hammersmith Camp, situated 35 kms north of the Muttlah Ridge, the forward base for the British troops. At the same time, the team set up BFBS TV for one of the small units based in this forward area.

During the next month, the engineers installed FM transmitters at Camp Rhino, Camp Fox, the APOD, the SPOD, Arifjan and Al Jaba, also as many DTH satellite TV systems as were available.

The next problem was to find a broadcast site and Chris Pratt and Dave Ramsay decided to use containerised units supplied by the Kuwaiti-style Portakabins as a temporary solution. One was immediately adapted with a studio

Sean Ridley collecting voice messages during a sandstorm in Kuwait – March 2003.

(© Private Photograph)

at one end, an administration area in the middle and a sleeping area for the breakfast show presenter at the other end.

The first live local breakfast show was broadcast on Monday March 3rd via an Inmarsat satellite terminal and the first record to be played was the aptly entitled 'The Boys Are Back in Town' by Thin Lizzy. Chris Pratt presented the programme but, due to technical restrictions, only the voice links were done locally: Darren Carrington in the UK played in the music. Soon the engineering team of Martin Richards, Jim Hardie and Darren Hobbs had replaced the Inmarsat terminal with a VSAT system. By now Chris Pratt had been joined by Sean Ridley, who presented an afternoon show and recorded dedications from the troops to be played back for families and loved ones in Britain. Sean recalls: "I had just finished recording dedications close to the front line when I was told about an incident when a generator in one of the front line British camps backfired and 20 or so Iraqi soldiers came over a sand burm in order to surrender to the coalition forces. They were promptly informed by some helpful British troops that the war had not started and so they should p*** off back to where they had come from."

When the British Forces deployed to Kuwait, it soon became apparent that an outlet for requests and dedications would be needed in the UK. Although local stations around the country were interested and wanted to help, it was felt that better exposure to the messages flooding back from the Gulf would be obtained if BFBS UK linked with a national network. Both BBC Radio 2 and Virgin Radio fitted the bill and were keen to become involved.

BFBS UK drew upon Glen Mansell's experiences from 'Calling the Balkans' to co-ordinate the requests and dedications and co-present 'Backing Our Boys' on Virgin Radio and BFBS Radio 1. The programme was simulcast nationally on Virgin and worldwide on BFBS every Saturday morning from the Virgin studios in London. Glen presented the first hour for BFBS listeners and then linked for a further two hours with Virgin's Ben Jones and Jezza: "The show was a mixture of requests, records and phone calls," Glen recalls. "Some of the calls were very emotional and needed delicate handling." As well as dealing with the requests and dedications, it was Glen's job to keep the other two broadcasters on the straight and narrow from a military point of view. "I did my best, but we did have a couple of Lance-Brigadiers mentioned!"

More requests between servicemen and women and their families were broadcast on BBC Radio 2 on Steve Wright's 'Love Songs' on Sunday mornings. Again, this was simulcast on BFBS Radio 1. Glen would call Broadcasting House early on a Sunday morning to confirm that none of the dedications were for servicemen and women whose names had been added to the casualty list overnight.

The last 'Backing Our Boys' was marked by a personal e-mail from the Prime Minister, Tony Blair, thanking everyone for helping those who were away to keep in touch with their families and friends.

The press noticed the exploits of the BFBS Middle East team. Daniel McGrory of The Times wrote an article on Friday March 7th with the headline 'Good Morning Kuwait, this is your desert DJ'. He went on: "The Americans may have more tanks than us, a lot more troops and more burger bars to feed them, but at least the British contingent has brought its own entertainment to this desert coalition. Every morning, thousands of US troops are roused from their sleeping bags by two British DJs broadcasting from a makeshift studio in a metal cargo container parked on the edge of one of the biggest and busiest camps in Kuwait.

Chris Pratt, the Station Manager, explained that when they bump into Americans in the queue for meals, they tell him that they listen to BFBS rather than their own AFN, which is holed up in a safe, air-conditioned complex thousands of miles from the front line. If the British Forces should end up in Baghdad, then Chris Pratt and his co-presenter Sean Ridley won't be far behind. As Chris said: 'We're not being foolhardy or trying to prove how brave we are, it's just that British Forces out in the field regard us as a way of staying in touch with home.'" On March 17th, St Patrick's Day, BFBS's Gulf War specialist, Jonathan Bennett, arrived and Chris Pratt made plans to return home.

Brigadier Shaun Cowlam, who had opened the new station two weeks earlier, wanted to know however, if the troops went into Iraq, whether BFBS could place a transmitter close to the front line so the men could hear the station's output in their off-duty moments. As a result, Chris Pratt put his return on hold.

The BFBS team was attending the daily J1 briefings on the morning of March 20th when the war broke out. No one was left in any doubt as to what would be required of them over the coming months. The briefing began with prayers from the Padre for both sides in the conflict and everyone at the meeting was given a pocket bible.

The BFBS team had experienced simulated missile attacks in training exercises before the war started, but it was very scary when it happened for real. As Chris Pratt put it: "Pulling on the NBC kit was a struggle to start with but soon we were slipping into it almost with ease. For two nights, though, we decided to sleep in most of our kit to give us a head start in moving to our bunker positions."

During one of the alerts, as the BFBS team of Jonathan Bennett, Sean Ridley, Jim Hardie, Darren Hobbs and Chris Pratt huddled in the centre of the hanger,

Jonathan Bennett in the BFBS Middle East Studios – March 2003.   *(© Private Photograph)*

an announcement was made that was more specific than before: "Two missiles incoming, expected to land in three minutes – take deep cover." They did not think a bunk bed was what they meant by deep cover, but it was the best they had. For three minutes, they waited, fearing that they might be making the ultimate sacrifice "for the love of working for BFBS". Of course, the missiles landed elsewhere and so it was back to broadcasting and some form of normality.

Jim Hardie, at the age of 22, was the youngest BFBS member of staff in theatre and he remembers being overwhelmed with "gut-wrenching, stomach-turning fear". Jim had only recently joined the engineering department from Southampton University and could not remember situations such as this being mentioned in the interview.

Sean Ridley remembers the arrival of Jonathan Bennett at Camp Arifjan. Not only had he done the lot in the first Gulf War but his expletive-rich comments about Saddam Hussein lifted everyone's spirits during the early days of missile warnings. "One particular night we had an alert warning and were waiting for the American all-clear message saying 'all missiles down'," said Sean. "However, the next voice to come over the Tannoy was not American and was not recorded.

Dave Ramsay on the Iraq/Kuwait border – March 2003 *(© Private Photograph)*

It was a British voice saying chillingly 'take cover for incoming ballistic missiles'. We were saved by the accuracy of a nearby American Patriot battery that successfully shot down each missile, but it made it clear to us that the Iraqis knew where we were!"

Several days later, Sean Ridley and Jonathan Bennett were walking into the dining facility when Sean remarked: "We have not had an air alert for over 24 hours.""As soon as I had closed my mouth, the alarm leapt into life and JB started hitting me over the head and shouting 'why can't you keep your bloody mouth shut!'" said Sean. "The Americans just looked on in amazement."

On 27th March, Stuart Holmes and Darren Hobbs, accompanied by Chris Pratt, moved into Iraq and installed a radio transmitter at Umm Qasr Port. As Dave Ramsay recalls: "The engineering team were now working at full stretch. Whilst living on the camp was safe enough, moving between locations could be dangerous." Stuart Holmes actually came under fire during the siege of Basra. Iraqi tanks broke out of Basra and headed towards his position just as he finished putting up the second transmitter in Iraq at Shaibah.

Captain David Ward, SO2 J1 OWP, described what happened. "Stuart Holmes was with the battle group who were advancing on Basra during the fighting phase of the war and was with the Artillery when they opened up on a breakout

Stuart Holmes and Darren Hobbs installing the Radio Transmitter in Umm Qasr Port – March 2003.

(© *Private Photograph*)

column of Iraqi tanks. The tanks responded and Stuart took shelter in the mosque at Shaibah Airfield believing this was the best place. He was sure the Iraqis would be loath to destroy a mosque! Shortly afterwards, when the British troops had taken Basra, Stuart was able to set up a transmitter that allowed them to listen to the second half of a football match involving Newcastle United. This gave them a morale booster to finish the job."

Meanwhile, Jim Hardie had travelled to Al Amarah believing he had two satellite installations to complete in two and a half hours while the Hercules turned round. Instead, he found he had eight systems to install but somehow he managed to complete the task in time. "Completing the radio and TV installations and seeing the difference it made to the morale of the troops was one of the most rewarding aspects of being in the Gulf," he said.

Members of the BFBS News and Features Department at Chalfont were also determined to serve the Forces audience. Six volunteers applied to be accredited as war correspondents and Rory Higgins and Susie Ferguson from BFBS Radio were accepted.

They were sent on a two-day NBC course at Winterbourne Gunner and were also required to attend a one-day field craft course with the RAF Regiment where they were lectured on what to do if the enemy captured them. Since

Stuart Holmes setting up the transmitter at Shaibah Airfield – March 2003.

(© Private Photograph)

neither of them had a service number and would be wearing civilian clothes, they felt they might confess they were reporters rather than spies!

Next came the issuing of kit, which included a very heavy flak jacket, helmet, NBC kit, a suitcase-sized communication's kit, a laptop computer, a bag with microphones and recorders and a Thuraya satellite telephone, which proved to be one of the most important items they had with them.

"I never intended to be a war correspondent so to get the opportunity to go to the Gulf as an embedded journalist was an unexpected development in my career," said Susie Ferguson. She only joined BFBS full-time four weeks before flying out to Kuwait to join troops from the 1st Royal Regiment of Fusiliers, part of 7th Armoured Brigade. At 25, she was the youngest embedded correspondent with the British Forces. This was the first time BFBS had sent journalists to cover a war at the front line.

To have them there was vital for BFBS to enhance and consolidate their credibility with the audience. "For the soldiers I was with, the radio was their window on the war," said Susie, "and that brought a great responsibility to tell it as it was." As Susie discovered, living with the audience was an added pressure to those at the front.

"The day before the land war started, I prepared to move north with the Fusiliers," Susie recalls. "As the soldiers made their final preparations, the Padre of the regiment spoke. Even those who weren't religious were riveted – he said nothing prepares you for blessing troops before they go into battle. The sense of anticipation was palpable and the atmosphere charged, as the soldiers gathered in the meal tent, sand whipping around as final words were said. For the first time, people spoke about how not everyone would come back; the gravity of the situation descended."

Susie and the Fusiliers were all wearing NBC suits and the rest of their protective equipment in case of chemical or biological attack. All the suits and body armour were marked with name, rank, nationality and blood group.

After final speeches by the Commanding Officer Lt Col David Paterson and OC Major John Swift, the men broke away to their own vehicles. "My last image before leaving," said Susie, "was of men playing volleyball, carefree and seemingly oblivious to the circumstances; a surreal final moment as we began down the road to war."

The fear of weapons of mass destruction was one of the reasons the troops were massing on Saddam's borders and, inevitably, there were suspected attacks on the first day of the war. Scuds were launched, and the alarms sounded. "We had all been through the training," said Susie, "but hearing 'gas, gas, gas!' for the first time, and the sense of urgency and panic in the soldiers' voices, the tinny clashing of metal and beeping of horns as the alarm was passed on, and reaching for your respirator, it hit home that this was real. Respirators are not comfortable at the

Susie Ferguson, Rory Higgins and Annie Haresign, BFBS' first embedded War Correspondents –
March 2003. *(© Private Photograph)*

best of times – in the desert heat they are sweaty and claustrophobic; but in the
circumstances, very welcome."

Susie's first view of Basra was at the university, and the looting that started
minutes after the forces arrived. "People were taking anything they could lay their
hands on. Everything from computers and televisions to fins from ceiling fans
were being wheeled away on office chairs," Susie recalls. "Iraqis streamed in over
the bridge near the university with wheelbarrows and donkeys. People poured
out – women carrying fridges on their heads and boys wrestling to keep hold of
wide-screen televisions."

She was struck at the response of the Iraqi people to the soldiers when they
entered Basra. From all sides people rushed out to greet them – waving, shouting,
laughing and giving thumbs up but what really stood out for her were the
women. "They were initially passive, eyes lowered and quietly went about their
daily business," she said. "But on the second day of being in Basra, they began to
respond to the troops. When the armoured vehicles went past, some women
would look up and smile, the kind of smile that lit up their faces and I was struck

Susie Ferguson interviewing Iraqi Civilians near the town of Basra – March 2003.

(© Private Photograph)

by their beauty. They remained doing their chores – washing clothes in the river, carrying baskets of food from the market – but their quiet acknowledgement was in many ways more touching than the loud response of the crowd."

Rory Higgins was embedded with 2nd Royal Tank Regiment Battle Group, who were on 15 minutes alert to move. On 20th March, they experienced at least 20 NBC alerts and several missile alerts. "The strain was very high," said Rory. "We were unable to work (as there was a comms blackout) and information of any sort was hard to obtain. It was anticipated that there would be a tank battle at some stage. No one slept that night, so it was a chance to write one's last letters."

For the next few days, 2nd RTR moved around frequently and it was during this time that Rory saw his first battlefield casualty. "It was a sight I shall never forget and I filed my report a few hours later."

During the first few days, most of the reporting had to be in the form of reports or 'two-ways' for the BFBS news and sequence programmes. "I know that having our own reporters on the ground made a big difference to our team in Chalfont," said Rory. "It had a remarkable effect on our audience and the families overseas, who heard what I hope was measured commentary on the events which enlightened and reassured where possible."

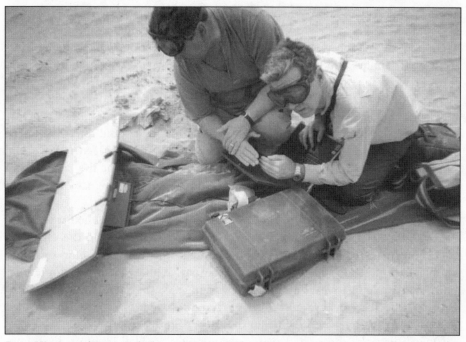

Rory Higgins and Terry Graham struggling to send an urgent report during a sandstorm in Iraq – March 2003. *(© Private Photograph)*

It was acknowledged by the military that the BFBS war correspondents more than held their own with the rest of the media. "I felt that our knowledge of the Forces allowed us to provide a unique service from a war zone to the rest of our audience," said Rory. Two particular highlights for him were telling a soldier in the field that he had just become a father, and recording messages with the Irish Guards in Basra in the back of a Warrior armoured car. The Guards had just spent a night fighting the Iraqis.

"As I was recording, a mortar round was heard heading our way," said Rory. "The shrapnel showered against a nearby building. The sergeant just said: 'Shut the door Scouse' and then we carried on. I stayed there for quite a long time."

On 3rd April, Sarah Donaldson wrote a feature in the Daily Telegraph, entitled: "The songs that inspire the troops on the road to Baghdad." She described the cult following enjoyed by Jonathan Bennett, the breakfast show presenter of BFBS Middle East. "Often, troops would knock on the studio door and thank him for playing a song, which for a moment, transported them away from the heat and sand and back to the familiar comforts of home. According to Jonathan Bennett, the troops can actually tune in while they are fighting if they wanted. BFBS had transmitters further forward than at any other time since the Second

World War. Jonathan knew when he went on the breakfast show in the morning he would be talking to guys who were resting, having come off the front line."

By now, the station was getting around 2,000 dedication requests a day. Most were from families and friends back home, but soldiers sent messages back and forth between the units. Popular inter-troop song requests included The Animals, 'We've Gotta Get Out of This Place'. On one occasion an armoured unit in Iraq mocked a battalion further away in the desert with the record, 'Things Can Only Get Better'. As Sarah Donaldson pointed out: "The best tonic for the soldiers' soul was a message from home, such as the Beatles, 'All You Need Is Love' and Norah Jones 'Don't Know Why'." The most popular song at the time of her report was 'Thousand Miles' by Vanessa Carlton, with its poignant lyric: 'You know I'd walk a thousand miles if I could just see you tonight'.

The BFBS studio moved to Umm Qasr from Arifjan and immediately was a great source of interest to the local servicemen. From 6.00am in the morning, bakers (normally based in Dulmen), pitched up with fresh bread, buns or bacon sandwiches. This continued throughout the day as individuals and sometimes units would pop in to leave a request or scrounge a cup of tea. It was obvious to Patrick Eade that the live and local programmes were exactly what the men needed and the presence of BFBS in theatre was greatly appreciated.

One of Patrick's most vivid memories was of a cocktail party on the Umm Qasr quayside. "The Band of the Scottish Division turned up to Beat Retreat. It was a bit like 'hey you'll never guess what I did last month, and where!' Here we were, on a broken down dockside in Iraq, with the Brits drinking non-alcoholic cocktails and eating curry followed by the pageantry of Beating Retreat as a

Frank McCarthy on detachment from BFBS Gibraltar in the Umm Qasr Studio – April 2003.
(© *Private Photograph*)

thank you to the Spaniards who'd helped with various logistics. The Provost Marshal came up to me and suggested that BFBS must be very proud of what we had done in theatre: 'you guys did a bloody good job for us on our exercise in Oman – but to be here providing round-the-clock radio and TV, and from an operational and still hostile theatre, is a remarkable achievement.' His remarks just about summed it up – it had been a real team effort, every piece in the jigsaw was vital or there would have been no complete picture. To be in Iraq gave us all in the BFBS team a tremendous sense of job satisfaction."

On the same quayside a few weeks later, troops gathered to meet the Prime Minister, Tony Blair. He emerged from a convoy of heavily guarded vehicles and strode over to the waiting crowd of khaki looking like a rock star. Later, aboard a Royal Navy minesweeper, he told Patrick Eade, in a BFBS exclusive interview of the gratitude that he felt for those he had met during his visit to Iraq.

When Michael Anderheiden, one of BFBS Germany's Special Operations Engineers visited Iraq in May 2003, he found himself on route for the capital Baghdad to install a transmitter for the British Forces. Like a good German

Michael Anderheiden on Saddam Hussein's throne, Baghdad – May 2003.   *(© Private Photograph)*

tourist, he decided to check out the local scene and discovered one of Saddam Hussein's thrones. Having been photographed sitting on the throne, he promptly placed his towel on it and the last we heard, the throne was still unoccupied!

One year earlier in Germany, one of the most popular summer events came to the end of the road. Patrick Eade, who was the Station Manager in Germany, recalls the Rhine Army Summer Show: "The RASS was always quite an occasion. This annual event aimed at bolstering Anglo-German relations, attracted most of the British Army of the Rhine to Bad Lippspringe for a cross between a funfair, military tattoo, beauty contest and a horse show. I remember the "Miss RASS" contest, taking place against a background of wolf whistles as timid young ladies paraded before an eager and predominately male audience, many of whom had exceeded their alcoholic levels! To present the RASS on air in a way that didn't portray something of a bear garden was a challenge. We put on a number of stage shows – one featuring the 2nd Bn Light Infantry's Barber's Shop Quartet, a knife thrower, sword swallower and a flame eater! Our insurers were mystified when we enquired about premiums, but all went according to plan. The RASS became a victim of its own success and finished in 2002 with over 100,000 people turning up for the event. It turned out to be just too big for the army to organise, finance and administer. But what a way to finish – in a three-day period we presented four live radio shows and nearly 30 stage acts from 10am to midnight including such favourites as Fish, Slade, Showaddywaddy, The Drifters, The Searchers, Ian Van Dahl, Honeyz, Phats and Small and Robbie Craig."

Glen Mansell presented 'Calling The Balkans' at Sunday lunchtimes from 1994 until 2002 from the studios of BFBS Germany. Frequently, the show came as outside broadcasts from all over Germany and indeed from the Balkans themselves.

The first live show from the Balkans was a transmission from the Konçar Factory in Split, Croatia, in 1996. 2 Battalion REME were based there and we had quite a collection of soldiers gathered for the broadcast on a patio outside the main factory building. As Glen Mansell recalls: "Before the show we had requested that the local rep in Germany be despatched to record requests and dedications from the children of the unit. During the show these were played over the satellite link to us in Croatia on a small loudspeaker. At the sound of the young voices wishing Dad, wherever he was, all the love and 'I can't wait until you come home so we can play fight', the normally brash and cheeky soldiers became fidgety and uncomfortable and a few openly wiped the tears away."

Glen Mansell, producer, presenter of 'Calling the Balkans' with Neil Carter, producer, presenter of 'Access All Areas', at a Families day at Stuckenbruck in Germany – 2002.   *(© Private Photograph)*

The show became more active as the Kosovo situation became tenser and Glen was deployed to Macedonia to broadcast from a field just north of Skopje that 4th Regt RA called home.

Just days after the push over the border from Macedonia, Glen presented the first live BFBS show from Kosovo. The programme was broadcast from the forecourt of a burnt out garage that had been commandeered by the Quartermaster for his stores.

"I must have read out hundreds of thousands of requests over the years while presenting 'Calling The Balkans'," Glen said, "but just a few stick in my memory. During one particular outside broadcast in Bosnia, I was tasked with delivering a bottle of Champagne and a dozen red roses to one soldier's wife back in Osnabrück and on many occasions I was the one to tell a serviceman that he was or had become a dad."

There was one dedication that repeatedly popped up on 'Calling The Balkans'. It was always signed off with… "PS Four Sticks". Glen was used to the saucy innuendos that used to pass across the airways and racked his brain trying to work out what 'Four Sticks' might mean. "I never worked it out but met the 'Four Sticks' lady at an outside broadcast in Hamlin. She swore me to secrecy and explained. To get them through the difficult months ahead, she and her husband had made a pact before he left that every night, at a certain time, they would stop whatever they were doing and just take a moment to think about each other. That time was 11 minutes past 11pm. Displayed on a bedside digital clock it became four vertical bars… or 'Four Sticks'. I hope she forgives me for telling the story now."

When 'Calling the Balkans' came to an end after a very successful 10-year run, a new programme called 'Access All Areas' took over. It was planned to provide a worldwide platform for our audiences' requests and dedications. Neil Carter, as the presenter and producer of the show, had the responsibility of organising and putting together live outside broadcasts for the families of units deployed under Op Telic. Welfare officers worked non-stop to put on entertainment for children and organise food, mini-buses shuttled backward and forwards from married quarters all over the garrison, engineers were desperately looking for another plug socket, while confused young soldiers tried to work out how to inflate a bouncy castle.

For Neil, his most memorable occasion came when he was asked to host a live show for the friends and families of 1st UK Armoured Division and Signal Regiment. "It was to be presented from a local school with well over 200 families expected to attend." Neil said. "During the lead up to the event, I was asked by a colleague's wife if I would kindly present a surprise birthday present to a little girl, who would be there on the day. Closer to the time, I spoke to her mother and was given a present which had been purchased by the girl's father prior to him going to the Gulf."

During the week preceding the event, the father called BFBS's 'Access All Areas' answerphone and left a message for his daughter to be played live at the event. "During the actual broadcast," Neil said, "I called the girl forward to wish her a happy nineth birthday then I asked her to listen to the message that her dad had recorded especially for her. As I played it live on air, the rest of the BFBS crew were already facing away from the audience and staring at the back wall, as everybody had a lump in their throat. Hearing her dad's voice coming out of the speakers reduced the little girl to tears and most of the audience as well. I then presented her with her father's gift and she went on to broadcast her own message to her dad in the Gulf through her tears."

Staff posted to Brunei have always had to put up with jibes about 'sunshine tours' and days spent sunbathing in between records, but Damian Watson, Station

Manager from 2001–03, recalls a week in January 2002 when swimming costumes were replaced by wellies.

"I was doing the breakfast show one morning and it was raining more heavily than usual, even though it was the monsoon season," said Damian. "I kept popping out of the studio during records to watch the water level rising and rising. Eventually, after a number of on-air flood warnings, I finished the programme only to hear the transmitter go 'ping' and the resulting sound of silence. By this point the whole area was under several feet of water, and although the actual radio station itself was raised above ground level, the transmitter hut was not."

Three days later, the equipment racks in the transmitter hut were a couple of feet higher than before and BFBS Brunei was back on air thanks to an emergency visit by Gary Searle, a UK-based engineer.

Brunei, on the north-west coast of the island of Borneo, has its fair share of tropical nasties. The floods of January 2002 washed a few unwelcome visitors out of the foliage and into the homes of Forces personnel and Shell Oil expats. "We were used to the little whip snakes and poisonous centipedes," Damian said, "but the black cobras that suddenly started to appear in married quarters were quite

Helen Finch preparing to transmit her report from the Oman – 2002.   (© *Private Photograph*)

Helen Finch in Afghanistan, with the Dog, who had been adopted by a British Unit and would
soon be on its way back to the UK – 2003.   *(© Private Photograph)*

another thing. One of my friends found a 5ft cobra in her sons' bedroom one
night while her husband was away in the UK on a course. Fortunately she
managed to get the boys out of bed without waking them and the snake was duly
dispatched by a neighbour."

Brunei Garrison actually had a contract with a local snake catcher. Many of
his victims were displayed in the conference room at the Jungle Warfare Wing. "The
BFBS Brunei Gurkha Programme Director, Binod Khadka, always maintained that
black cobra curry was a delicacy I should have sampled before I left Brunei," said
Damian. "Then again, Binod always did have a mischievous glint in his eye."

Twenty five years ago, the highlight of a BFBS reporter's life, apart from those
who lived in Hong Kong or Berlin where rock stars and politicians were
plentiful, would be the chance to become involved in a major military exercise.
However, the Falklands War changed all that. Suddenly, for the first time,
broadcasters and engineers were expected to work on unaccompanied tours in
difficult conditions. The chance of a three-year uninterrupted posting to Cyprus
was gone to be replaced with at least one unaccompanied tour of the Falklands
or Belize during the three years.

Following the first Gulf War, the members of BFBS became involved in the Balkans, originally as reporters and then as staff members based in the region. Today, the reporters and engineers can find their diaries filled with trips to the Oman, Afghanistan, Kosovo, Sierra Leone and Iraq.

Alan Phillips and James Forster were among the first members of BFBS to go to Afghanistan. The RAF had just leased four C17 Globemaster Transport Aircraft to help with the heavy-lift needs of the military. The C17 is a little like a warehouse with wings. Alan Phillips remembers quite clearly arriving in Kabul: "All landings take place at night with lights extinguished and a very steep and I am told, spiral descent to avoid the threat from surface-to-air missiles. On the ground there were no external lights and everything was ink-black. It was February and that meant it was bitterly cold at night, though pleasant enough, during the day." Alan and James were billeted in a 10 x 12 tent with no ground sheet. "That first night it was minus 15 inside the tent," said Alan, "certainly, I have never tried to brush my teeth with frozen toothpaste before, as I had to the following morning."

Helen Finch was sent to Afghanistan as a BFBS reporter to cover, amongst other things, a football match involving a British Forces team and an Afghan side. She was amazed when more than 100,000 people turned up to see the match, held in a stadium that was once the scene of public executions. She was able to beat the best of Fleet Street with her report on the game. Later she covered the story of the dog that was adopted by one of the British units and later flown back to England to go into quarantine. She was sent to the Oman to cover the Parliamentary Defence Select Committee's visit and found that flying in a helicopter did not agree with her! It was then off to Sierra Leone to report on the Defence Minister's visit to the country at the time of the first major elections.

Following her exploits in the Gulf War, Susie Ferguson went to Afghanistan following the war against the Taliban. Because of the security situation, it was only possible for her to go to Kabul and Mazar-e-Sharif where British soldiers were based as part of the international peacekeeping force.

Kabul was relatively safe, but beyond the city limits the warlords ruled the country. The drugs trade still had a significant hold and the Taliban and al-Qa'eda terror network were regrouping. Mines laid over decades were washing down the mountains into residential areas, and unexploded ordnance was everywhere. "Despite that, I was struck by the attitude of the people during my visit," said Susie. "They were keen to have Westerners in their homes, and to talk to the soldiers on their patrols."

"On one foot patrol when I accompanied the soldiers, we were invited into a house in Kabul. With the awe-inspiring backdrop of the Himalayas, children were playing amongst the few mud brick houses. Curiosity brought people out

– the children began following the soldiers, eyeing their guns, and women cautiously looked out from behind their house doors. Through the male interpreter Emal, I began talking to a teenage Afghan girl called Terana. She invited me into her family house and introduced me to her mother and sisters. They were all unveiled, but weren't fazed by Emal or the British soldiers. She told me that life had changed enormously in the last two years – she can now go to school, no longer lives in fear and that they are pleased that there are British troops in Afghanistan."

While all the activity and excitement was going on overseas, back in Chalfont in September 2001 the decision was taken to re-brand the three BFBS Radio Networks: Forces Radio BFBS, Radio 2 and the Gurkha Service. All three were to be given a stronger image and the timetable for the re-launch was set. Forces Radio BFBS was to become BFBS Radio 1 in September 2002, BFBS 2 was to become BFBS Radio 2 in April 2002 and the Gurkha Service was to become BFBS Gurkha Radio in February 2003. Marc Tyley, former General Manager in Germany, was posted back to Chalfont to take up the new position of General Manager BFBS Radio. "What we required was, not just a review of the programmes but new, clear and appropriate air-branding for each network," Marc said. "Andrew Wright was tasked with sifting through most of the main jingle makers in the UK and America to produce a short list of promising composers and producers, whilst Kishore Gurung searched for the same in Nepal. The outcome could not have been more diverse, with production teams being lined up in Billericay, Los Angeles and Kathmandu. Whilst the latest digital technology, multi-tracking and studio trickery was used to produce the new sound of BFBS Radio 1 and 2, it was a team of 17 musicians and the original composition of commercial producer Sachin Singh that gave BFBS Gurkha Radio its strong new identity."

Forces Broadcasting has come a long way since that former pirate's harem in Algiers in 1943. In the past 60 years, they have operated 92 different radio stations in all parts of the world. Although there have been moments when its future has looked uncertain, the enthusiasm of the men and women who kept the service going, often in adverse conditions, has never wavered.

Charles Foster, the present Controller of BFBS Radio, assesses this amazing organization: "It is remarkable that BFBS has survived 60 years. So many opportunities were presented to close the service, for many comprehensible and incomprehensible reasons, but still it goes on, and now includes three radio services broadcasting from radio stations and transmitters in countries from Brunei to Canada, a set of television channels and Internet streaming.

"The success of Forces Broadcasting is thanks to the work of hundreds of broadcasters, engineers and support staff who battled against local conditions, politics and impossible challenges to produce an outstanding model of the best of British broadcasting abroad, endured, tolerated and loved by the British forces and foreign eavesdroppers alike. It is unique – no other nation engages civilians to broadcast such a service.

The combination of sensitivity to the audience, ego, some incredible personnel situations, luck, ingenuity, love, affection and good old British grit have produced this service that drives the lives of many and has changed the destinies of others.

The future is as challenging as the past. BFBS grew out of the dying embers of the Second World War, and war and its aftermath still provides the impetus for its mission of providing Britain's forces with a link with home, a mission that is as important now in 2003 as it was in 1943 and will be in 2043."

Charles Foster, Controller BFBS Radio and Peter McDonagh, former Director of Broadcasting of BFBS discussing whether broadcasting was easier in the 'good old days'.   *(© Private Photograph)*

The SSVC's New Patron, HRH The Duke of York visits the Broadcasting Headquarters of the SSVC

The Duke with SSVC Chairman David Hatch and Managing Director, David Crwys-Williams.
(© Private Photograph)

HRH chats to Colin Livingstone, BFBS Forces Action Editor and Alan Phillips, BFBS Radio Managing Editor.   *(© Private Photograph)*

RADIO STATIONS OPERATED BY
THE FORCES BROADCASTING SERVICE
1943 – 2003

BFBS Aden	1962 – 1967
BFES Algiers	1944 – 1945
BFBS Akrotiri (Cyprus)	1976 –
ABS Athens	1945 – 1947
FBU/FBS Baghdad	1944 – 1945
BFBS Banja Luka	2002 –
ABS Bari (B 2)	1944 – 1945
JFPA/ No 6 FBU/FBS Basra	1944 – 1947
JFPB/No 6 FBU/FBS	
Basra broadcasting for the Indian Forces on 345 metres	
No 2 FBU/FBS Battisti, Libya	1946
BFBS Belize	1984 –
No 5 FBU/FBS Benghazi (incl: break of two years)	1946 – 1967
JCLA/FBU/FBS Beirut Site No 1 at Khalde near Damour.	1944 – 1946
Later the Station moved to Mount Carmel, Haifa	
BFBS Berlin – operating full time 1963	1961 – 1994
BFBS Bielefeld	1975 – 1990
ABS Borgo San Lorenzo	1945
BFBS Brunei	1979 –
FBS Cairo	1943 – 1946

Canal Station JCFA broadcasting on 215.4 metres
   The Station covered Kabrit and Fayid and had its transmitter
at Kom-Al-Dik, Pyramids Road, Cairo. The Studios were in
Shawarbi Pasha Street in Cairo City. This was also the
Headquarters of the . Middle East Broadcasting Unit
(MEBU) and FBS.

Cairo Station JCFB broadcasting on 316 metres
   The Station was initially at Abbasieh Barracks, Cairo, and
later moved via JCPA to Beit Jala, Jerusalem.

No 3 FBU/FBS Canal Zone	1948 – 1954
BFBS Chalfont (UK)	1997 –
BFN/BFBS Cologne	1954 – 1990
JCCA FBU/FBS Cyrenaica	1945 – 1947
JCLB Damascus	1945 – 1946

All India Radio Delhi (All Forces Programme)	1943 – 1946
BFBS Dharan (Nepal)	1982 – 1991
BFBS Dhekelia (Cyprus)	1964 – 1991
BFBS Dortmund	1992
No 3 FBS El Ballah (operated for six months)	1955 – 1956
Also known as No 3 FBS Omar	
BFBS Episkopi (Cyprus)	1969 – 1991
No 3 FBU/FBS Fayid (Egypt)	1954 – 1956
BFBS Falklands (with FIBS)	1983 – 1985
BFBS Falklands – Lookout Camp Stanley	1985 – 1986
BFBS Falklands – RAF Mount Pleasant	1986 –
ABS Florence	1945
BFBS Gan (Maldives)	1970 – 1976
No 3 FBU Gaza	1944 – 1945
BFBS Gibraltar	1961 –
ABS/FBS Graz (Austria)	1946 – 1955
BFBS Gutersloh	1994 –
JCLA/No 4 FBU/FBS Haifa	1946 – 1948
(JCKW The Short Wave Station 41.55 metres)	1945 – 1947
BFN Hamburg	1945 – 1954
BFBS Herford	1958 –
Originally operated by Sgt Tony Plummer on an occasional basis. This system continued until 1990 when it became the Headquarters of BFBS Germany.	
BFBS Hohne	1988 –
JCPA/No 1 FBU/FBS Jerusalem	1943 – 1948
The first Station was based at RAF Quastina, it then moved to RAF Gaza and finally settled at Beit Jala, near Jerusalem	
No 3 FBU/FBS Kabrit (Egypt)	1944 – 1948
BFBS Kathmandu (Nepal)	1997 –
No 18 FBU Khartoum	1944 – 1946
No 7 FBS Klagenfurt (Austria)	1946 – 1955
No 4 FBS Kato Lakatamia (Cyprus)	1948 – 1952
FBS/BFBS London (Kings Buildings)	1961 – 1983
BFBS London (Paddington)	1983 – 1997
FBS/BFBS Malta	1948 – 1979
BFBS Middle East (Al Jubyal)	1991
BFBS Middle East (Arifjan)	2003 –
ABS Milan (B 1)	1944 – 1945
No 2 FBS Mombasa	1948 – 1949

ABS Naples (B 6)	1944 – 1946
FBS Nairobi	1948 – 1964
No 4 FBS Nicosia (Cyprus)	1952 – 1964
BFBS Northern Ireland	1992 –
BFN Northern Italy	1945 – 1948
BFBS Norway at Boemon Camp near Voss	1994 – 1996
BFBS Osnabruck	1988
ABS Padua	1945 – 1947
BFBS Pristina	1999
Opened September 13th	
BFBS Rheindahlen	1980 –
ABS Riccione	1945
ABS Rome (B 5)	1944 – 1945
No 1 FBU/FBS Sarafand	1948
Radio SEAC (Ceylon)	1946 – 1949
BFBS Sek Kong (Hong Kong)	1971 – 1996
BFBS Sennelager	1989
BFBS SHAPE	1997 –
BFBS Sierra Leone – unmanned station broadcasting	
in Freetown	July 2000 – July 2002
BFBS Singapore	1967 – 1976
BFBS Skopje	1999
BFBS Suffield,Canada	2000
BFBS Tamar (Hong Kong)	1985 – 1997
changed to BFBS Prince of Wales Barracks - 1994	
No 6 FBS Tobruk (El Adem)	1964 – 1969
No 1 FBS Tripoli	1948 – 1966
FBS Trieste	1947 – 1954
ABS Udine (B 4)	1945 – 1946
BFN UK (Forces Radio)	1999
Catterick	
FBS Vienna	1946 – 1955
ABS Zeltweg (Austria)	1953 – 1955

BFBS – British Forces Broadcasting Service
BFES – British Forces Experimental Station
ABS – Army Broadcasting Station
FBS – Forces/Field Broadcasting Service
FBU – Forces Broadcasting Unit

JFPA – JCLA were call signs of transmitters in Palestine and the Lebanon and were linked to the various stations i.e. JFPA/FBS Basra.

BFN UK (Forces Radio) went on air 12th April 1999 in Bulford followed by Catterick Garrison, Colchester and Aldershot. This was a one month trial at each location.

The first example of broadcasting by the Military to the Military was in Iceland in 1940 when a group of servicemen persuaded Radio Reykjavik to let them broadcast a programme in English. It was called 'The Hour in English for the Forces in Iceland.' The operation was not fully resourced by the War Office.

A limited number of programmes for the Forces were also transmitted from Radio Cairo (Egyptian State Broadcasting) and The Palestine Broadcasting Service in Jerusalem as well as Radio Levant in Beirut, and Radio Baghdad in Iraq. These Stations were relatively high power for their time. When JCPA at Quastina went on air, there were two or more Forces Programmes being transmitted in the Cairo and Palestine areas. The final Jerusalem Beit Jala Station JCKW broadcasting on 7.5 kw shortwave was actually borrowed from Sharq-Al-Adna, the HMG Station for the Arab Broadcasting Service. It later moved to Zyggi in Cyprus.

The Beit Jala Transmitter Station had a history of its own. It originated during the war as part of the Royal Signals Force 133. "The British Mediterranean Station" was set up to broadcast to the Balkans and the Studios were at St. Pierre en Gallicante, Jerusalem. Later both the Studios and the Transmitter were handed over to FBS and Sharq-Al-Adna.

The first Middle East Forces Experimental Station to go on air was Station JCJC which was run by two Army Majors – Kidd and Vast - from the Royal Signals. It was sited at Abbasieh Barracks, Cairo. It is believed this Station was operational in 1943.

The setting up of Forces Broadcasting in the Middle East was through Army Welfare 5 and the Signals Experimental Group. The Family Tree went from AW 5 – MEBU – FBU – FBS.

In the Middle East, FBS operated a Station for the Indian Troops in Basra – JFPB No 6 FBU. They also broadcast special programmes for Troops from East and West Africa, Ceylon, Mauritius and South Africa. In Benghazi in 1946 they allowed German Prisoners of War to broadcast programmes in German for the POWs who were still awaiting repatriation. Occasionally Polish troops broadcast from the studios in Jerusalem to their colleagues, who were also waiting to return home.

A programme for Greeks who were working in the Canal Zone, was broadcast by No 3 FBU Fayid. In 1948 No 4 FBS in Lakatamia Cyprus broadcast programmes in Greek and Turkish for the men of the Cyprus Regiment and in 1956 FBS Nicosia broadcast programmes in French for the French Armed Forces who were involved in the Suez Affair.

In Italy, during World War II, Forces Broadcasting used Mobile Radio Stations B 1 – B 6. Most became static but B 3 and B 4 continued their mobile role until the end of the war.

During the invasion of Northern Europe, Forces Broadcasting again used Mobile Stations British Liberation Army Units - BLA 1 – BLA 4. They ceased to operate after BFN Hamburg went on the air in July 1945.

Radio Tiger in Swaziland 1963 – 65, was run by the Army and Radio 540 in Masirah 1972 – 78, was run by the RAF. Both were supplied with programmes from BFBS London.

In 1968 following the closure of BFBS Aden, it was decided to open a BFBS Station at RAF Sharjah but after protests from the Royal Air Force, the Station was not finished and its equipment was sent to a variety of BFBS Stations around the world.

BFBS Banja Luca (Bosnia) opened for two weeks in 1996.

BFBS Pristina, which went on air in September 1999 transmits two 24 hour Radio Services and one 24 hour Television Service. The bulk of this material being relayed by satellite from BFBS Headquarters in Chalfont. BFBS Pristina has two locally presented shows per day.

INDEX